# THE AUTHORS

RALPH RIEGEL:

Ralph Riegel is the southern correspondent for Independent Newspapers, Ireland's biggest newspaper group, covering the region for the *Irish Independent*, *Sunday Independent* and *Evening Herald*. A graduate of DIT-Rathmines, his work has also featured in *The (London) Independent*, *The Daily Telegraph* and *The Irish Examiner* while he is a regular contributor to RTÉ, TV3, BBC, Channel 4, NewsTalk and C103FM. This is his sixth book. Three were best-sellers. The fourth, *Three Kings*, was long-listed for the William Hill 2008 Irish Sports Book of the Year and the fifth, *Commando*, is now the focus of a Sky TV documentary. He lives in Fermoy, County Cork with his wife, Mary, and three children.

JOHN O'MAHONY:

John O'Mahony is a veteran of Ireland's 35th UN Battalion which served in the Congo in 1961. Having completed his army service, John became a successful cereal farmer and rose to become Chairman of the Irish Farmers Association's (IFA) powerful National Grain Committee, taking part in EU farm talks in both Belgium and France. A keen amateur historian and meteorologist, John is now active in the Fermoy-based Post 25 of the Irish United Nations Veterans Association (IUNVA). John lives in Tallow, County Waterford with his wife, Sheila. His two sons now live in Tipperary and Oklahoma in the US.

MERCIER PRESS

Cork

www.mercierpress.ie

Trade enquiries to CMD BookSource,
55a Spruce Avenue, Stillorgan Industrial Park,
Blackrock, County Dublin

© Ralph Riegel and John O'Mahony, 2010

ISBN: 978 1 85635 694 7

10 9 8 7 6 5 4 3 2 1

A CIP record for this title is available from the British Library

Printed and bound by ScandBook AB, Sweden.

RALPH RIEGEL & JOHN O'MAHONY

# MISSING IN ACTION

## THE 50 YEAR SEARCH
## FOR IRELAND'S MISSING SOLDIER

MERCIER PRESS
IRISH PUBLISHER – IRISH STORY

# CONTENTS

*To the memory of Trooper Patrick Mullins and the extended Mullins-Kent-Dwane-Kelly family.*

'I can't promise you that I will bring you all home alive. But this I swear, before you and before Almighty God, that when we go into battle, I will be the first to set foot on the field and I will be the last to step off – and I will leave no one behind. Dead or alive, we will all come home together. So help me, God.'

*Lt Col Hal Moore, 7th Cavalry, US army, in a public address to his troops before the battle of Ia Drang, Vietnam.*

# ACKNOWLEDGEMENTS

This book would not have been possible without the incredible support of a great number of people.

Foremost amongst these are the extended Mullins-Kent-Dwane-Kelly families who, for half a century, have loyally kept the memory of Pat Mullins burning bright. The family never, despite innumerable setbacks and disappointments, faltered for a second in their determined campaign to locate Pat's body and bring his remains back home for a Christian burial. As the old German military proverb goes: 'The finest monument a soldier can have is carved not in marble or bronze but in a cherished memory.'

The family were hugely supportive of the idea for this book from the very start and were unfailingly generous with their recollections of Pat and access to family photos and letters. It is our cherished hope that this book, in some small way, does justice to their courage and dignity. We are honoured that they entrusted us with this project.

Secondly, a heartfelt 'thank you' to Art Magennis who, more than any other person, has battled over the years to see justice done for Pat Mullins and his family. His dedication has gone above and beyond the call of duty – and reflects all that is best about the Defence Forces. Art's fascinating memoirs were of enormous assistance in tracing the sequence of events back in 1961 and his personal photographs offer a vivid glimpse of what it was like for the soldiers of Ireland's 35th Battalion. Linking up with Art at his Blackrock home in Dublin was also one of the unexpected pleasures of working on this book.

Special mention must also be made of retired Sgt Tim Carey, whose heroism at the Radio College in September 1961 – despite an horrific injury – stands as testimony to the finest military traditions of loyalty, courage and honour.

Another stalwart supporter of this project was military historian Paudie McGrath. Paudie has been a good friend to the Mullins family for many years and very kindly provided some key photographs for this book. Paudie has also been a tireless campaigner for military service and sacrifice to be both recognised and commemorated.

Thanks also to the former soldiers who agreed to be interviewed, supplied vital material or simply lent moral support for this book, including Des Keegan, Danny Sullivan (RIP), Martin O'Keeffe, P.J. O'Leary, Bill Maher, Michael Boyce (RIP), Tommy McCarthy, James Ronan, Brigadier-General Paul Pakenham and Liam Nolan. Thanks also to former Minster for Defence Willie O'Dea and his staff. Thanks to *Irish Independent* assistant news editor, Don Lavery, and Jonathan Healy of NewsTalk for their expert opinions on the manuscript. Don's late father Jim served in the Congo as an officer with the Irish 33rd and 36th UN Battalions and alongside Art Magennis on UN duty in Cyprus. Jim Lavery was awarded a DSM for his actions in 1962 at the Battle of Kipushi in the Congo. Armoured cars under his command fired 60,000 rounds from their Vickers guns in just a single day.

The background details to events in the Congo and Katanga in 1959–61, as listed in Chapter 4, are recreated thanks to reference to some superb historical and political works. All are listed in the bibliography, but special mention must be made of Martin Meredith's *The State of Africa*, Ludo de Witte's *The Assassination of Lumumba*, David O'Donoghue's *The Far Battalions*, Raymond Smith's *The Fighting Irish* and Thomas Pakenham's *The Scramble for Africa*. The BBC, *The Irish Times*, *The Guardian* and the *Irish Independent* were also valuable sources.

The photographs included in this book are courtesy of the extended Mullins family, John O'Mahony's collection, Art Magennis' coloured slides of the Congo, Paudie McGrath, Bill Maher and Keith Dransfield.

We have taken the liberty to 'interpret' events from Pat Mullins' perspective in the eight hours between the ambush and his death, particularly in Chapters One and Eight – but this dialogue is strictly based on the available evidence as to what most likely happened on 14/15 September 1961. All other events are as detailed in memoirs, journals, newspaper reports and books from the period, as well as government reports and the Defence Forces special 2010 review on the circumstances of Tpr Pat Mullins' death.

This entire project hinged on the support of Mercier Press – and our thanks to Clodagh Feehan and Mary Feehan for their faith in this book from the outset; to Wendy Logue for her excellent editing; to Catherine Twibill for her fantastic cover design and to Patrick Crowley for his marketing expertise.

Thanks to the staff of Cork Library's reference section for their unstinting support in accessing archival and research material for this book.

It should also be noted that while Tpr Pat Mullins is Ireland's first soldier of the modern era to be 'Missing In Action', he is not alone. In this regard, special mention should also be made of Private Kevin Joyce who was kidnapped and killed in Lebanon in 1981 while on UN duty. The Joyce family find themselves in the same traumatic position as the Kent-Mullins family in mourning a loved one whose remains have yet to be repatriated.

Finally, a heartfelt 'thank you' to our respective families for supporting this project since it was first mooted in January 2009.

In John's case, thanks to my wife, Sheila, and sons, Brian and Desmond, daughters-in-law, Tara and Mary, granddaughter Maeve, and sisters Anna-May and Peggy, without whose help, support and encouragement I would not have been able to play a part in producing this book. Thanks also to everyone in Post 25 of IUNVA for being such great comrades and friends.

In Ralph's case, thanks to my wife, Mary, my children, Rachel, Rebecca and Ralph Jnr, my mother Nora, as well as Rorey Ann, Craig, Conor, Cian and Caiden. Thanks also to everyone in Independent Newspapers for their staunch support over all the years.

Special mention also to Joe Kearney and the staff of The Grand Hotel in Fermoy, County Cork, who provided the coffee to vitally refuel this project at regular intervals. Special thanks also to Fermoy GAA and Pitch & Putt Club for kindly agreeing to host the launch of the book.

Ralph Riegel & John O'Mahony
Fermoy & Tallow
June 2010

# CHAPTER ONE

*14 September 1961, Elisabethville, the Congo*

PAT MULLINS' EYES flickered open to a scene straight from Dante's *Inferno*. The interior of the old Ford armoured car stank of sweat, blood and acrid smoke. Pat's eyes desperately struggled to focus in the gloom of the biting cordite fog. Worse still, his head felt as if it had just been hit with a jack-hammer – he had a roaring sound in his ears and his temples felt as if they were going to explode from the inside.

As Pat's eyes slowly focused, he gazed groggily around for a clue as to what the hell had just happened. Corporal Michael 'Mick' Nolan (22) lay sprawled on the floor of the armoured car – apparently unconscious – blood slowly soaking into his uniform blouse.

Pat knew instantly that his friend was gravely injured. But what had caused the injury?

Painfully, he eased himself up off the car's cramped metal floor and looked around in a daze at the interior of the armoured vehicle for some clue as to their plight.

A chink of dull light was visible from the lower portion of the cupola, the raised armoured viewing lip in the turret where the old Vickers machine gun was angled mutely at the sky. There was something vaguely wrong about that. The Ford's chassis was made of heavy plate steel obtained from an old boiler at the Liffey Dockyard facility in Dublin. While this wasn't plate-hardened steel, it was still almost three-quarters of an inch thick on the hull front. Yet something had just torn a hole through the steel plating like it was nothing more than wet cardboard. Pat realised the armoured car had been hit. But was it by a missile or a recoilless rifle round? Was this just a potshot or had their patrol stumbled into an ambush?

Pat slowly shook his head in a desperate bid to try to clear his thoughts. He gingerly tried to rouse the injured radio operator, but he got no response. Mick was from Colbinstown in County Wicklow and was just four years older than Pat. Always full of lively talk, he now lay still and silent on the ground. His eyes were closed and his face was getting paler by the second.

Desperately Pat looked around for the armoured car's other two occupants, his commanding officer, Cmdt Pat Cahalane and the driver, Sgt Tim Carey (27). Surely they would know what had happened and what they were supposed to do next? They were nowhere to be seen.

There was only himself and Mick Nolan in the armoured car, which, Pat realised with a sudden jolt, was eerily silent. There was no familiar rumble from the old Ford V8 engine; although, craning his neck he could see no obvious damage to the dashboard plate that controlled the car's ignition, lights and steering. The driver's armoured visor plate was still locked in the 'up' position.

Looking at the driver and commander's positions, Pat saw further signs of combat. There was a pool of slowly congealing blood by the driver's seat from where Sgt Carey had, just two hours earlier, steered the modified Ford out of the Irish UN Battalion's base at Prince Leopold Farm on the outskirts of Elisabethville.

Pat remembered that they were supposed to be helping check on the Irish troops guarding the Radio College building – nothing more than a routine resupply patrol they had been told. So what had gone wrong? The heavy fighting was supposed to have been over when UN units, comprising Irish, Indian and Swedish troops, had moved to seize Katangan positions around Elisabethville over the course of the previous day. This was supposed to be nothing more than a resupply and 'fly the flag' operation. They were to check on the position of the Irish detachment, then drive to 'The Factory' where another Irish unit was based and, if everything was OK, head back to base.

Pat knew the fighting the previous day had been fierce because the rifle and machine gun fire coming from the city centre had echoed for more than thirty-six hours around the Irish base. There had even been fighting several hours before their patrol had been sent out, but everyone presumed this was merely part of the mopping up operations. A few Katangan gendarmes – the paramilitary force, which supported the secession of Moise Tshombe and his government from the rest of the Congo – had taken potshots at the Irish base, but there had been no attempt to mount a serious assault on the fortified UN position. Everyone assumed that this was merely the precursor to a phased withdrawal by the secessionist forces in the face of the UN mission.

UN troops had successfully taken the Elisabethville Post Office and the Radio Katanga building the previous day. There had been rumours of heavy losses by the Katangan gendarmes when the Indian troops stormed both and there had also been gossip about the nature of Katangan losses at Radio Katanga. But it was all just rumour. The Irish operations had gone relatively smoothly and the only loss had been Trooper (Tpr) Edward Gaffney who was killed when the Bedford truck he was driving got caught in crossfire. There had also been a lot of gossip about heavy fighting involving Irish troops in the north of Katanga near Jadotville. But as far as Pat knew the battle had gone well for the UN.

The truth was that no one seemed to know precisely what

was happening, which made the plight he now found himself in all the more alarming. Were the Katangans and their mercenaries now mounting a counter-offensive? Had the UN forces found themselves caught in a Katangan trap? If so, where the hell was the rest of the Irish patrol?

All Pat could remember was standing in the gunner's position inside the cupola and suddenly, without warning, everything went black just as they drew level with the Radio College building. He vaguely recalled a loud bang and then everything dissolved into blackness.

Pat tried to clear his throat to call for help, but his mouth seemed burned by the smoke that still hung inside the armoured car like a choking mist. His mouth felt coated with the toxic stuff. Mercifully, darkness had now fallen and the oppressive, sticky heat of the Congo day had begun to ease into the welcome cool of night. But it was still gallingly hot inside the armoured car and sweat was pouring off his forehead. As Pat's head began to clear he frantically wondered what to do next. His eyes fell on the radio and he wondered whether it had been knocked out by the shell impact.

Suddenly, a shout came from somewhere outside the car. It ran like an electric current through Pat's mind, jolting everything back into focus. There was someone else here. He couldn't make out what was being shouted, but it seemed as if the shouts were intended for the occupants of the armoured car. Pat shook his head, trying to clear his thoughts and his eardrums. Who was shouting? It didn't sound like any member of his platoon – he couldn't understand what was being shouted but he could make out that the voice was accented.

It was an ambush, he thought. Our patrol drove right into a trap. There was no other alternative. But who was outside now and what did they want? He raised his head and, glancing through the driver's slits, realised it was pitch black outside. What the hell had happened to all the other lads?

Pat realised that he had to get Mick to a medic before he lost any more blood. Yet, he worried that other members of the patrol might be pinned down nearby and need the fire support of the armoured car. There were two armoured cars, a jeep and a bus full of troops in the patrol that had departed the Irish base. He had left the Irish UN operations camp about two hours earlier in the second, open-topped armoured car but, as part of a patrol re-arrangement, had been transferred to the forward armoured car to man the Vickers machine gun in its enclosed turret. They had left base around 9.30 p.m. but what time was it now – and how long had he been unconscious?

The old Vickers, dating back to the First World War, was the Irish patrol's main defensive weapon. Without the old machine gun the lads only had the Browning machine gun in the open-topped armoured car to the rear of the patrol and a few rounds for the single recoilless anti-tank rifle in the jeep. But the recoilless rifle rounds weren't much use on their own in an ambush scenario – anyone trying to use them in the open would probably be cut to pieces, particularly given the rumours that the mercenaries now leading the Katangan gendarmes had brought with them heavy weaponry and the skills to use it.

The old Vickers was a weapon to fear, but it was heavy and its water-filled cooling jacket was vulnerable to damage. Some idiot had forgotten to install a trap inside the armoured car for the hot cartridges ejected from the breech after firing – a factor which meant Pat and the other crewmen had to dodge hot shell casings. They also had to be wary of stepping on the steel plate floor in case they slipped on the casings, which rolled and rattled around the hull interior.

A dull throbbing pain suddenly penetrated the fog in Pat's mind and he gingerly felt for the source. As he rubbed his chest, his hand ran over a large set of keys in the upper pocket of his jungle blouse. He must have been lying on the damn keys and they'd left a painful bruise on his chest. As he removed the keys, he saw the back of his hand and realised it was smeared with blood. Was it his blood or Mick Nolan's? Absent-mindedly Pat ran his hand over his face and traces of fresh blood were left on his hand. The blood must be coming from a head wound or his ears. But he felt okay so it mustn't be too bad.

Someone shouted again from outside the armoured car. But whether it was the armoured hull or the damage to his ears, Pat still couldn't make out precisely what was being said. He shook his head in a vain effort to get rid of the roaring noise in his ears and listen to what was happening outside. All he knew for certain was that the voice definitely wasn't Irish. His training took over and he remembered his Carl Gustav sub-machine gun. In a smooth motion Pat grabbed the Swedish gun, checked its magazine of 9mm shells and flipped off the safety. At least he was now in a position to defend himself and Mick. He had to find out exactly who was outside.

Just metres from the armoured car, a White Missionary priest, Fr Paul Verfaille, wondered what to do next. He had repeatedly shouted for the occupants of the armoured car to get out of the vehicle and follow him to the safety of the missionary house just up the road. At his side stood a local doctor, Dr Jean Defru, who was also trying to help the occupants of the armoured car. His first shouts had been from the relative safety of the roadside verge, but he wasn't sure that his voice would carry to anyone inside the armoured car.

If they were still alive the soldiers must understand that their best chance of safety lay in getting out of the armoured car and following him. But maybe they were dead or so badly injured they couldn't respond to his entreaties. The missionary stared intently at the damage to the armoured car, which he guessed must have been hit in the opening exchanges of the ambush. The shell had sliced through the car's armour leaving the hull looking pockmarked. Surely no one was alive inside the car now, he thought.

Brave as he was, Fr Verfaille was reluctant to get too close to the armoured car in case he was shot by mistake by either the UN troops or the gendarmes. He knew that the other members of the Irish UN patrol had already taken shelter in a building adjacent to the communications complex. Their vehicles now lay strewn across the roadway in front of the Radio College. But there were dozens of Katangan gendarmes now swarming around the area and he knew that he was being carefully watched. The gendarmes were acting under the orders of mercenaries who had been flown into the country by Moise Tshombe to defend his regime. The cleric also knew that, at this very moment, there were probably guns trained both on him and the armoured car.

The missionary understood that the Katangan gendarmes were now specifically acting under the orders of the mercenaries – but he wasn't quite sure if they were French, Belgian, British or South African. Whoever they were, these men knew how to use the heavy weapons that had just crippled this armoured car. Smouldering behind him was the blackened hulk of the bus that had transported the UN troopers to Radio College.

The cleric glanced carefully around him. Just down the road the second UN armoured car lay abandoned, though it did not appear to have been too badly damaged. The jeep and the bus were also still where they had braked to a halt. There was no sign of any of the UN personnel and there were no bodies lying near the vehicles. Fr Verfaille prayed that no one would die this night.

The fighting, which had been going on for almost two hours, had now been reduced to an ominous silence. Less than an hour ago it had seemed as if the very gates of hell had opened such was the violence of the ambush. It was so bad that the occupants of the mission lay huddled for shelter on the floor behind concrete walls. But slowly, the balmy calm of an early African evening was returning.

The missionary prayed silently that the soldiers would negotiate a truce and end the bloodshed. The peace of the previous decade now seemed a long-distant memory and, like his fellow missionaries, he was caught up in a hurricane of violence beyond both his control and understanding. He made up his mind to make one final effort to talk to whoever might still be alive inside the armoured car before withdrawing to safety. He edged closer to the armoured car and banged on the heavy steel door and he shouted out his identity one more time: 'I am missionary.'

'Mercenary'. Pat Mullins was sure he could make out the word that had been shouted above the din of the roaring in his ears. It was muffled and heavily accented, but surely that was what had just been shouted at him from outside the armoured car. As he glanced over at Mick Nolan, the icy ball in his stomach transformed into a red cloud of rage. Surrender was out of the question and yet there was no way he could defend all four sides of the armoured car while it was stranded almost in the middle of the road. If it stayed motionless the old Ford was a sitting duck for any anti-armour weapons the Katangans possessed.

Besides, if he surrendered, what would happen to Mick? No one knew what the Katangans' policy was towards wounded soldiers and Pat didn't want to find out. Fresh in his mind was the realisation that the Katangans had themselves suffered heavy losses in the UN operations the previous day. They obviously weren't going to take too kindly to the UN soldiers they held responsible for those losses.

Pat decided to adopt the cavalry squadron adage that movement was the best strategy. He had to get the old Ford started up and moving again. He realised that he first had to get the gendarmes and mercenaries back from the car, then start the engine and try to limp back to base where Mick could get medical treatment. With his mind made up, Pat eased his aching body into a standing position to put his plan into action.

The White Father stood and listened intently for any indication that someone was still alive inside the car. He had shouted 'missionary' as loudly and as clearly as he could but there had been no response. The silence of the evening was broken only by the distant 'crack' of small arms fire. He knew that his English wasn't the best but surely it could be easily understood?

Suddenly, the cleric heard the distinct 'clink' of metal against metal from within the armoured car. While he was a man of the cloth, he had been in Africa long enough to know what the cocking of a gun sounded like. Without thinking, he stepped back to see what would happen. A single, short burst rang out and the missionary and doctor turned and ran for their lives. He had done all he could, Fr Verfaille thought, as he ran for his life to the safety of the church building. Whoever was in the armoured car, they were now on their own.

Pat fired a single warning burst into the air, desperate not to hurt anyone but to get everyone back from the blind side of the armoured car and buy himself a few precious minutes. He didn't wait to see what happened and painfully swung himself into the driver's seat to get the old Ford fired up and moving. He had trained as a driver back in the cavalry squadron in Fermoy, County Cork, but had shipped out to the Congo with the 35th Battalion before he had fully completed his training. His official rank was gunner-driver rather than specialist driver, but he knew the old Ford as well as most men and prayed that the legendary reliability of the V8 engine wouldn't let him down.

Pat pressed the starter – nothing happened. In desperation he tried again, and this time the V8 turned over but didn't catch. He tried again and relief flooded over him when the engine bellowed into life as its ignition caught. There was nothing like the deep roar of the V8 rumbling into life he thought, as he eased the armoured car forward, careful not to let it stall. It took some time to get used to handling this 4.5 tonne chassis, but the Ford's greatest strength was its brute of an engine.

From the safety of the church building, the cleric stole a careful glance back to the road and saw the old armoured car slowly rumbling away. He wasn't sorry to see it go. Maybe the Katangan forces would chase the car and leave him and his fellow missionaries in peace to tend the wounded. He noted the car slowly gaining speed as it jolted down the road towards the junction north-west of the Radio College where Avenue Wangermee met Avenue Drogmans. But, as he turned away, the missionary failed to realise the full significance of the armoured car awkwardly swinging to the left onto Avenue Drogmans instead of to the right. Had he known, the cleric would have prayed again for those inside the car. A right-hand turn onto Avenue Drogmans would have brought the car back to Rue de Liege and Avenue du Luxembourg, both of which were less than one kilometre from Prince Leopold Farm where the Irish UN detachment had established their base. The right-hand turn meant safety and medical treatment. A left-hand turn onto Avenue Drogmans – after a second swing to the left near the River Lubumbashi – brought the car directly away from the Irish battalion base and instead towards the headquarters of the local Katangan gendarmes less than four kilometres away. As the armoured car rumbled on, fate sealed the death warrants of both Pat Mullins and Mick Nolan.

# CHAPTER TWO

FEW THINGS MAKE military life appear easy – but farming on Ireland's Cork-Limerick border in the late 1950s is undoubtedly one. For the average farm labourer it was a never-ending litany of backbreaking, poorly paid, thankless and generally miserable work. Those that had jobs considered themselves lucky to be employed such was the grim economic situation – and those that complained about wages or work conditions were bluntly told they could easily be replaced.

After twenty-five years working as a general farm labourer, most men were left either inured to the hardship or physically broken from it all. Others sought escape from the drudgery of working someone else's land – with little or no chance of securing their own holding – in the bottle.

For thousands of men, after a few years working as a farm labourer, joining the army or emigrating to Britain, Australia or the United States came as a blessed release. When Seán Lemass finally secured the position of Taoiseach in June 1959, emigration from Ireland had reached levels never experienced since 'the Black 1880s'. Over the course of a decade, more than 400,000 Irish people emigrated and, between 1956 and 1961, net emigration had peaked at 42,401. The most damning indictment of just how brutal rural life could be came from the fact that, of the men who emigrated from Ireland in the 1950s, an astonishing seventy per cent described themselves as small farmers and agricultural labourers.

The economy's stagnation under Éamon de Valera had reached the point where analysts realised that without the 'safety valve' of emigration, Ireland would face social turmoil. By 1956, Ireland's balance of payments deficit had reached IR£35.6 million – an astonishing increase of almost 650 per cent in the space of just three years. Should Ireland face a national crisis, there was little fiscal guarantee it could be coped with. In Irish cities like Dublin, Cork and Limerick, poverty was a grinding, soul-destroying fact of everyday existence. In Limerick, the appalling hardship spawned childhood memories that led Frank McCourt to write his 1990s international bestseller *Angela's Ashes*.

In June 1959, Pat Mullins (16) was thinning turnips on a farm not far from his home at Boher in Kilbehenny on the border between Cork and Limerick. On a bright summer morning the view from the pastures he worked was nothing short of breathtaking. To the north the Galtee Mountains rose to dominate the landscape with scudding clouds casting varying hues on its myriad crags and valleys. Above it all loomed Galtymore with its deceptively flat-topped summit. From up there you could gaze all over Cork, Limerick and Tipperary. On a clear day you could even see Waterford in the distance.

To the south the countryside opened up into a rich panorama of farms, fields and forests. Some of the best land in Ireland was here and it had been fought over by Celtic tribes and Anglo-Norman families for more than 2,000 years. If you stared hard from Boher, you could make out the spires of Mitchelstown's churches and, in the distance, the Kilworth Mountains that shielded Fermoy from view. Pat knew that in those distant mountains was Flagstaff Hill, which marked the biggest military firing range in the south. It was a realm of soldiers in a landscape dominated by farming.

To the east, the River Tar and River Suir carved their way

through forests and farms, overlooked by Slievenamon Mountain, so beloved of all in Tipperary. In the west, the Galtees gradually gave way to the Ballyhoura Mountains, which formed a northern bulwark for the majestic River Blackwater. The river traced its source all the way back to Kerry and nothing quite underscored the value of the local land like the Blackwater.

Pat knew that the old Anglo-Irish aristocracy had nicknamed the Blackwater 'the Irish Rhine' and had built their sumptuous grand houses along its banks in the eighteenth and nineteenth centuries, usually alongside the crumbling remains of old Norman and English castles. Each great house was the centrepiece of the famed Anglo-Norman estates that often encompassed tens of thousands of acres of prime farmland. The great landowning families in that area were the Kingstons, the Mountcashels, the Moores, the Hydes and the Barrymores.

Not that Pat knew much about the grand houses. The only great house near Boher – Mitchelstown Castle – had been burned down during the Civil War in the 1920s and not even its scorched stones were still in place. They had been sold to the Cistercian monks for the construction of Mount Melleray Abbey in west Waterford and transported over a period lasting from 1925 to 1931. Pat, like everyone else in north Cork, spent his life in the fields rather than the marbled hallways of the great houses.

Bright as this June morning was, it was still cold in the shade, although early summer was beginning to chase the chill of winter from the ground. Pat's back was aching from hours spent on his hands and knees thinning the turnips. Of all the difficult jobs in farming, this was one of the worst. It was an annual task that Pat hated with a passion. By 6 p.m., when it was time to go home, Pat's back and knees would be in spasm from hours spent crouched over. And all for the princely sum of £2 per week. It was hardly enough to maintain Pat, let alone a girlfriend or, God help us, a wife and children. Pat painfully straightened and sighed, 'there has to be an easier way to make a living'. One of the other workers, thinning a line of turnips just yards away, overheard the young man and smiled to himself. Young lads always dreamed of better wages, shorter hours, pretty girlfriends and even being able to afford a car. And then they learned that in Ireland this was not the way things were.

In the Ireland of 1960, the majority of people were happy just to have a job and an income. Ireland, along with Portugal, was the poorest country in Europe and farming was the poorest sector of the economy. With an average of six workers chasing each job, it was an employers' market – hours were long and wages low. If you didn't like it, well, there was always someone else willing to do the work. Without a job, little else beckoned except the boat to Britain, the liner to the United States or, if you were lucky, an aeroplane to New York or Boston.

Pat's £2 per week wage was the standard national payment for a farm labourer. It came with the promise of three meals a day to be supplied by the farmer and these varied in quality depending on the individual landowner involved. In this regard Pat was very lucky – he worked for neighbours, so the food was excellent and he was treated every bit as well as if he was a member of the family. But not all farm labourers were so fortunate.

Pat's week still involved six days of hard work and the hours were long, usually from 7.30 a.m. to 6 p.m. Workers were also asked to work on Sundays at harvest time, particularly if the farmer himself was not available for milking cows or feeding livestock. It was tough for labourers – but it was also tough for the farmers who were struggling with artificially low prices as a result of being tied to Britain's cheap food policy for exports, as well as high input costs due to a lack of domestic competition. This meant that Irish farmers were forced to accept low prices for their produce which was being exported to Britain, Ireland's biggest export market. Britain could dictate terms and prices because of our over-reliance on them as a customer. On top of this prices at home for consumer goods like clothes and footwear were artificially high due to the lack of true competition and import tariffs.

Tractors were slowly becoming commonplace, but the majority of farm tasks still had to be done by hand – including milking and ploughing. A fifteen cow herd took a single man two and a half hours to milk by hand in the morning – the labourer then faced the same task each evening. Most farmers, particularly the small to medium operators, still took their milk to the local creamery by horse and cart.

To make matters worse, Pat, like all other Irish labourers, was entirely responsible for his own work clothing and equipment. The disastrous economic policies pursued throughout the 1950s by Éamon de Valera's government had driven consumer prices sky-high in Ireland. At this time, a basic pair of Wellington boots cost the princely sum of £1 and 10 shillings – almost two-thirds of an entire week's wages. In 2010, it would be the equivalent of asking a farmer to pay €250 for a single pair of wellies. In 1960, a good quality pair of Wellingtons with heavy soles could cost as much as £2, yet labourers like Pat would be lucky to make a single pair last for more than three months.

It was the same with work clothes. Clothing was carefully stitched and mended to make it last as long as possible – but Pat, when he couldn't use hand-me-downs from his older brothers Dinny and Tom, had no option but to purchase his own work clothes. Most people considered themselves fortunate to have one pair of good shoes and one suit, which had to last for years and were reserved for special family events, Mass on Sunday and the odd dance.

To make matters worse, there was no such thing as holidays or overtime. If extra work needed to be done on the farm, you just rolled your sleeves up and got on with it. The power of the church ensured that holy days inevitably meant a day off – but extra work to compensate had to be done both the day before and the day after. In that respect, Sunday came as a treasured relief. Afternoons were almost always free to attend a local GAA match, but money had to be saved to fund these activities. If one of the lads was lucky enough to have a car, everyone was expected to chip in towards the cost of petrol. Otherwise, distant GAA matches required a good bicycle and strong leg muscles.

Living at home spared Pat some expenses, but he was still expected to make a financial contribution to the Mullins' household. That left only a modest sum each week for social spending. Even the traditional Christmas bonus – a vast payment of £5 which was made in lieu of an entire year's worth of overtime and late working – seemed to disappear on clothes, shoes and sundry expenses.

Pat was the youngest of Ned and Catherine Mullins' children. Ned farmed a medium-sized holding just over two miles from Kilbehenny village. Ned's holding at Boher was typical of the period – he milked cows, kept sheep, tilled a few fields with potatoes and turnips and even kept a few pigs for extra food and income. While his farm was decently sized for the period, its location at Boher in the foothills of the Galtees meant that its land varied in quality – there were some top-quality pastures off the Kilbehenny road, but there were also some poorer hill fields. Yet Ned was a shrewd farmer and a hard worker throughout his life, resulting in the Mullins' farm being regarded as one of the best run in the area.

Pat was born on 19 November 1942 at the height of Ireland's 'Emergency' and just as the German 6th Army was fighting its way to an icy grave at Stalingrad. The Second World War meant shortages of most things and even after the war ended in 1945, Ireland's consumer industry was bleak to say the least. Most families considered themselves well to do if they had enough food for the table and if one family member was employed. Emigration was part and parcel of Irish life.

Despite this it was a happy childhood for Pat who, like other youngsters, revelled in the outdoors and the myriad local sports clubs. When he was old enough Pat attended Kilbehenny National School, just over two miles walk from his Boher home. His older brothers, Tom and Denis (Dinny), were already farming, while his sisters, Mary, Peggy and Nelly helped around the house until they got jobs, married and moved away.

Dinny focused on helping his father work the family farm, while Tom pioneered the route that Pat would soon follow – working for other farmers in the general Kilbehenny area. Tractors were almost unheard of on most small to medium Irish farms, so all the Mullins boys knew how to work with horses – a handy skill when it came to getting work from outside farmers.

Life in the 1950s in Boher was anything but easy. There was no running water and supplies had to be drawn each day from a well some distance from the farmhouse. Similarly, there was no electricity. While the ESB had connected power to Kilbehenny village by the 1950s, Boher – some two miles away – did not get its supply until the early 1960s. Telephones, like televisions, were simply unheard of in most country homes. Even householders who could afford a telephone and were close enough to an existing Post & Telegraph (P&T) line to apply for one had to wait for the privilege. Sometimes the wait for a connection lasted as much as four years.

After completing his national school studies, there was little question of Pat attending secondary school. He could have cycled the six miles to Mitchelstown to attend the Christian Brothers secondary school but, such was the economic climate of the time, an immediate job and income appeared far preferable to both him and the Mullins family. A secondary school education meant money for books, pencils and clothes – and that was something that was in short supply in Ireland in the late 1950s.

When his son was old enough to work, Ned Mullins made a few enquiries at the creamery and mart, at local cattle fairs and amongst his neighbours. One local farmer, Jack O'Brien, had a slot open for a general labourer and, such was the Mullins' reputation for hard work and diligence, Pat was offered the job the minute he expressed an interest in it. Jack O'Brien was a good, kindly employer and he looked after Pat as if he was his own son. The O'Briens were well known in Kilbehenny because Jack's brother Tim ran the local hostelry, The Three Counties Bar.

Pat's job was officially that of 'yardman'. The ploughman – or more senior farm labourer – was Tom Kiely. Pat settled in quickly and was blessed that he had learned so many farming skills from Ned, Dinny and Tom. But it was hard work, because farming in Ireland had yet to become mechanised. Milking was done by hand and ploughing was a backbreaking task that usually started in November and continued until late February. If the weather was good, the ploughman was skilled, the horses willing and everything went well, a man could plough up to one acre a day. 'But that would be a very good day,' Dinny recalled.

For two years Pat worked and saved. But at times it was like trying to swim up the River Blackwater against the current in the middle of a winter flood. It just couldn't be done. No matter how hard he tried to save, there always seemed to be a bill on the horizon that had to be paid. Pat realised that there was very little money to be made from farming – and yet there was very little else available.

Jobs in Mitchelstown Co-op did offer better pay, but were as scarce as hen's teeth, such was the demand for positions. A German pencil firm, Faber-Castell, had opened in Fermoy, but any extra money he would make would be wiped out by the cost of having to either travel to Fermoy on a daily basis or secure lodgings in the town.

Tom had worked for several years for farmers around Kilbehenny and decided he'd had enough. 'If I couldn't get a job in the creamery, I decided I'd head off to England,' he recalled. But one of the farmers that he'd given loyal service to had connections with the creamery board and knew Tom was a dedicated and hard worker. He intervened to ensure Tom got a job with the creamery.

Life was tough for everyone in pre-1960s Ireland. Pat's sister, Mary, recalled that even attending dances was unheard of. 'It just wasn't done. We didn't have a car in the 1950s let alone a tractor. We walked the two miles to school in Kilbehenny and if it was raining or frosty, our father would take the horse and cart and maybe meet us to bring us home. Sometimes we would catch a spin with him on the horse and cart to school in the morning if he was heading to the creamery.'

Pat, as the youngest in the family, grew up seeing at first hand the limited social and economic options available to his siblings. 'We had one radio and no one outside Dublin had a television set. We had an old wireless that had the usual wet cell and dry cell batteries. Our father would listen to the news and a match on a Sunday. Once in a while, we could listen to a short music programme, but when the adults came into the room, the wireless was switched off. If you were lucky, you got two weeks out of the battery before it had to be recharged.'

Mary recalled how Pat's social outlets were almost exclusively focused on sport and music. 'When you had your jobs done, like drawing water from the well and bringing in turf and timber for the fire, you could go down to the crossroads where there'd usually be someone either playing hurling or football. Sometimes there might be a game of skittles or handball going on in the village where the boys would go.

'In the summertime, a stage would be set up in Kilbehenny village and there would be traditional dancing and Irish music. We would sit on the grass outside our home at Boher if the weather was fine and hear the music playing in the distance. But if we wanted music ourselves, we had to play it in the house. Pat was a very good singer and he had learned a few Jim Reeves songs from the wireless. Sometimes you'd play the accordion or the tin whistle as an accompaniment.'

Pat's other great love – like so many boys of his generation – was the cinema. It was like a window onto an alien, forbidden world. A world of western gunfights, fearless pirates, courageous soldiers and wicked Chicago gangsters that Pat could only marvel at. The problem was that the only local cinema was in Mitchelstown and getting to go there was a rarity. Hence the local saint's day – St Fanahan's Day, which fell on 25 November – was a special treat because it meant a trip into Mitchelstown to go to pray at the local holy well dedicated to the long-dead holy man. But it also meant Pat and his friends could check out what shows were playing at the local cinema and marvel at the glitzy posters outside.

'We were a very close family and Pat, being the youngest, was looked out for by everyone else. But he wasn't spoiled – he was expected to work as hard as the rest of us. But he somehow had a great confidence about him – and you could see that on the hurling or football field where he was a fine player,' Mary added.

By April 1960, Pat had finally had enough. He was tired of working as a farm labourer and decided it was time to consider his options. He'd seen how Tom had tired of the backbreaking grind and been fortunate enough to get a creamery job. Maybe he could follow suit. But above all else, Pat was determined not to spend another winter as a farm labourer. Pat realised he had one major alternative – the army.

It was an alternative career path that Pat shared with another young man who, that very same month, a mere thirty miles away, was struggling with the same harsh realities of Irish economic life. John O'Mahony from Tallow in west Waterford was similarly disillusioned with life as a farm labourer and, at seventeen, was also wondering if he had other options available to him. 'You had three choices at the time if you were a young lad from the country who didn't want to work as a farm labourer – you could try for a job in a factory, but they were like diamonds in a coal mine. You could emigrate to England or America, but that was seen as a last resort because, like hundreds of other lads, you might never again make it back home. Or you could join the army,' John explained.

The financial arguments in favour of a life in uniform were very persuasive indeed. Compared to a farm labourer earning just £2 a week for six days of backbreaking labour, a young man in his very first week in uniform could expect to be paid £2 19s 6d. After a six-month training period, that would rise to £3 10s. Recruits had a uniform and boots provided for them – and received three square meals each day.

But it was the social benefits that made the army seem like a godsend. Soldiers were off every weekend unless they were on special duties – and rarely worked beyond 5 p.m. unless they were on guard patrol. And the offer of promotion to corporal, sergeant or even sergeant major offered the tantalising prospect of even better pay.

'My parents weren't too keen on the idea of me joining the army,' John explained. 'It wasn't that they had anything against the military, it was just that they thought the best career for me was in farming. But I was seventeen and thought there was more to life than working from dawn to dusk and never really having any money of my own. To us, the army was a different world – going to Collins Barracks in Cork for basic training, maybe being sent to Spike Island on guard duty, or even going to Dublin or the Curragh. In those days they were almost exotic assignments.'

Pat Mullins travelled to Collins Barracks and signed on to become a soldier on 9 May 1960 with the Recruit No. 810552. The trip to Collins Barracks was Pat's first ever trip on a bus and his first ever trip to Cork city. John O'Mahony made the same journey the week before, signing up on 5 May. The two young men ended up on the same No. 6 training platoon. Given their backgrounds and ages, it was hardly surprising that they quickly became friends.

For Pat, it was a decision that took great courage. He didn't tell his father that he was going and, eventually, the recruiting staff – realising Pat's age – made contact with Ned back in Boher and asked what they wanted him to do?

'My father said: "Look, if you send him home he'll probably go across the water and join the army for John Bull. He wants to be in the army so it might as well be the Irish army." My father told them to keep Pat above in Collins Barracks if they could. That's how it happened,' Dinny explained.

But if Pat and John thought army life was going to be exotic, they were quickly disabused of the notion. The pay was good but the training regime was tough. Recruits were relentlessly drilled on parade ground procedures, marching orders, kit and uniform discipline. Both Pat and John were assigned to Block 6 at Collins Barracks' Command Training Depot. The assigned platoon sergeant was Sgt John Cusack who worked alongside Corporals Bill Sisk, Joe Hunt and John St John. They were tough but fair – with Sgt

Cusack determined to ensure his recruits, no matter their age or ability, were turned into competent soldiers.

Within a matter of days, Pat Mullins and John O'Mahony had become confidants and spent most of their social time together. 'Pat was a country lad like myself. We had both worked on farms and I suppose we had a lot in common. Pat was only seventeen but he had a quiet confidence about himself. He always seemed to be smiling and in good humour – and that's very important when you're training and the sergeants and corporals spend most of the day roaring at you for getting things wrong,' John recalled.

After a few weeks, the recruits were deemed to have learned the basics of parade ground discipline and were introduced to the weapon that they would now train on – the venerable Lee-Enfield Mk IV rifle. The Lee-Enfield – itself a development of the earlier Lee-Metford rifle – had equipped the British army in various guises throughout both the First and Second World Wars. The rifle might be more than fifty years old, but it was every bit as deadly now as it had been when British troops opened fire on German infantry in Flanders in 1914, making the German troops think they were under machine gun fire.

The army had huge stocks of the Lee-Enfield rifles – many of which dated back to the 1914–1916 era. Regular units were soon to be equipped with the Belgian-made FN assault rifle, but army recruits still learned their infantryman's craft on the old .303 calibre Lee-Enfield.

'Pat was probably the most natural soldier amongst us. He always seemed to be happy, it was impossible to faze him and he took to army life like a duck to water. But it was his quiet confidence that astonished us all. Most of us recruits were fascinated but terrified of women – remember this was Ireland of the late 1950s. But Pat was a smooth operator and, within weeks of basic training starting, he was going out with a gorgeous-looking girl called Esther from Sunday's Well. I walked out with him one evening when he was meeting her and I watched, from a distance mind you, as he met up with her. I was green with envy because she was a smashing-looking girl,' John recalled.

By October, Platoon No. 6 had finished its basic training rotation and the recruits were ready for their assignments. Not surprisingly, Pat and John were earmarked for assignment to Fitzgerald Camp in Fermoy, with the then 1st Motor Squadron. The north Cork camp was Ireland's inheritance of the vast British army base that had been built up there between 1800 and 1914. At its peak, the Fermoy-Kilworth military complex was second in size only to the Curragh Camp in Kildare. During the War of Independence the British even based Bristol and Martynside spotting aircraft at the base – earning it the nickname of 'the Aerodrome', which lasted for decades after the last British aircraft went home.

Pat and John were joined by six other recruits: Pat Crofton, Mick Casey, Jimmy Burke, John Murphy, Joe 'Josie' O'Grady and John Clifford, for an assignment that seemed more like an early Christmas present. (Josie O'Grady was an accomplished sportsman and went on to play League of Ireland football with Cork.) Pat and John knew that an assignment to Fermoy meant training either on armoured cars or motorcycles as dispatch riders – and being close enough to home to visit family and friends.

'Fermoy was our dream assignment because we were close to home and because we'd be training on some of the most serious equipment the army possessed. A BSA, Triumph or Jawa motorcycle cost a full year's wages for a working man – maybe more. And here we were being sent out to train on them – how to handle the bike at speed, how to cross a river without stalling and how to negotiate over fields and forest tracks. We had been ordered to report for training to Sgt Paddy Fraher who was a tough taskmaster but as nice a man as you could ask to serve under. We were having the time of our lives and being paid for it,' John recalled.

Pat's sister, Mary, had by now married and was living at Caherdrinna with her husband, Tom Kent, not far from Lynch Camp in Kilworth. With Pat and John on regular duties at the camp, it was inevitable that the Kent's would become a 'home from home' for both young men.

'The dispatch riders course took three months and we had both passed with flying colours by late February [1961]. It was around this time that we all began to realise that the Congo was more than likely going to be an overseas assignment for some of us. Eleven soldiers had been killed the previous November in the Niemba ambush and I think that shocked every single person in an Irish uniform as well as the entire country,' John added.

With no immediate dates for a Congo deployment, the duo got on with being young men. Pat was a handy hurler and was immediately recruited by teams that played on the camp sports field in Fermoy. He quickly graduated to the cavalry senior team and, despite having just turned eighteen in November, was tough and wiry enough to hold his own on the field of play. On occasion, both Pat and John would be asked to 'guest' on some of the interfirm teams that played GAA leagues in Mitchelstown on weekend mornings.

'We'd seen Pat play in Kilbehenny, but I don't think we realised just how good he was until we started seeing him on the army teams. He was quite young compared to the other soldiers but he was wiry, tough and had a great touch with a hurley,' his brother Tom recalled. It wasn't long before army and Fermoy sides were seeking the GAA services of the young Boherman.

The army commanders encouraged sport because it not only

kept the men fit, but also served to promote the army as a career. The young troopers spent the rest of their social time trying to meet girls at local dances, going to the cinema and listening to albums of their favourite singers, usually Elvis Presley, Jim Reeves or Johnny Cash. A few went drinking but, even with the subsidised cost of pints in the army canteen, given his wages there was a limit to how much a young trooper could spend. For Pat and John, the lure of the cinema and dance halls was vastly greater than that of the pub.

'In Fermoy, the Ormonde cinema was hugely popular. But Cork was the real attraction. That was where the real nightlife was and, I suppose, where the greatest number of girls was. Whenever we were based in the city we would go to the Gaylord dancehall or, if a good film was showing, to the Capitol, the Pavilion, the Palace or the Savoy. That's where you went if you were taking a girl out and wanted to impress her. If it was just a night out with the lads, you'd go to the cheaper places like the Assembly Rooms or the Lido in Blackpool. They were a bit more downmarket than the other cinemas and you did occasionally run the risk of getting cigarette butts flicked at the back of your head from up in the gallery. But the Assembly Rooms and the Lido always had great westerns and war movies showing which was good enough for us,' John explained.

Pat was a good singer and he became famed within his platoon for his more than capable versions of 'Red River Valley' and 'Mona Lisa', which he would sing on marches or in the army canteens. He particularly loved Jim Reeves and never needed an excuse to break into his favourite songs and ballads.

With the Congo increasingly dominating headlines in news-papers like the *Irish Independent*, *The Irish Press* and *The Cork Examiner* and seemingly omnipresent on RTÉ radio news bulletins, the feeling began to spread that another deployment to Africa was now inevitable. The only question was when would the troopers from Fitzgerald Camp be again asked to volunteer now that the 32nd and 33rd Battalions had finished their tours of duty and the 34th was about to rotate back to Ireland?

'By the end of February, we were almost finished our dispatch riders course. We were in a large storage shed one day listening to an instructor when a sergeant arrived over with a clipboard and said he was looking for volunteers for a six-month tour of duty in the Congo. Pat and I couldn't get over to him fast enough to volunteer and sign on,' John said.

Interest in the Congo had rocketed since the deployment of the first Irish battalion – the 32nd – to the UN mission in July 1960. The euphoria and excitement over Ireland's first overseas military mission had been tempered by the tragedy of the ambush at Niemba in November of that year, where nine Irish soldiers had been killed. Yet that hadn't put young soldiers off the idea of serving in the Congo – in fact, the return of veterans of the 32nd and 33rd Battalions had whetted the appetites of serving soldiers back home who were determined to make it to the Congo before the UN mission ended.

The impact made by the Congo veterans on their return to Ireland shouldn't be underestimated. Back in Fermoy, P.J. O'Leary was just eight years old and living on Barrack Hill when the first detachment of troops arrived back from Africa. He recalls being mesmerised by their tropical uniforms, suntans and nonchalant banter about the Congo and such exotic places as Stanleyville, Leopoldville, Kamina, Jadotville and Elisabethville. Overnight, the Congo veterans became local superstars.

'I think I decided then and there that I wanted to join the Defence Forces. I think every youngster in the town was absolutely fascinated by the lads who had just returned from the Congo – we had never seen tropical uniforms before and everyone wanted to hear the stories about the jungle, the Balubas and Katanga. The lads whose fathers had served in the Congo were really proud of them and stories about Africa were all we wanted to hear about in the schoolyard. I can still recall how the troopers were dropped off at Fitzgerald Camp and marched down the town, all in tropical kit and each one in perfect step, as they headed to their homes. I think the Congo changed not only the army but Ireland itself,' P.J. explained. The sight of the Congo veterans was sufficiently impressive to ensure that just over a decade later, P.J. would himself join the army and proudly serve on repeated UN missions in Lebanon.

The youngsters weren't the only ones inspired by the Congo veterans. Ultimately, almost sixty personnel volunteered at Fitzgerald Camp for overseas service – though it was expected that only twenty-five men would be required. Army commanders wanted a good cross-section of troops and they tried to weld experience with youth and various skill specialities. Because it was Ireland's first major overseas deployment, only volunteers were being accepted, and strict medical and fitness standards were being insisted upon.

'I think a lot of the younger soldiers were very gung-ho,' John recalled. 'Most of us had never even been to Dublin before let alone outside Ireland. Going to the Congo was viewed as a once-in-a-lifetime opportunity. I remember a few younger soldiers excitedly talking about going to the Congo in front of Pat. He turned and said to them: "It is all right to go out but will we come back?" I still wonder to this day whether Pat had some kind of premonition about what was going to happen. But, like me, he was determined not to miss out on what we all thought was a great adventure. Despite the lesson of Niemba, none of us thought that anything would happen to us. I suppose like all young lads we thought we were bullet-proof.'

After three months of the rigorous training and selection process, the list of twenty-five Congo-bound troopers was pinned on the

Fitzgerald Camp noticeboard. John was absolutely devastated to discover that he wasn't among them.

'Pat was chosen – and I wasn't surprised by that because he was a great soldier, a natural trooper. If anyone was going to be selected for the Congo it was Pat. But I thought I would surely make the cut too. I couldn't understand how I wasn't chosen and, to be honest, it put me on a bit of a downer for a few weeks,' John added.

It was a painfully awkward situation for Pat Mullins. On the one hand he was thrilled at the prospect of a Congo adventure and intensely proud that he had been selected from the gruelling selection process, but on the other hand he was devastated for his friend and the disappointment he felt. Then, one day, their prayers were answered when a revised selection list was pinned on the camp noticeboard.

'I had been on guard duty for the night and had gone to a barrack room in a quiet part of the camp to try and get some sleep,' John explained. 'The next thing, Pat Mullins tore into the room and shook me awake. "John, you're going to the Congo – you're going to the Congo."'

Waking with a start, John stared crossly at his friend and said: 'What the hell is wrong with you, Pat? You know I'm not going.'

But Pat Mullins excitedly explained how six of the selected soldiers had just failed the medical assessment for the Congo – and six new names, including that of John O'Mahony, had been added to the Congo detachment list to join the now-forming 35th Irish Battalion.

The two friends tore out of the barrack room and ran to the noticeboard, where John danced an impromptu jig of delight when he saw his name on the deployment list. Just like two of the young characters in a Pavilion western or war movie, Pat and John were proudly heading off together in pursuit of adventure.

# CHAPTER THREE

NOTHING ECHOES AROUND the cavernous interior of a United States Air Force (USAF) Douglas C-124 Globemaster II transport quite like the sound of young soldiers engaged in an energetic bout of vomiting. The veteran USAF loadmaster smiled to himself at the obvious distress of the young Irish troopers, who grimly sat in the paratrooper-style webbing seats, the green hue of their faces almost perfectly matching their green wool uniforms. The plane carried almost 100 soldiers – virtually all of whom sat with their backs to the fuselage sides, grimly staring across the floor at each other.

A few stared out the window at the landscape beneath them, but that only added to the nausea when the turbulence suddenly hit and the plane plummeted up to 100 feet before regaining altitude. It was a hard lesson, the American sergeant thought to himself, but one that had to be learned by every infantryman who thought that a life in the air force was easy.

The seats, which resembled canvas buckets, were quickly dubbed 'hard arses' by the soldiers, who found that, after eight or ten hours strapped into one, they lost all feeling below their waists. One soldier – distressed by constant vomiting and the turbulence – ignored the directions from the USAF loadmaster, unstrapped himself and insisted on walking up and down the central aisle of the plane. One sergeant acidly queried whether the young man 'was going to fucking walk all the way to Africa?' For others, the experience was clouded by a fog of ignorance and innocence. One trooper was shocked to realise that the Belgian Congo was actually in Africa and not in Europe.

The Globemaster rumbled on southwards over the African continent, the brown sprawl of the Sahara Desert spread out below it like a vast mosaic. The giant Douglas military transport was a good aircraft with an enviable safety record. Her four giant Pratt & Whitney Wasp Major piston engines could drive the aircraft, and up to 200 troops, at almost 250 miles per hour over a range of 4,000 miles. Since immediately after the Second World War, the Globemaster had been the US military's transport aircraft of choice.

The California-built plane could carry light tanks, armoured cars, artillery and even disassembled aircraft. But, unlike her newer jet-powered rivals, she had a substantially lower maximum altitude. This meant that she had to cruise through turbulence rather than climb over it like the newer jet counterparts from Douglas, Boeing and Lockheed. But, in terms of reliability and rugged build, the Globemaster still dominated the skies.

The aircraft occasionally shuddered and dropped like a stone as it hit a pocket of turbulence caused by the hot air currents sweeping up from the desert below. This added to the discomfort of the soldiers, several of whom were now gripping Rosary beads as sweat poured from their foreheads. Their wool uniforms didn't help matters either. A few soldiers would pause between bouts of vomiting to mouth silent prayers for deliverance. No one had said it would be like this back in Dublin or Cork – and they weren't even in the Congo yet. Flying had seemed such a great adventure back at Baldonnel Air Base that no one had anticipated this kind of agony.

The USAF sergeant would have smiled even more broadly had he realised that, but for a handful of soldiers, this was the first time the Irish troops in front of him had ever been on an aeroplane. Almost none of them had left Ireland before – and the few who could claim to be global travellers had merely taken the ferry across the Irish Sea to visit relatives in the UK. What was a routine delivery mission to the Congo for the veteran USAF personnel was akin to a journey on the *Starship Enterprise* for the inexperienced Irish troops.

A few hardy souls who managed to ignore the sound of sickness and pervading smell of vomit around them suddenly realised that they were hungry. They tentatively began to inspect the standard US army ration packs that had been handed to them back at the giant USAF base in Tripoli before the final leg of their journey to the Congo.

'It was the closest thing to *Babes in the Wood* that I have ever seen,' John O'Mahony recalled. 'One soldier turned to Cmdt Pat Quinlan and pointed out that there was meat in the sandwiches and, as this was a Friday, should they be allowed to eat them given the Catholic Church regulations? Cmdt Quinlan turned to him and smiled: "You're in the field now, lad, and you eat whatever you like." For most of us, it was our first experience of such staples of US military life as Hershey chocolate, rye bread and doughnuts.

'I struck out because my sandwich had this kind of sticky purple jam in it. I'd never seen anything like it before let alone tasted it and thought it was a strange kind of blackcurrant. I asked the American sergeant what it was and he grinned at me and said it was beetroot jelly. I was so hungry I ate it up without question but, in the next bout of turbulence, I threw it all back up again. That was June 1961 and I've never eaten beetroot jam since then,' John smiled.

THE JOURNEY FOR the soldiers began back in February when those who volunteered for the Congo had been selected and confirmed following medical assessments. All soldiers then underwent a special four-month training rota – largely based on the lessons that were slowly being digested from the Niemba tragedy. Niemba taught the tragic lesson that indigenous populations who might initially appear friendly could turn hostile in a matter of seconds. In future, all Irish patrols would exercise extreme caution when dealing with roadblocks. Central to the new training was how to deal with roadblocks – and, crucially, how to defend a convoy while a roadblock was being removed.

Soldiers were shown how to properly approach a roadside obstacle – with half the patrol adopting defensive positions and half working to clear the roadblock. Soldiers were also drilled in policing techniques, crowd control skills and protecting and reassuring refugees. One of the ironies of the Irish training regime was the recognition that Irish troops would most likely have to protect Baluba refugees – despite the fact it was Balubas who were responsible for the fatal Niemba ambush.

In early June, a deployment date was confirmed. For Pat, John and the other soldiers of the Southern Command, it meant going to Collins Barracks for a special march-past parade and blessing. They were then transported to the Curragh – with a brief stop back in Fermoy for some final farewells. Having spent a night in Connolly Barracks at the Curragh, the troops were ordered into full dress uniform and transported to McKee Barracks for a second formal march-past parade and blessing on 19 June. It was a major occasion for the young troopers as the dress parade was formally reviewed by Taoiseach Seán Lemass, Foreign Affairs/External Affairs Minister Frank Aiken and Defence Minister Kevin Boland.

Pat, who knew he would spend his nineteenth birthday in Africa, had told his family and friends to find their way to any house in Kilbehenny village that had a radio, as the McKee Barracks parade was recorded by RTÉ to be broadcast as a key part of that night's main Radio Éireann news bulletin. The soldiers were thrilled to see cine-cameras at McKee Barracks – and realised that newsreel footage of their parade might even make it into the interval slots at local cinemas like the Ormonde.

Advance parties of the 35th Irish Battalion – which was now bound for a six-month tour of duty in the Congo – had already flown out to Africa on 10 May. The bulk of the battalion would fly out (via Malta/Tripoli and Kano, Nigeria) between 20 June and 2 July in various 'chalks' – a term coined by paratroopers for a planeload of troops. Some of the Globemaster flights would involve the shipment of the battalion's armoured cars, Landrover jeeps and logistical equipment.

The troops in the first transports that stopped in Kano to refuel were shocked by the formality of their welcome. Nigeria – which was still a British colony at that point – had its Kano Air Base run by Royal Air Force (RAF) personnel, supplemented by British army support units. The British commander – realising that the Irish troops were undertaking their first ever UN deployment overseas – insisted on providing an honour guard for the bemused Irish soldiers as they got off the plane.

Pat, John and the others from Fitzgerald Camp now formed part of the new Armoured Car Group, which was the 35th Battalion's primary support unit. They had excitedly posed for a photograph at Fitzgerald Camp before their journey to the Curragh – and the proud smiles of the twenty-five men led by Captain Seán Hennessy reflect the fact that they regarded themselves as elite soldiers and ready for anything that Africa might throw at them.

An ordinary infantryman might be a private, but Pat and John were intensely proud of the fact they were 'Troopers' as in the old cavalry parlance. While they didn't exactly broadcast the fact, Pat and John believed they were following in the same tradition as the US cavalry troopers that had fought and won the battles for the Wild West, as well as the Irish dragoons that had played such a key role in helping Wellington defeat Napoleon. They would move fast, strike hard and protect those in their care.

The boyish romance of the mission quickly began to fade under the sheer logistics of getting to the Congo and the discomfort of the arduous flight. 'A lot of the lads swore that they would never, ever fly again after that trip. It would have been bad enough for experienced fliers but it was a horror-show for us. I think there were only a handful of people on board who didn't end up throwing up their dinners,' John recalled. 'We had to fly from Baldonnel in the USAF Globemaster II because our own Air Corps had nothing remotely capable of flying us out to Africa. We were in regulation wool uniforms and the only weapons we carried on board were the Carl Gustav sub-machine guns that we were normally issued with. The regular infantry lads used the FN assault rifle, which was a Belgian gun and had only recently been introduced into Irish service. But while it was a fine gun it was too long and awkward for us to use in the confined space inside an armoured car. That's why we had the Swedish Carl Gustav which was short, stocky and used the 9mm cartridge,' John said.

If the Congo represented a coming of age for the Irish army, the adoption of the FN assault rifle was the first effective admission that soldiers could no longer be expected to be equipped with the weapons from a previous generation. The Lee-Enfield had equipped the Irish army for forty years. First produced in its Mark II form in 1907, the Lee-Enfield was superbly accurate, legendary for its reliability and weighed a portable 3.9 kg. But the rifle was a bolt-action design where the rate of fire depended on the skill of the individual soldier.

In contrast, the FN was an assault rifle design that, like the Kalashnikov, was in the process of revolutionising infantry combat. Manufactured by Fabrique Nationale (FN) in Belgium from 1953, the weapon was properly known as the FN-FAL. It weighed half a kilo more than the Lee-Enfield but introduced a whole new era of lethality. The FN boasted a firing rate of 650 rounds per minute and had a twenty-round magazine – ten greater than that of the Lee-Enfield. It was rugged, reliable and extremely accurate – traits that ultimately resulted in it being adopted by ninety countries worldwide as their army's primary infantry weapon. The FN could also be produced in selective fire or semi-automatic forms, and it was so powerful that a heavy-barrelled model was manufactured which could take the place of a squad machine gun. The adoption of the FN meant that, for once, the Irish army was at the cutting-edge of military technology.

All of this combined to make the younger soldiers in the nascent 35th Battalion almost sick with excitement – although they maintained their calm exteriors lest they be mocked by their sergeants. Repeated delays merely added to the tension and excitement. 'The flight was delayed for a while due to weather before the pilot was finally able to take off at 11 a.m. I don't think I was ever so excited in my life and the only downside was that Pat and myself were assigned to travel out on different flights. We eventually arrived into Tripoli at 7.30 p.m. and I still cannot believe the size of the base that we landed at,' John said.

In the era of King Idris I, before the advent of Muammar al-Gaddafi, Libya was a key US ally. The major benefit of this relationship for the US was the use of a huge air base outside Tripoli that was strategically located to effectively dominate the southern Mediterranean. At the time, Wheelus Field Air Base was one of the largest air force bases anywhere in the world. Just seventeen years before, US armoured units had helped defeat Rommel's fabled Afrika Korps over these same north African sands. Since then, the US had maintained a very strong strategic presence in the region, which, given the growing military strength of the Soviet Union and their accelerated warship building programme, was now deemed vital to US national interests. Since the era of the Romans, north Africa was a location that could, in the wrong hands, threaten control of the Mediterranean.

Wheelus, originally called Mellaha Air Base, was built by the Italians in the 1930s. Having seized the facility from the Germans in 1943, the US renamed the base Wheelus Field and supplied it with massive concrete runways to handle the giant long-range nuclear bombers and strike-fighters that the USAF wielded. To further complement Wheelus' facilities, a vast gunnery range was developed at El Watia to help air crews hone their bombing and strafing skills.

At its peak in the late 1950s and early 1960s, a staggering 4,700 US personnel were stationed at Wheelus and El Watia – and, in line with US military doctrine, the base was developed to offer troopers a 'home from home' complete with ice-cream parlours, hamburger restaurants, a cinema and sports facilities. An impressed US Ambassador to Libya, John Wesley Jones, having toured Wheelus in 1959, referred to it as 'a Little America – on the sparkling shores of the Med'. In common with other major US overseas bases, from Ramstein in Germany to Diego Garcia in the Pacific, Wheelus was designed to offer homesick soldiers and airmen all the comforts and attractions of Main Street USA. But the major drawback of Wheelus was the harsh north-African summer where noontime temperatures could soar to a sizzling fifty degrees Celsius (120 degrees Fahrenheit).

If the young Irish soldiers weren't awestruck enough with US military might, their arrival at Wheelus Air Base settled matters. 'I didn't believe that military bases could be so huge,' John recalled. 'We landed and our runway was so far from the accommodation complex that we had to be taken there by a special shuttle bus. Stepping off the plane was like stepping into an oven – everyone was astounded by the heat. But when a US orderly ushered us to the canteen to get some food, we walked into a room that was beautifully air-conditioned. None of us had experienced anything like it.

'I laugh today when I remember what it was like. None of us knew what a self-service restaurant was – so we sat down and wondered what to do next. No one wanted to look foolish so we watched to see what was happening around us. The next thing we saw a US serviceman stick his hand into an ice-filled bin and grab three or four cartons of milk. He then queued at a cooking area and was served his hot dinner. Eventually, we all did the same thing.

'I remember it like it was yesterday because it was the first time in my life I had ever eaten a hamburger. We were absolutely starving so we helped ourselves to whatever was on offer, including the fantastic dessert trays of ice cream, apple pie and chocolate cake. There were bins full of ice and all kinds of soft drinks from Coca-Cola to Dr Pepper's. We knew what Coke was but no one wanted to try Dr Pepper's because we were genuinely worried that it was a drink made from pepper-spice. We were still young lads and it was like finding yourself locked in a sweet shop. It was also a bit like finding yourself in one of the Hollywood movies that we marvelled at back home. At home it was all bacon and cabbage – here it was hamburgers, French fries, milkshakes and ice-cream sundaes. We'd never even dreamed a military base would be like this.'

What shocked the Irish troops most of all was that soldiers could help themselves to food – if you felt hungry after your main course, you simply queued up and helped yourself to another. Such largesse was relatively unknown in Irish army dining halls, where soldiers fought to get decent helpings – particularly extra meat and potatoes – for their main course because they knew that it was all they would get. Return trips to the serving staff were unheard of and were likely to generate serious consequences.

'You never, ever saw food like this back in an Irish army dining hall. It wasn't that the food in Ireland was bad. Far from it. But this was the kind of food we all expected to be served in restaurants not army canteens. The food was really good and when we complimented one of the US servicemen who was sitting and eating beside us, he looked at us to see if we were serious or trying to make fun of him. When he realised we were genuinely impressed, he just said: "It ain't home cooking, Paddy, but it sure will keep you going."'

The self-service canteen underlined how much more the Irish army had in common with its British counterpart than its American host. The Irish army maintained a subtle social distinction between officers and enlisted men – a trend that dated back to the days of British rule. When one of the Irish transport planes arrived at Wheelus, the officers proceeded to sit at a table in the canteen – separate from their men – and patiently waited to be served. After a while, a US serviceman noticed what was going on and walked up to the senior officer and said: 'Bud, everybody queues for their food here – there ain't no table service at Wheelus.' Privately, the ordinary Irish soldiers were delighted, although they took care not to show any outward sign of enjoyment at their officers' loss of face.

Wheelus was an absolute revelation for the soldiers: it resembled a hotel more than a barracks. In the accommodation blocks, soldiers were ushered to proper barrack beds in blissfully air-conditioned rooms. For twelve hours, they were offered a reprieve from the oppressive cargo hold of the aircraft and the scorching heat of the Tripoli tarmac. Yet most of the Irish troops – including John O'Mahony and Pat Mullins – were too excited to sleep and recounted a journey that had already exceeded their wildest dreams.

The Irish also proved a huge attraction for the US servicemen, most of whom were only too willing to boast about their Irish roots. Several US personnel kindly offered to show the Irish troops around, while others, meeting up with Irish troops heading home on leave several months later, generously threw parties in their honour. Such extravagance didn't last long as one Irish soldier somewhat spoiled their welcome by trying to steal cowboy boots from the room of one Texan soldier. The young Irishman was absolutely fascinated by the Texan's boots – which looked like they had come straight from a Hollywood western – and waited until the American had fallen asleep after a drink-fuelled party before trying to secure a prized memento.

However, for John O'Mahony, Pat Mullins and the outward-bound troops, the stopover on the way to the Congo was all too short. Just twelve hours after they arrived at Wheelus, the Irish troops re-boarded the Globemaster II for the final – and most daunting – leg of their marathon journey to the Congo. But not before they enjoyed a mammoth breakfast and each received lunch ration packs from US servicemen.

Now, the troops would get a taste of just how truly vast the Dark Continent was. The plane took the soldiers across the Sahara Desert before landing to refuel at Kano in Nigeria. Modern transport planes might make the trip in a single hop from Baldonnel, but the venerable Douglas had thirsty engines and limited fuel capacity, necessitating numerous stops on long-haul delivery flights. In Nigeria, the plane would only be on the ground for a matter of hours before taking off again for the Congo, so the weary soldiers were told to stay by the aeroplane – a fact made all the more difficult by the searing heat and all-pervasive stink of kerosene fumes, which tested even the most hardened stomachs.

Having refuelled, the Globemaster lumbered back into the air for the final leg of the trip into Leopoldville in the Congo. The journey took them into the continent's interior. As darkness fell, the characteristic flames from the exhaust of the giant Pratt & Whitney engines were all the more pronounced. One Irish trooper – having fallen asleep as the plane took off from Kano – awoke and suddenly reeled back in horror as he noticed the flames dancing outside the window. He shouted in panic to the USAF loadmaster, who immediately approached the trooper to see what was wrong. 'The engine is on fire – there's flames coming from the engine,' the panicked Irish soldier pointed out. The bemused crewman stared for a second out the window, turned back to the Irish soldier and smiled calmly: 'Buddy, it's when you don't see the flames that you better start worrying.'

Finally, they reached Leopoldville – the city formerly known as Kinshasa, which the Belgians had insisted on renaming in honour of Leopold II, whose colonial dreams had dragged the small European country into African affairs. Leopoldville was the administrative capital of the Congo and the seat of the central government now trying to hold the sprawling country together. The city was framed by the vast Congo River, which the Irish troops craned their necks to gaze out at through the plane windows. Darkness seemed to fall fast in Africa and the river merely appeared as a snake-like meander of blackness against the twinkle of lights from the city below.

It had taken almost four days of travel, but John and the weary Irish troops finally arrived at Leopoldville shortly after 7 p.m. It had been a long, arduous journey from Fermoy, but the soldiers were grateful just to be back on *terra firma*. One Irish officer – perhaps better acquainted with the parade ground than field assignments – immediately ordered one of his NCOs to do a head count on the plane. The sergeant snapped to the task and began counting the soldiers who were now eager to get out of the vast cargo plane. But an amused US pilot – stretching his legs nearby – wondered aloud how even the Irish could possibly have managed to lose any soldiers while the plane was in mid-air.

A UN liaison officer greeted the 35th Battalion elements at the airport and the troops – after collecting their kit – were transferred by waiting lorry to a special transit base where they were issued their tropical kit and briefed about their six-month mission. John, Pat and the other members of the Armoured Car Group also learned precisely where in the Congo they were about to be stationed. Their great adventure had begun.

# CHAPTER FOUR

THE VAST AFRICAN country in which the young Irish soldiers landed that steamy day in June 1961 resembled a giant powder keg with multiple lit fuses.

Just one year earlier, the enormous country – seventy-five times the size of Belgium, its colonial overlord – had celebrated its independence with a ceremony that echoed with the tragedies of both the past and future. Belgian and Congolese alike gathered in the Palais de la Nation in Leopoldville in stifling heat on 30 June 1960 to usher in a bright, independent future; instead the ceremony provided the spark that would doom the fledgling Democratic Republic of the Congo to years of bloodshed.

The Congo had been Africa's worst run and most brutal colonial outpost for decades and the seeds of impending tragedy had been sown well over 100 years before. The miracle was that, sixteen years after the Second World War, the Congo had still not exploded in an orgy of violence.

In 1960–61, Irish troops – alongside soldiers from sixteen other United Nations member states – were pouring into a country bigger than western Europe to ensure that a humanitarian tragedy did not occur. Most crucially of all, they were trying to ensure that Congolese independence did not lead to a fragmentation of the vast country and jeopardise other former colonies in the region.

Reforms did occur in the Congo, but at a pitifully slow pace. To many, including veteran French and British colonial officials, the

Congo's vast potential wealth stood in tragic contrast to the fate of its people.

The Congo started out as a late-nineteenth-century private enterprise controlled by Belgium's King Leopold II, who was enthralled by the reports of the famed Welsh-American explorer David Stanley. Stanley – who successfully found the missing missionary David Livingstone – became an ardent exponent of colonial expansion in the Congo and raved about its vast natural resources.

But unlike Livingstone, who was beloved of the African tribes for his gentility, Stanley was a harsh man who never shied away from brutal punishments and punitive expeditions if he believed tribes were thwarting his plans. Stanley eventually became known to tribes in the Congo basin as 'Bula Matari', a Kicongo phrase meaning 'breaker of rocks'. It was not a term of endearment for Stanley who, by the time he had finished his Congolese 'explorations', had persuaded more than 350 tribal chiefs, none of whom could write or speak English or French, to sign away sovereignty over their lands.

Britain and France – leery of each other over existing colonial developments – effectively declined a Congo entanglement amid concerns it could spark a fresh war in Europe in a century where numerous wars had already been fought. Germany, then forging itself into a Prussian-led empire, was directed by Otto von Bismarck's foreign policy, which shunned colonial baubles as a distraction from the strategic European theatre.

King Leopold, however, became a staunch supporter of Stanley and the development of the Congo. The Belgian king's dreams were answered when his Congo Development Company was given international sanction over the vast territory. The decision came at the Berlin Conference in 1884 when von Bismarck secured

Leopold as an ally by backing his Congo plans – a measure he happily took to ensure the French did not add another huge colony to their overseas empire.

All 2.34 million square kilometres of the Congo fell under King Leopold's personal control – not that of the Belgian state. It was a situation unique in the annals of colonial history and made Leopold II, at least on paper, the greatest landowner on the planet. The Congo initially struggled to make any profit for its new Brussels-based master, but thanks to the world's discovery of the automobile, which depended on rubber tyres, the Congo suddenly became a goldmine for Leopold. Wild rubber was one of the Congo's greatest natural resources and in the decades before the true extent of the country's mineral wealth was realised, this raw material transformed the sprawling African colony from a financial liability into a profitable asset.

Having initially failed to harvest the financial rewards he had expected from the Congo, King Leopold and his advisers were now determined to exploit the rubber boom for all it was worth. The world's growing love affair with the automobile meant riches beyond compare for King Leopold. In 1890, the Congo exported just 100 tonnes of wild rubber – but, just a decade later, the country was shipping 6,000 tonnes to Europe to help shod the new cars rolling off the production lines in Britain, France and Germany. However, the rubber boom meant misery, torture and death for millions of Congolese who were forced to harvest the crop without pay and with impossibly high harvest quotas to meet.

Leopold was initially an ardent supporter of free trade and the civilising mission of colonialism, but he was persuaded by the new riches on offer to make a subtle and highly secret switch. Instead of fostering free trade, the Congo became a vast monopoly for Belgian-controlled firms – all of which paid profits to Leopold. Everything from rubber to ivory and minerals to timber was Leopold's export preserve, although the Belgian monarch was careful not to alienate French or British interests.

But Leopold made two crucial errors: by fostering a monopolistic culture in the Congo, Leopold inevitably risked the ire of the powerful British merchants to whom protectionism was anathema; and, by effectively fiddling the export figures for the Congo to hide the true scale of his profits, he handed a potent weapon to the missionaries and reformers who were appalled at the stories of atrocities and brutal punishments now filtering out of the vast country.

The initial reports of abuses came from missionaries including the American, William Morrison. His recounting of the savage punishment of Congo tribes followed damning claims by the Anglo-French journalist, Edmond Morel, that King Leopold was duping European merchants and, most specifically, the powerful African importers-exporters in Liverpool, London, Bristol and Manchester. Morel's revelations ensured that the missionaries' abuse claims went right up to the cabinet table in Westminster.

London was loath to alienate an ally in Belgium, but the government was sensitive both to protectionism and the voting power of Britain's Christian reformist lobby. Just forty years earlier, London had been hugely sympathetic to the Confederate cause in the US civil war, but had stayed neutral because of the overwhelming opposition of British reformists to the slave trade which the Union was fighting to abolish.

Westminster decided it had no option but to request the British consul in the Congo to investigate the reports of abuse from the missionaries. Roger Casement – who had personally known Stanley – set to work with diligence and passion. His report, submitted in December 1903, caused an international outcry and eventually resulted in Casement, an ardent Irish nationalist, being knighted.

The savage manner in which Leopold's overseers and soldiers punished the Congolese workforces unable to meet harsh rubber targets became a cause célèbre for international civil rights campaigners for decades to come. The brutality was so appalling that it shocked a world already inured to brutality, where capital punishment was accepted as a norm of civilised society. Punishments in the Congo for trivial offences were savage in the extreme. They included the preservation, by smoking, of severed African hands by Congolese soldiers for presentation to Belgian overseers to prove that punishments had been meted out and bullets had not been expended.

The Congo quickly became a byword for the evils of colonialism and the exploitation of African peoples. Stung by international criticism, Belgium eventually took formal control of its king's African possession in 1908 and launched a process of reform, though it proved painstakingly slow.

Józef Konrad Korzeniowski, better known to the world as the Anglo-Polish author Joseph Conrad, who was a first-hand witness of events in Leopold's colony, penned the book *Heart of Darkness* in 1902. The novel immortalised the horrors of both colonial brutality and exploitation, and instantly became one of the most revered books in English literature. In later years, Conrad said that what happened in the Congo in the last decade of the nineteenth century stained the conscience of all humanity. It is impossible to put an exact figure on how many Congolese died to sate Europe's rubber demands but the figure could be as high as eight million.

By the First World War, Belgium's wild rubber industry was in rapid decline as the world turned to cheaper alternatives for automobile tyres. But the Congo's vast natural resources still continued to pour north to Brussels to fund lavish buildings, palaces and gardens throughout Belgium. Congolese exports now included diamonds, copper, uranium, timber and ivory – all of which dramatically helped boost the Belgian economy.

Interest also switched south to the Congolese province of Katanga where vast mineral resources were discovered. Led by the giant Anglo-Belgian mining multi-national, Union Minière, Katanga became a magnet for European and American mining and mineral firms and vast fortunes were made. Leopold's monopolistic approach to the Congo was transformed into a corporate free trade onslaught, which targeted everything of value in the sprawling state.

The vast mineral wealth of Katanga made it one of the most profitable mining locations in the world. The preservation of these wealth streams suddenly became a cause for concern both in Brussels and in corporate boardrooms around the world. Yet, there was little official concern for Congolese natives who, the colonial authorities argued, were well served with missionary schools and the efficient white-run administration.

The advent of the post-colonial world after the Second World War – largely under American direction – meant that nationalism could no longer be ignored in sub-Saharan Africa. The problem was that whereas the British and French – albeit reluctantly – had recognised the impossibility of maintaining colonial administrations in the face of a tidal wave of nationalism, Belgium was largely ambivalent. In the 1940s, one Belgian official proposed a move to independence for the Congo over a thirty-year period. He was laughed at by colonial experts who thought a figure of eighty to one hundred years was more apt. Disastrously, the disdain shown for independence by key Belgian personnel led, in turn, to more radical rhetoric from Congolese nationalists and their leaders.

All the while, the British and French moved to put structures in place to ease the rapid transfer of their former colonies to independence. The Suez crisis had been proof-positive that the old imperial world was now dead. Britain and France had combined to try to crush Egypt over the nationalisation of the Suez canal in 1956. Yet, despite the support of Israel and dramatic military victories for the old colonial powers, the United States had forced Britain into a humiliating climbdown, and both France and Britain withdrew from Suez. Egypt's President Abdel Nassar hailed the event as a triumph and both African and Asian colonies looked on in amazement at the changing world order. Meanwhile Paris and London, still recovering from the shock of the Suez crisis, worked to ensure that Africans had experience in positions of administration before the transfer of power.

Tribal rivalries and the fact that Europe's colonial powers had often carved out African states with little or no regard for history or ethnic concerns meant that the move to independence was always going to be fraught in many countries. Yet London and Paris, despite repeated mistakes, ignorance and arrogance, at least recognised that preserving the status quo was now impossible. Belgium, on the other hand, did little or nothing to accelerate preparations for independence in the Congo. Belgian administrators – supported by powerful industrial interests – were anathema to the new breed of pro-independence politicians who were likely to emerge as the Congo's new leaders.

Africans were excluded from all senior positions of authority in the Congo, while parts of the capital, Leopoldville, were restricted to white Europeans only. The highest rank a black Congolese soldier could rise to in the army was that of sergeant – and the 25,000-man Force Publique, or Congolese army, was commanded by 1,135 Belgian officers. In the entire army there was not a single commissioned Congolese officer in 1958. In the Congolese civil service in 1955, there were just three African managers in positions of any semblance of power. Many Belgians automatically presumed that after independence the new fledgling country would simply retain its existing administrative and commercial cadre out of sheer necessity.

Writing in David O'Donoghue's excellent collection of essays, *The Far Battalions*, one Congolese clergyman, Rev. Daniel Diafwila, described King Leopold II as little more than a thief and warned that the single worst element of the Belgian administration was its blunt refusal to place Africans in any position of responsibility. 'One of the worst aspects of the colonial system was the total exclusion of African people from politics and urban administration. In 1959, the French President Charles de Gaulle, delivered a speech in Brazzaville calling for the start of the emancipation process for the African nations. The Belgian colonialists were greatly surprised by this and would not agree to hand over control of the country's riches to the people of the Congo,' he wrote.

But riots in Leopoldville badly frightened the Belgian administration in 1959. In an effort to ensure the Force Publique would maintain its discipline after independence, its commanding officer, Lt General Émile Janssens, bluntly – and insultingly – spelled out to Congolese soldiers what would happen. He simply wrote on a blackboard in a military briefing room: 'Before Independence – After Independence'. In other words, there would be no change. Badly paid, worried about their futures and furious over the lack of promotion opportunities, soldiers in some military units chose to revolt.

Brussels then looked south to Paris and saw that even the mighty French were struggling to cope with a vicious civil war in Algeria. The lesson was obvious: if Paris could not militarily contain a revolt in one of France's own departments (Algeria was not considered a colony but an actual part of France), then what hope did little Belgium have in fighting a nationalist uprising in a country bigger than western Europe?

Having dragged their feet on independence for decades, Belgium now moved with astonishing, if not reckless, speed. It was announced that the Congo would receive its independence within twelve months. On 30 June 1960, Congo celebrated its independence day and Belgium's King Baudouin attended a special ceremony at the Palais de la Nation in Kalina, a district of Leopoldville which, in colonial times, was strictly reserved for white Europeans. The final part of the ceremony saw Congo's newly elected Prime Minister, Patrice Lumumba, a well-educated trade unionist and former post office clerk, deliver a key speech.

King Baudouin – who had been on the Belgian throne for a decade – was still a relatively young man and delivered a speech prepared for him by his courtiers and advisers. In it he wished the Congo well in its independent future but, controversially, he chose to exalt Belgian achievements and particularly the legacy of King Leopold II. Baudouin chose to publicly endorse the family version of Leopold's achievements while ignoring the African opinion that he was a ruthless robber baron. 'The independence of the Congo constitutes the culmination of the work conceived by the genius of King Leopold II – undertaken by him with tenacious courage and continued with perseverance by Belgium. Do not compromise the future with hasty reforms. Do not replace the structures that Belgium hands over to you [today] until you are sure you can do better,' the king declared.

The speech may have salved Belgian consciences, but it infuriated the Congolese who regarded Leopold as the worst face of European colonial exploitation. However, most Congolese leaders realised that the Palais de la Nation ceremony was a dangerous place to debate history and politics. Congo's president, Joseph Kasavubu, swallowed his anger and delivered his mundane prepared speech. His only concession to the occasion was to omit a special thanks to King Baudouin for having agreed to attend the ceremony.

Patrice Lumumba – visibly shocked by the king's speech – had taken copious notes and, with the ceremony about to conclude, stunned everyone present by striding to the rostrum. Lumumba had been omitted from the official programme, but encouraged by a Belgian friend, Jean Van Lierde, decided to walk up to the podium and make an impromptu speech – one of the most important, if not most consequential, speeches in modern African history. Lumumba had been irked by the Belgian king's condescending remarks and launched a fiery attack on the exploitative nature of the colonial system. He roundly criticised Belgian actions over the years, particularly those of King Leopold II, a direct ancestor of the current Belgian ruler. The prime minister laughed at Belgian claims of having ever helped the Congo and described the past century for the huge African country as one of 'humiliating slavery which was imposed upon us by force. We have known harassing work, exacted in exchange for salaries which did not permit us to eat enough to drive away hunger, to clothe ourselves, or to house ourselves decently, or to raise our children as creatures dear to us.

'We have known ironies, insults, blows that we endured morning, noon and night, because we are negroes. We have seen our lands seized in the name of allegedly legal laws, which in fact recognised only that might is right. We will never forget the massacres where so many perished, the cells into which those who refused to submit to a regime of oppression and exploitation were thrown.'

Lumumba's speech was a disastrous miscalculation. As he strode angrily from the rostrum, the room erupted in consternation. The Congolese present cheered Lumumba to the rafters, but the Belgians seethed in outrage at the prime minister's claims and the fact that their king had been so publicly humiliated. King Baudouin was deeply embarrassed and his courtiers initially pressed him to stage a walkout in protest. A gala luncheon had been prepared, but this was stalled for almost two hours while Belgian officials went into a conclave to debate what to do next.

The king eventually emerged and attended the reception, but the atmosphere – despite the steamy summer heat – was icy. Lumumba and the royal entourage pointedly ignored each other until the king retired to his official residence. Powerful Belgian military and industrial officials were incensed and decided then and there that if Lumumba was the face of an independent Congo, then that face urgently needed to be changed.

'The king was very angry. The Belgians wanted nothing to do with him [Lumumba] after that. People say it was this speech that brought his end,' Van Lierde later told the BBC World Service.

Lumumba – a magnetic figure whose emergence as one of the Congo's independent leaders had upset other more established rivals – revelled in the congratulations he received for his speech from fellow Congolese. He even took steps to ensure the speech was typed out in the form of a press release and distributed to various parts of the country. However, the prime minister had tragically misjudged the moment. Rather than assessing the most politic course of action, Lumumba indulged his emotions and decided to hold a mirror up to Belgian actions in Africa over the previous century. However justified those emotions and sense of outrage at colonial exploitation might have been, the royal ceremony was an exceptionally dangerous place to engage in fiery rhetoric. While he may not have instantly realised it, Lumumba had just played directly into the hands of his sworn enemies – both European and Congolese.

In 1956, Patrice Lumumba was a humble post office clerk about to launch a doomed career as a beer salesman. Within four years he was ranked amongst Africa's most charismatic post-independence leaders and was prime minister of one of Africa's biggest countries. Lumumba had emerged in Congolese politics as the head of the Mouvement National Congolais (MNC) which, unlike other pro-independence groups, aimed more for a national Congolese settlement rather than a deal which favoured one tribal group over another. A talented orator, Lumumba quickly outshone his leadership rivals and such was his popular support that a meeting in Belgium in January 1960 to discuss the independence proposal could not take place because other Congolese leaders refused to take part unless Lumumba, who was serving a six-month sentence in prison for inciting a riot in Stanleyville, was released.

However, Lumumba had an unfortunate talent for making enemies – particularly amongst powerful Belgian commercial interests who felt his emotional stump speeches heralded African communism. Lumumba made no secret of wanting the Belgians out of the Congo immediately and repeatedly said so in speeches to thronged Congolese political rallies. He saw no reason for the retention of white officials and was determined that the Congolese would fully take charge of their own affairs.

He also managed to alienate several key figures within the Congolese nationalist movement – several of whom viewed this young charismatic man, who appeared to have a long career ahead of him, as a direct threat to their own future leadership ambitions. Worst of all, Lumumba's contacts with the Soviet Union – which, viewed with the hindsight of half a century, were naïve and innocent enough – were sufficient to worry the United States. This ultimately ensured that Lumumba had few friends with influence in the administration of the most powerful country on earth. In the end, the CIA seemed as eager as the Belgians to get rid of Lumumba. CIA Director Allen Dulles – one of President Eisenhower's closest confidants – dismissed Lumumba as 'a mad dog'.

Lumumba was so frustrated at the ongoing failure of the US and UN to force Belgium to fully withdraw from the Congo – and specifically the rich province of Katanga – that he accepted an offer of help from Moscow. A consignment of Soviet transport planes, military trucks and, the CIA suspected, Kalashnikov guns was dispatched to the Congo. It was only token support, but was enough to push CIA analysts over the edge. Even the American ambassador in Leopoldville began referring to the prime minister in correspondence as 'Lumumbavitch'.

Chief amongst the prime minister's domestic rivals was Joseph Mobutu, a would-be journalist who was attending college in Belgium when the independence movement accelerated. Mobutu lacked Lumumba's oratorical skills and populism. He also lacked, by 1959/60, any major credibility within the Congolese independence movement. Unlike Lumumba and others, Mobutu hadn't been jailed nor had he suffered for his anti-colonial views in the 1950s.

However, Mobutu was shrewd enough to perceive that the powerful interests Lumumba had alienated were fully capable of destroying him, so he slowly set about building a power-base should Lumumba fall. Crucially, Mobutu also recognised that the dominant power in the world was the United States – and that US backing was vital for any African regime that wanted to enjoy longevity.

Mobutu boasted an oft-underestimated intellect as well as a deep appreciation of the power the army offered. He had been one of the best students at a Christian Brothers missionary school before he ran away and was forcibly enlisted in the Congolese National Army (ANC) for a seven-year term. Here he obtained a different kind of education and learned at first hand just what a powerful weapon the military presented to those willing to wield it.

During his term in the army Mobutu was an avid reader and secured old newspapers and books from his Belgian superior officers. By continuing his studies in this way, he was able to secure work as a journalist when he left the army. It is interesting to note that Mobutu's favourite books were those by Charles de Gaulle, Winston Churchill and Niccolo Machiavelli – men who had grasped the true meaning of political power and knew precisely how to properly wield it. What very few people knew was that Mobutu had also worked as a police informer, reporting to Belgian colonial officials on the activities of some of his Congolese nationalist colleagues.

Ironically, the decision to promote Mobutu was made by Lumumba. It was an action that ultimately destroyed him. The prime minister was badly shaken by unrest within the Force Publique and determined to rid himself of all its Belgian officers. Congolese soldiers who had never risen above the rank of sergeant now suddenly found themselves promoted to that of major and colonel. Lumumba's cousin, Victor Lundula, was plucked from obscurity to become a major-general while Lumumba, impressed by Mobutu, appointed him chief of staff, holding the rank of colonel. It was an incredibly short-sighted and, ultimately, disastrous move for Lumumba. With one stroke, he had placed the single most important source of power in the Congo outside his own direct personal control.

Should Mobutu prove a loyal ally, all would be well. But should Mobutu prove ambitious or ruthless, he had just been handed the keys to the state. The changes resulted in chaos and the Force Publique, more than anything else, contributed to the carnage that spread throughout the new republic. Mobutu wasted no time and, as chief of staff, ensured that the new Congolese officer class was loyal to him and not Lumumba or the fledgling government.

Within months, Mobutu had used the military to undermine Lumumba, isolate the prime minister's remaining allies and strip him of all real power. Lumumba was now effectively defenceless in the face of his enemies. Mobutu – unheard of before 1959/60 – was now Congo's 'Cher Colonel' (Dear Colonel) and beloved of the troops whose futures he now promised to massively enrich.

Lumumba was also held personally responsible for the horrific orgy of violence that unleashed itself across the Congo. White farmers in isolated rural areas were the first targets of the Congolese who were determined to take revenge for decades of colonial abuses. Reports of murders and rapes flooded into Leopoldville, Elisabethville and ultimately Brussels. Belgian politicians later determined that 291 European women – mostly Belgians – had been raped by Force Publique troops who were now rampaging throughout parts of the country. Thousands of Belgian estate owners abandoned their holdings and fled for their lives to Congo-Brazzaville, northern Rhodesia, Uganda and Angola. In Brussels, responsibility for the carnage was laid at the Congo prime minister's door.

Lumumba had been weakened from within by rivalries carefully nurtured by the US with emerging Congolese officials including Joseph Kasavubu, Mobutu and others. These rivalries would be crucial in leaving Lumumba vulnerable and isolated when his enemies chose to strike. Belgian interests also fostered a growing separatist movement in Katanga to the south, where a pro-Brussels administration was deemed preferable to the 'radicals' who were taking the helm in Leopoldville.

Central to the Belgian and European ambitions in this regard was Moise Tshombe, the leader of the Conakat movement and a former sergeant in the Belgian-run Congolese army. To the Europeans, Tshombe represented stability and a pro-business administration that was compliant to European concerns. Tshombe made it clear he was willing to be a loyal Belgian ally, which secured him all the backing he needed to make Katanga independent. Tshombe also enjoyed the full confidence of Union Minière and other major mining multi-national companies.

In July 1960, Belgian forces took up positions in Katanga where they had boosted their troop numbers from 3,800 before independence to 9,400. Tshombe, who was the provincial governor, declared the region's independence from the rest of the Congo. With the loss of Katanga, the Congo lost more than half the sources of its foreign currency earnings, a potentially catastrophic blow to the fledging Congo state. Patrice Lumumba instantly appealed to the international community – and specifically the United Nations – for help to preserve the integrity of the state. His plea met with immediate UN support and it was agreed that UN forces would be installed in Katanga to help keep the peace.

The move served to accelerate the pace of Congo's internal confrontation. While the international community refused to recognise Katanga as an independent state, the chaos within the Congo itself steadily mounted. Tshombe exploited this fact by claiming Katanga had chosen to secede from chaos.

Within six months of delivering his controversial speech in front of King Baudouin, Lumumba was dead. In the final months of his life, Lumumba was effectively under house arrest as Mobutu used the army to tighten his grip on power. Lumumba had become such a controversial figure that rumours swirled around the Congo that the Belgians, the CIA and even MI6 were all conspiring to secure his assassination.

In late December 1960, Lumumba, realising the danger he was in, decided to try to escape. He evaded the guards surrounding the prime minister's villa and attempted to make it to Stanleyville, his main support base, where he hoped to either set up a rival regime or allow his allies to arrange for safe asylum in a friendly African country or possibly Europe. Lumumba left his villa in a Chevrolet car on the pretext of dropping servants home. He then headed towards Stanleyville – but, disastrously, he decided to make several stops on the way to deliver political speeches to local village elders on how he had been treated.

Mobutu had planned for just such a move and had a fast-response corps of troops ready. They hunted Lumumba to Kasai near the River Sankuru where he was trapped and captured. Despite a two-hour head start, the prime minister's leisurely progression took him just over halfway to the safety of Stanleyville before he was captured. Lumumba's end mirrors the tragedy of the Congo itself. He was savagely beaten by the Congolese troops who had received orders from Mobutu to show his political rival no mercy. One of the last photographs of Lumumba shows him being hauled out of the back of an army truck, hands bound painfully behind his back. He is being dragged by the hair and is surrounded by laughing and jeering soldiers. Lumumba may have had a premonition of what was to happen when several weeks beforehand he quipped to a friend that the Congo had need of martyrs. 'If I die, tant pis [too bad],' he is alleged to have said.

UN troops – aware of what was happening – did not intervene. Some of the troops who spotted Lumumba were Swedish and they were appalled at what was going on. It later emerged they had received direct orders from UN headquarters in New York not to interfere in what was viewed as an internal Congolese matter – ironic given the speed with which the UN had intervened in the first place to prevent Katanga seceding. Brigadier Indarjit Rikhye, a UN officer, was deeply disturbed by what was happening. 'He [Lumumba] was chained in the back of a truck. He was bleeding, his hair was dishevelled, he had lost his glasses. But we could not intervene,' Rikhye later explained.

Lumumba was flown to Leopoldville where he was beaten again, humiliated in front of reporters and photographers, and then transferred to Colonel Mobutu's personal base. Congo's new strongman was operating from Binza, a fortified para-commando facility outside the city. Mobutu ordered Lumumba brought before him, and the protégé studied his former mentor. Mobutu is reported to have laughed, spat in Lumumba's face and warned him: 'You swore to have my skin – now it is I who have yours.'

Further humiliation followed as Mobutu's young officers punched, kicked and whipped the prime minister. The army revelled in Lumumba's fall and the rise of their own leader. Unconfirmed reports indicate that some of the abuse was even filmed for subsequent viewing by army leaders. But the tragedy had not yet reached its climax. Mobutu was determined that, whatever about humiliating his rival, he did not want Lumumba's blood on his hands. The Belgians wanted Lumumba dead, so an arrangement was secretly agreed whereby Lumumba would be delivered to Katanga and to those who hated him most.

What happened next has largely emerged through the award-winning work of Flemish investigative journalist, Ludo de Witte, who tracked down many of those involved. His book – *Die Moord Op Lumumba* (*The Assassination of Lumumba*) – became a bestseller and prompted a formal inquiry into the events of 1961 by the Belgian parliament. De Witte argued that not only was Belgium complicit in Lumumba's murder, but President Dwight Eisenhower's administration and the CIA were also supportive of the assassination.

On 15 January 1961, Belgium secretly instructed President Tshombe and Katanga to accept custody of Lumumba. Tshombe

– who fully realised it was coded language for a death sentence – is said to have hesitated for only a moment before agreeing. One Belgian official later commented that Lumumba's death was 'a public health measure'. On 17 January, Lumumba was flown from Leopoldville to Elisabethville in the heart of Katanga. On the flight, he was savagely beaten again by Baluba soldiers who were specifically assigned to the mission because of their tribal hatred of Lumumba.

The bloodied prime minister was taken from the military jail at Thysville and handed over to Katangan soldiers – commanded by a Belgian officer – who ushered the politician to the Villa Brouwe, a secure compound on the outskirts of the city. Katangan and Belgian soldiers took it in turns to beat Lumumba while Tshombe visited to view his deposed rival at first hand.

Later, after some discussion between Tshombe and the Katangan cabinet, Lumumba and two of his staunchest supporters who had also been arrested, Maurice Mpolo and Joseph Okito, were taken to a remote location in the bush some fifty kilometres outside Elisabethville by an armed squad commanded by Belgian officers. A Belgian soldier, Captain Julien Gat, commanded the firing squad. In the presence of Tshombe and the Belgian police commissioner in Katanga, Franz Verscheure, the three prisoners were placed against a tree. Lumumba had been so badly beaten that, according to accounts, he was hardly able to stand. Lumumba spotted the graves, which had already been dug, and he turned to one of the Belgians and said, in French, 'You're going to shoot us?' Lumumba was executed by firing squad and then shot at close range through the head. He was the last of the three friends to be executed. It was 9.40 p.m. on 17 January 1961 and Congo was about to enter another dark age.

The bodies were dug up two days later amid mounting Belgian

concerns about the political fall-out from the execution. The corpses were hacked to pieces before being dissolved in sulphuric acid obtained from local mining firms. Belgian policeman, Gerard Soerte, was ordered to take charge of the exhumation and to help cover up all traces of the killing. Later he admitted, 'He [a Katangan Minister] said "You destroy them – you make them disappear. How you do it doesn't interest me." We were there for two whole days. We did things an animal would not do. That is why we were drunk – stone drunk.'

The final earthly traces of Patrice Lumumba and his friends – anything the mining acid could not destroy – were then placed on a huge funeral pyre with the ashes later scattered along a local road and river. The only things left after the process were bullets recovered from Lumumba's corpse, which were kept as grisly souvenirs.

Mobutu, as he had shrewdly predicted, was the only beneficiary from the killing. Far from securing recognition of Katanga's independence – and protecting Belgium's puppet state – Lumumba's death reinforced Congolese determination not to lose their wealthiest province. It also enraged Lumumba's supporters who now staged a military coup of their own. The prime minister's killing would forever stain Tshombe's breakaway regime.

However, Lumumba's death did not immediately derail Tshombe's separatist movement. Rather, it increased the stakes in the short term, and Katanga suddenly saw an influx of Belgian, French, American, German and even South African mercenaries eager to defend the statelet. These guns for hire – many of them veterans of the bitter colonial conflicts in north Africa and south-east Asia – were regarded as the 'steel' in the rapidly expanding Katangese army or gendarmerie.

The availability of hard cash ensured that the gendarmerie had access to the very best in weaponry. Katanga even secured Fouga

Magister jets for its air force, instantly giving it a major advantage over any UN troops to be deployed. Katanga also acquired some ex-US army armoured cars, including a number of Staghound T17E1 vehicles, which boasted a 37mm gun.

THE FIRST UN troops from Ireland entered the Congo in July 1960 – one month after Patrice Lumumba's doomed speech – in a desperate effort to hold the country together and prevent a civil war over Katanga. Niemba, an isolated outpost in Katanga, then claimed the lives of nine Irish soldiers in November 1960 and forever dispelled the thought that Ireland's first major United Nations mission overseas would be little more than a parade ground exercise.

Those responsible for the Niemba killings – members of the Baluba tribe – never understood that the Irish soldiers were in fact there to help them. The Balubas were one of the African tribes left most vulnerable by both independence and the threat of Katangan secession – to them there appeared to be no difference between Belgian mercenaries and Irish or Swedish UN troops.

By the time Pat Mullins, John O'Mahony and the members of the 35th Battalion descended the steps of the Globemaster II at Leopoldville in June 1961, the Congo stood on the precipice of all-out civil war. The UN was deployed to keep the peace between armed groups determined to destroy each other or anyone who got in their way, but the Irish soldiers realised that the situation was much more dangerous than they had realised.

'We arrived in the Congo to discover that we were the meat in the sandwich. The UN was there to keep the warring sides apart – the only problem was that some of the warring sides outnumbered and outgunned us,' John O'Mahony said.

# CHAPTER FIVE

WHEN PAT MULLINS, John O'Mahony and the other members of the 35th Irish (UN) Battalion stepped out onto the tarmac of Leopoldville Airport they might as well have set foot on Mars. Most of the soldiers who gratefully scrambled out of the Globemaster II that evening had never been abroad before, let alone experienced a culture as exotic as that of the Congo. Most of the men had never even seen a black person at first-hand before – now there were Congolese porters, ground crew, airport attendants and drivers curiously gathered everywhere to watch the new arrivals.

'We stepped out into the heat of Leopoldville in our normal wool uniforms – and I'd say within a few minutes you could have fried eggs on our foreheads we were so hot,' John recalled. 'We didn't get our tropical kit until the following day when we began to organise ourselves at Camp Limiate on the outskirts of Leopoldville. This was the old Belgian colonial capital and it was quiet and pretty safe. Katanga was far to the south and Leopoldville seemed totally unaffected by what was going on.'

The city was known as Kinshasa to the Congolese and Leopold-ville to the Belgians. Leopoldville/Kinshasa was the true centre of power in the vast country – and also offered concessions to the Europeans who came to the Congo looking for fame, fortune, adventure or simply escape.

Kinshasa was a vastly older settlement than its upstart rival to the south, Elisabethville. Whereas Kinshasa had been a settlement of some form or other since about 500 BC, Elisabethville had been founded in 1910 by the Belgians to assist with the development of the newly discovered mineral riches in Katanga. Located on a strategic stretch of the Congo River, Kinshasa offered both access to the coast via steamboat and to the interior, upriver along the Congo.

The settlement, discovered first by Stanley and then King Leopold's agents in the 1880s, was just a rudimentary trading post located on the river and surrounded by a vast collection of African villages one of which was named 'Kinchassa'. The major tribes of the region were the Humbu and Mfinu, and they received a share of the profitable trade that passed through, whether it was slaves, ivory, timber or foodstuffs. Slaves – usually the unfortunate losers in the latest bout of Congolese tribal warfare – were shipped to the coast where there was a ready market with European and Arab slave traders.

Africa's west coast was one of the 'points' of the infamous slave triangle trade. This involved African slaves being shipped by Europeans to North America and the Caribbean for work on the cotton and sugar plantations. The ships then brought tobacco, sugar, cotton and rum from North America back to Europe. They then loaded up with European trade goods for Africa, including cloth, ironware and weapons. Having unloaded in the Congo or the other slave depots along the west African coast, the triangular process started all over again. Of all the Congo's exports, it was slaves that generated the most wealth and the greatest misery.

Stanley was the first to grasp that Kinshasa was a vital hub that offered control of western, northern and central Congo. Crucially, it was the first navigable port above the Livingstone Falls, some 300 kilometres to the west. While Boma – located in the Congo estuary near the coast – was initially chosen as the capital of King Leopold's new territory, it was soon clear that Kinshasa offered far greater strategic advantages.

The French, who established Brazzaville – the capital of the other Congolese nation, the Republic of the Congo – on the north bank of the vast Congo River, also appreciated those strategic advantages. Eventually, the French made Brazzaville the capital of their vast new entity, French Equatorial Africa (AEF). This huge colony comprised the modern-day Republic of the Congo, Gabon, Central African Republic and Chad. The two booming capitals now stared across at each other over the brooding Congo River.

For a decade, the Belgians had to use vast teams of porters to carry export goods from Kinshasa to Matadi, the next navigable port below the falls. But the king was adamant that the Congo had to develop and, in 1898, a railway was finally completed linking Kinshasa/Leopoldville with Matadi. It was a prodigious achievement given the terrain and the climate, and the death toll of workers is still only estimable. The railway slashed shipment times – particularly for wild rubber exports – and the city suddenly began to expand at a ferocious pace.

As the Irish troops gazed around at their surroundings that June day in 1961, it was clear that Leopoldville was a city of enormous contrasts. There were wide, graceful tarmac boulevards lined with beautiful colonial houses and manicured lawns dotted with exotic flowers. There were also grand colonial buildings housing the organs of the Belgian administration – and there were bistros, restaurants and hotels. Leopoldville had spacious parks and its own Parc Zoologique. But nearly encircling the city, there were also vast shanty towns where the native African workers lived, most in varying degrees of squalor. While Leopoldville was only a fraction of the size it would soon become under President Mobutu, it was clear to all the Irish troops that, already, the vast contrasts in lifestyles did not bode well.

For the young Irish soldiers, it was a sensory overload –

everything was so strange, exciting and exotic that the troops weren't quite able to take it all in on that first ride from the airport to their staging barracks. Yet, what every single Irish soldier noted was that the Congo was armed as if it was expecting imminent trouble. There were Force Publique or Congolese army troops stationed throughout the city, while UN military police patrols swept around the streets in jeeps ensuring that UN peacekeepers stayed out of trouble.

Camp Limiate was everything that the USAF Wheelus Field base was not. There were few concessions to comfort. The barracks were basically old sheds and all the cooking had to be done in field kitchens set up by the UN logistics corps. The weather was also oppressively hot and sticky. Irish soldiers, totally unaccustomed to humidity, wilted in the ferocious humidity generated by the Congo basin. The soldiers made the welcome swap to tropical kit and soon everyone took to wearing shorts because of the heat and humidity. But mosquitoes made life hell for everyone.

'I think we were all a bit stunned by what a huge contrast it was to home. We'd seen films about Africa, but until you experienced the heat, the noise and the smells for yourself, there was no way of preparing for what an incredibly different place it was. It truly was a different world. But we were young, full of beans and determined to enjoy ourselves,' John O'Mahony said.

After a few days, the members of the 35th Battalion began to acclimatise. The Irish troops now had the opportunity to meet up with members of the 34th Battalion who were about to rotate back to Ireland. 'The lads in the 34th were desperate for news of home while all we wanted to do was talk about the Congo. What was it like? Was the security situation bad? How many mercenaries were there in theatre [in the area]? But I think we were all a bit surprised when the lads in the 34th described the situation as quite peaceful.

They had had a pretty uneventful tour and there had been nothing like a repeat of Niemba. But a few of the older hands admitted that there were tensions there and warned us that trouble could flare up in a matter of hours depending on the political situation,' John explained.

As they prepared for their deployment south, the 35th were told that their tour of duty was likely to be entirely spent within the greater Elisabethville area – though a detachment of two rifle companies from the 35th would spend four weeks in north Katanga. The entire Armoured Car Group would operate from Elisabethville and would act in support of Irish, Swedish and Indian peacekeepers if required.

The trip south involved another air armada. The transfer involved a stopover in Kamina where the Irish troops transferred to a smaller aircraft, the ubiquitous twin-engined Douglas DC-3 Dakota, which had proved a war-winner for the Allies in the Second World War. No one told the Irish soldiers, but the DC-3 was regarded as less of a target than the Globemaster II should the Katangan gendarmes suddenly decide to open fire. It was also judged better able to evade ground fire. The troops later heard that Moise Tshombe had forbidden the use of Globemasters in Elisabethville – perhaps fearful they might be used by the UN to bring in heavy weaponry including tanks.

The 35th, once fully assembled, quickly settled into a pattern of military duties. The month of July was an exhausting succession of training drills, exercises, patrols and guard duty rotations. Some of the NCOs insisted on the gruelling parade ground discipline of Dublin, Cork and the Curragh being maintained. For example, one soldier, who had won a Distinguished Service Medal (DSM) for his courage in the Congo the previous year with the 33rd Battalion, was threatened with arrest because he had the impudence to erect a flag pole which was slightly crooked. There was little concession to the fact the soldier had toiled all day to dig a hole in the concrete-like earth just to mount the pole.

Part of the problem was that since the Second World War, veteran NCOs and junior officers had dominated the army with tales of duty during 'The Emergency' (Ireland's euphemism for the Second World War) and now their tales were suddenly being rivalled by young soldiers who had served in the Congo in 1960 with the 32nd and 33rd Battalions.

Suddenly NCOs who proudly boasted of night marches from Fermoy to Mallow in County Cork and emergency cycles across Munster to prepare for an invasion by German paratroopers that never came, found themselves faced with seventeen-year-olds who had seen more action than they had. 'I remember one NCO [non-commissioned officer] screaming at a trooper who was missing his webbing belt. "Where's your webbing belt?" the sergeant roared. But the trooper just replied: "I left it at Kamina, Sergeant." The sergeant just didn't know what to say. The truth was that there was no substitute for having seen action and all the NCOs knew that,' 35th Battalion veteran Des Keegan explained.

One of the great strengths of the Irish army was the respect accorded to the equipment they had – possibly because it was so precious given the chronic under-investment in the Defence Forces at the time. A lot of the gear may have been old and unsuited to some of the tasks asked of it, but it was immaculately maintained. Most Irish soldiers could strip a Vickers machine gun in a matter of minutes, and the Lee-Enfields now being retired were so well maintained they looked like they had when they had just left the production line in 1912. The new FN-FAL assault rifles were treated as if they were the Crown Jewels – soldiers took greater care of the FNs than they did of themselves.

Slowly but inexorably, the excitement of being in the Congo faded under the onslaught of monotony. Drills were followed by patrols and endless rounds of guard duty. The unfamiliar heat also took its toll on troopers totally unused to such conditions. Insect bites and stomach upsets became part and parcel of the daily grind. Part of the problem was that the Irish soldiers arrived during a bout of relative calm in Katanga – though a few of the shrewder soldiers realised there were storm clouds brewing on the horizon.

Sometimes the only respite from duty was the prospect of periods of leave in Elisabethville or the occasional unusual duty. John O'Mahony was one of those assigned to a detachment travelling to Kamina on 13 July 1961 to escort two Irish armoured cars back to Elisabethville by train. The mission was so out of the ordinary that dozens of other troopers had volunteered for it.

'The return trip was really slow, taking three whole days and nights to complete. I remember standing in the turret of an open armoured car as the old train lumbered through the night with the African jungle on either side of the track. You could see fires in the distance out in the brush – it was a thrilling experience and, at times, I almost felt like I had been transported into a movie like *The African Queen*. In all those times sitting in the cinema back home, I never dreamed I would see Africa this way. We stopped at every single local town along the way and the Irish soldiers threw sweets and candy to the children who ran alongside the train to gaze up at us. We finally got back to Elisabethville on 20 July at 8 a.m.,' John recalled.

The young Irish troopers were shocked – but delighted – to hear that they would be allowed into the cities, either Leopoldville or Elisabethville, on short periods of leave should the security situation permit it during their tour of duty. Both Leopoldville and Elisabethville were hives of activity. Thousands of UN soldiers, diplomats, Belgian administrators and foreign corporate deputations were now passing through the cities – and the local bar, restaurant and hotel owners were doing a roaring trade.

Houses of ill-repute were also thriving with so many soldiers in town. The Irish troops, warned of the dire consequences of fraternising with the local females by both their officers and chaplains, were more cautious than most. Stories of incurable venereal diseases were circulated amongst the soldiers, although a few hardy souls decided that, with the easy availability of penicillin, a romantic local liaison might be worth the trouble. In one episode, an officer was asked to intervene by an outraged Irish expat living in the Congo, who had spotted a couple of young Irish soldiers in a local bar with two buxom and scantily clad Congolese ladies, one of whom was wearing her apparent 'payment' – a Scapular Medal. The Elisabethville 'ladies of the night' were focused on two things – cash and white Europeans. Their prime targets were the Irish and Swedes, and several enterprising women even took to visiting the hospital to see if wounded soldiers required anything other than medicine.

But for the majority of Irish soldiers, R & R simply involved getting leave to go into town – whether it was Leopoldville or Elisabethville – for nothing more than a few beers, a good meal and maybe a chance to go to the cinema. The Belgians boast one of the proudest brewing traditions in the world and they had brought their expertise to the Congo with the establishment of several quality local breweries that produced beers called 'Simba', 'Primus' and 'Timbo'. They were excellent brews and quickly won a popular following amongst the Irish troops, although given the local climatic conditions, certain precautions had to be taken. One Irish soldier – while off duty – took an ice-cold bottle of beer from a fridge and placed it on the floor beside him. A short time later, he leaned over to pick up the bottle and it exploded in his face, almost costing him an eye. The temperature variation between the ice-cold bottle and the heat from the sun-baked floor tiles had caused the beer to explode.

The local tensions in Elisabethville also had to be taken into consideration when deciding where to go for a beer. 'In Elisabethville, you did have to watch yourself. We were allowed into town on evening passes and we would have a few drinks or look for a little fun. But there were almost always a lot of mercenaries and Katangan gendarmes around the town as well. Usually there were no problems but, if you were on your own or even if there were only two of you, you did run the risk of getting involved in a row with them,' John said. To avoid such problems, UN military policemen regularly circled the city centre to either bring single soldiers back to barracks or else reunite them with larger groups of their comrades. Irish soldiers were repeatedly urged to socialise in groups of at least four.

Perhaps an indication of the innocence of the era was that one of the favourite activities of the Irish soldiers was visiting the modern swimming pool complex at the Lido Hotel in Elisabethville, which had been built for the use of the European settlers and Belgian military personnel. Most of the soldiers had never seen anything like such a facility back in Ireland, where swimming was usually done either in the sea or in local rivers. The cool water was a blessed, if temporary, relief from the steamy heat of Katanga.

One of the things that most shocked the soldiers was the level of development in Katanga as compared to Ireland. 'Of course it shocked us – there was a dual carriageway with a fine tarmac surface between Elisabethville and Jadotville. You had no road like that back in Ireland in 1961 and this was supposed to be poor, deepest, darkest Africa,' Des Keegan explained. 'We arrived in

Elisabethville and there was no smoking in the cinemas – remember this was fifty years ago – and there was air conditioning in restaurants, refrigerators in most buildings and urinals in toilets. It was hilarious to hear a few of the more innocent younger Irish lads chatting amongst themselves about what they thought the urinals were really for.'

Those Irish troops nearing the end of their tours were fixated on finding a freshly arrived UN soldier to swap their Katangese francs for a convertible currency. 'We were paid in the local currency which wasn't recognised outside Katanga, so you might as well have tissue paper in your wallet. The trick was to keep all the francs you hadn't spent and swap them with a newly arrived UN trooper for either Irish pounds, Swedish Kroner, Belgian Francs or, best of all, US dollars. At least you had something to spend when you went home,' John O'Mahony added.

The other obsession was 'mingi' or souvenirs to be brought home. 'Mingi' was the Swahili word for 'plenty' – and rapidly became one of the most important words in the entire vocabulary for every Irish soldier. Goods ranged from African shields, knives, masks and arrows, to Katangan flags, jungle helmets and ivory carvings. The Irish troops carefully guarded their 'mingi' hoard and woe betide anyone caught interfering with another man's 'mingi'. In one case, when a tent accidentally caught fire from a stove, the troops raced to save their 'mingi' from the flames – only focusing on their uniforms and weapons once their souvenirs were safe.

SINCE THE DEPLOYMENT of Irish troops the previous summer, the ambush at Niemba had been the only major conflict. Throughout Katanga an uneasy peace prevailed. UN troops, mercenaries and Katangese gendarmes eyed each other with respect but also with extreme caution. The irony was that while the rest of the Congo threatened to descend into chaos amid army revolts, tribal loyalties and political machinations, Katanga was relatively stable and it was business as usual for the mining operations.

In Katanga, there was no challenge to Tshombe's regime beyond the claims of the Leopoldville-based Congolese government. But the Leopoldville regime was facing challenges from various army insurrections, and Lumumba loyalists established their own rival administration in Stanleyville. Repeated revolts within the Force Publique led to Katangans viewing their poor northern neighbours with increasing alarm. Stories of army mutinies and the rape and murder of western plantation owners seemed, in Katangan eyes, to justify their going it alone. Outside Katanga, the Congo teetered on the brink of anarchy, with Mobutu playing the staunch US support as his trump card.

Politically, the UN's mission in Katanga was in Irish hands. Up-and-coming young Dublin diplomat, Conor Cruise O'Brien, was stationed in Elisabethville and was entrusted by UN Secretary-General Dag Hammarskjöld with trying to persuade Tshombe and his mercenary-led army to peacefully reintegrate with the Congo. Cruise O'Brien was an intelligent, determined and opinionated man who, as the UN's special representative, now found himself in a hugely influential role in Katanga.

Cruise O'Brien hailed from a family deeply immersed in Irish literature and politics. His father worked as a journalist with *The Freeman's Journal (Irish Independent)*, while his grandfather had been a member of the Irish Parliamentary Party. Cruise O'Brien's aunt was married to Francis Sheehy-Skeffington, the pacifist who was murdered in Dublin in 1916. Cruise O'Brien attended Sandford Park School and Trinity College Dublin (TCD) and his impressive academic record earned him a position within the civil service. When he was posted to the Department of External

Affairs his abilities were recognised by Seán MacBride, who assigned the young man to several prominent diplomatic duties. This, in turn, brought him to the attention of the United Nations' Secretary-General, Hammarskjöld, who requested his secondment. The Fianna Fáil government – leery of allowing Irish personnel to become directly involved in as contentious an issue as Katanga-Congo – allowed Cruise O'Brien to be assigned to the UN but requested he only go to Africa via a short spell of duty at the UN's New York headquarters.

Once in Katanga, Cruise O'Brien quickly lost respect for Tshombe, who repeatedly promised to comply with all UN requests, but then fudged, determined to try to maintain an independent Katanga. Tshombe knew he had Belgian support and, unless the US was going to directly intervene in Congolese affairs, clearly felt he could out-last the UN commitment provided he could keep his army intact and well armed. Tshombe worked to frustrate the UN while, at the same time, trying not to give them an excuse to take armed action against him. Relations between the two men deteriorated, with Cruise O'Brien determined to bring the secession to an end and Tshombe equally determined to keep Katanga independent.

Between January and July 1961, the UN desperately sought a negotiated solution for the crisis triggered by Katanga's secession, Lumumba's killing and Mobutu's seizure of power in Leopoldville. But the exhaustive peace talks – staged in both Leopoldville and a special conference in Madagascar – ultimately failed to break the deadlock. Mobutu felt he had tacit US support for the way in which he had handled Lumumba in late 1960, so was not willing to compromise, while Tshombe, with backing from Belgium and the mining companies, saw no reason to abandon plans for a breakaway state. One year into the UN mission – now referred to as ONUC (Organisation des Nations Unies au Congo) – there was no sign of Katanga indicating its willingness to reintegrate within the Congo. Equally, the chaos within the Congo itself was worse than the previous year as the factional fighting continued.

By late July, elements within the UN began to question what would happen should the talks drag on and fail to deliver a political settlement to the Katangan crisis. Some UN officers felt that as long as Tshombe and the Katangan regime had a mercenary-led military force, there was little motivation for them to make concessions at the talks table. Several UN military officials began to discuss the possibility of moving against Katanga's gendarme leadership and their foreign mercenaries.

On 28 August, the UN finally decided to try and defuse the secession by reducing Katanga's military power. The UN gambled that without their mercenary advisors and senior officers, the Katangan gendarmes would not be as threatening a force. It was also hoped that the move would persuade Katangan politicians that the UN was serious about ending the secession, which, in turn, would cause the Katangans to negotiate with greater earnestness.

The Swedes called it Operation Rampunch – but it subsequently became corrupted to 'Rumpunch' in English-language reports of the Katangan operation. The operation was also called Rampunch in both the 35th Battalion's record and the ONUC orders for 1961. Operation Rampunch allowed mercenaries to be detained in Elisabethville and its surrounding area and then deported. Key Katangan positions were also disarmed by Irish, Swedish and Indian UN troops.

Cmdt Pat Quinlan and his 'A' Company troops successfully took the Katangan gendarmerie headquarters in an operation that lasted just fifteen minutes – Cmdt Quinlan distinguishing himself by being the first to march into the building. *Irish Independent* journalist,

Raymond Smith, who soon earned the affectionate nickname 'Congo' Smith for his reports, quoted the modest Quinlan: 'I would not ask any of my men to do what I would not do myself'. 'B' Company under Cmdt Alo McMahon successfully seized control of the Air Katanga facility at Elisabethville Airport, while the remaining Irish troops under Lt Col Hugh McNamee took the hospital, which had been serving as a temporary base for Katangan mercenaries. Hopes began to rise that Operation Rampunch would bring an end to the secession and the threat of civil war.

The Armoured Car Group played a distinguished role in supporting the UN operations. Pat Mullins and his Ford AFV crew were part of a unit that on 28 August helped disarm and capture a Katangan detachment which had tried to dig in beside Elisabethville Airport in order to disrupt UN flights. The order came from the 35th Battalion commander, Lt Col Hugh McNamee, who was determined that the Katangans should not threaten the airport as it was one of the UN's main supply arteries. Two companies – supported by two Ford armoured cars – encircled the Katangans at first light and secured their surrender after a brief standoff. They captured forty-five gendarmes, two European mercenaries and one Congolese officer. In this swift action the Irish also captured a quantity of weapons, including assault rifles, pistols, two mortars and two squad machine guns, which had already been mounted in firing pits. It was an encouraging action for the Irish as their objective had been achieved without bloodshed.

'I remember Pat was really excited when he was telling me about the operation after it was over and he came back to camp. At one point, they were ordered to close down the airport because there were fears some of the mercenaries might try to flee capture and fly to a rural air base to link up with Katangan forces. So two Irish armoured cars – one with Pat at the Vickers machine gun

– dramatically drove out onto the runway to stop planes taking off. But one pilot was determined to make it and he revved his propellers ready for take-off. Pat and the other Irish gunner simply turned their turrets and aimed the machine guns directly at the cockpit. The pilot had no option but to stop the plane. Pat was laughing as he told me how the pilot was furious and kept shaking his fist at the two Irish gunners,' John O'Mahony recalled.

However, for John, Operation Rampunch was a frustrating experience. Just eight days before the operation was launched, he had been on guard duty when, as the evening got cool, he marched back to his accommodation block to get a tunic for warmth.

'On the way back I noticed some of the off-duty soldiers were engaged in an impromptu game of football. Passing by, I could not resist an opportunity to join in for five minutes or so. But this was to be my undoing as during a scuffle for the ball I pushed someone too hard and fractured a bone in my right hand. I heard the "crack" of the bone and felt a jolt of pain in my hand. But I continued the night on guard duty and did not report the matter for a couple of days as I hoped it would clear up by itself. However, the hand remained painful and then started to swell up in the heat. Finally, I simply couldn't use it properly and couldn't operate the turret handles in the armoured car to rotate the Vickers machine gun. At the UN hospital in the city, an Italian doctor fitted a plaster and ticked me off for not reporting the matter sooner. I remember him saying: "What were you waiting for – the hand to fall off?" So for the next few weeks I would be on light duties with my hand in a cast,' John explained. The injury kept him off patrol duty for several weeks.

Within forty-eight hours of Operation Rampunch being launched, the UN disastrously undermined its potential success by agreeing to allow local Belgian officials to complete the measures the UN had initiated. It was a fateful miscalculation, because the UN allowed the benefits of their bold intervention to be frittered away by Belgian officials operating to a different agenda – and then found themselves in precisely the same position as they started. Except now the Katangan populace had begun to regard the UN as more of an army of occupation than a peacekeeping force.

As promised by the Belgian authorities, regular Belgian officers duly left Katanga – but the mercenaries who had previously been deported quietly slipped back across the border. Additional mercenary reinforcements were discreetly flown in and nothing further was done to disarm the mercenaries now leading the Katangan gendarmes. The UN finally realised in early September that Operation Rampunch had failed to reach its targets and it was decided that firmer measures would have to be put in place.

The second UN assault on Katanga was earmarked for 2 a.m. on 13 September 1961. It was called Operation Morthor – the name apparently having been chosen by Conor Cruise O'Brien after learning from his Indian military advisor that 'Morthor' was a Hindu word for 'smash' or 'hammer-blow'. It was a calculated gamble that the Katangan gendarmerie, weakened by the deportation of its Belgian officer corps, would not resist the UN troops as they seized key installations around Elisabethville.

Conor Cruise O'Brien and his military advisers estimated that Tshombe originally had 208 Belgian officers and 302 European-African mercenaries in Katanga. The arrests and deportations were believed to have whittled the number down to just 104 – and it was not thought likely that this small force would stand and fight. During Operation Rampunch, Irish troops alone had taken forty-one officers and mercenaries into custody. But the UN failed to appreciate that Tshombe – through his own military experience – placed enormous faith in the skills of European soldiers and had been secretly hiring further mercenaries to stiffen resolve within his Katangan army. They ranged from ex-French-colonial paratroopers hardened during the brutal Algerian civil war, to adventurers from South Africa, Rhodesia, the US and even (reportedly) one Irish-American. Critically, there were also a number of former German Wehrmacht troops who had served with the French Foreign Legion.

These mercenary recruits soon earned the nickname 'Les Afreus' – 'the Terrible Ones' – a monicker first used for French paratroopers during their anti-rebel duties in Algeria. The mercenaries clearly loved the notoriety, and some of them dressed to fit the 'Les Afreus' description. They wore their hair long, they grew scrub beards and they appeared in a variety of well-worn combat fatigues and were never seen on the street unless they were heavily armed, sometimes with ammunition belts draped around them. Some of the experienced mercenaries had been recruited with the offer of a £200 signing fee – the equivalent to a €20,000-plus payment in modern currency. It was an astonishing amount that dwarfed the salaries of senior engineers and diplomats. They were provided with whatever arms they required, as well as free accommodation and lodging. 'Les Afreus' were assigned to specific units of the Katangan gendarmes and they knew their primary targets would be the UN should a second move against the secessionary forces be attempted.

Tshombe was an enthusiastic supporter of mercenary recruit-ment and, having seen how the Congo's Force Publique had disintegrated into a riotous mob over the previous twelve months following the loss of its European officers, told his senior Belgian military adviser, Major Guy Weber, 'I only trust whites.'

Tshombe also knew that his army needed hardware and money had been spent acquiring Staghound armoured cars. The US vehicle was Second World War vintage, but was ideally suited to the Congolese conflict. It was fast, being capable of speeds of up to ninety kilometres per hour, it had a great range of almost 800 kilometres on one tank of fuel and, with eight millimetres of hardened armour, was able to withstand hits from virtually all light weapons. Its 37mm gun also meant it outgunned anything the UN could currently field against it.

Critically, Tshombe had also secured three Aerospatiale Fouga Magister jet-trainers. While effectively obsolete as a combat aircraft, the Magister ruled in the Congo because it had no rivals. The Magister – distinctive with its butterfly tail – could cruise at 750 kilometres per hour and had a range of 925 kilometres. The latter meant that, when operating from Elisabethville, virtually every isolated UN post was within its strike radius. The Magister was really a training aircraft, but could be equipped with 7.62mm machine guns, rocket pods, 500 kilogramme bombs and even napalm. Because it was designed as a jet trainer, it had docile handling characteristics and was a stable gun platform. Against vulnerable ground targets it was a lethal foe.

With no UN jet fighters in the theatre, the Magister dominated the skies. It instantly rendered the UN helicopters, on which isolated posts often depended for communications and supplies, hugely vulnerable. If, as local rumours hinted, Tshombe had secured Belgian mercenary pilots to fly his Magisters, then the skies belonged to the Katangan secessionists and not the UN.

For Operation Morthor, the UN decided on a more robust repeat of Operation Rampunch – but without the previous mistakes. This time the UN would see the operation through to the finish itself and would not involve the local Belgian or Katangan authorities. But the Katangans had also learned a harsh lesson and they were determined not to be caught off-guard a second time. Katangan propaganda – later blamed by Cruise O'Brien for dangerously inflaming tensions – claimed that the UN would replace Katangan soldiers with Congolese Force Publique troops, with obvious implications for the local population. 'We tried every means to assure them on this point but this particularly destructful [*sic*] piece of propaganda was one of the reasons there was such bloodshed,' Cruise O'Brien later claimed.

Operation Morthor's aims were quite simple – it would quash secession by cutting the sinews of power in Katanga. UN troops would surround Tshombe's presidential palace and then they would seize and occupy the Telephone Exchange-Post Office and the radio centre. The Katangan interior security and communication ministries would be surrounded and raided, and key documents would be confiscated. UN troops would also raise the Democratic Republic of the Congo's flag on all major Elisabethville buildings. It was then expected that Tshombe could be persuaded to abandon the secession.

The UN would see the operation through to the end and not entrust seized arms or key prisoners to either Belgian or Katangan interests. Mercenaries would be immediately shipped out of Africa and Katangan heavy weaponry would be placed in secure UN storage pending an end to hostilities. But there were already ample signs that Operation Morthor would not go as smoothly as Operation Rampunch.

On 5 September, there were anti-UN riots in Elisabethville by a group of 500 youngsters who were pro-Tshombe and dubbed themselves 'The Katanga Youth'. They staged their rally outside the UN headquarters and UN hospital, and it escalated to the point where they stoned the armed UN sentries on duty. Police eventually had to fire shots into the air to disperse them. Radio Katanga, an installation that had been seized and then handed back by UN troops the previous week, began broadcasting virulent anti-UN news reports. For the first time, UN soldiers found themselves being berated by the white European population in Elisabethville, who accused them of making things worse, not better. The atmosphere in the city was fast becoming poisonous.

Matters continued to escalate in the wake of Operation Rampunch. On 6 September, Quartermaster Sergeant Seán Hamill almost lost an eye when he was struck in the face by a stone which was thrown at the jeep he was travelling in near Avenue Usoke on the outskirts of the city. The same day, a thirty-strong Irish platoon suddenly found itself being stoned by a crowd of protesters. The soldiers, unwilling to use lethal force on the crowd, sustained two casualties from the thrown stones. Irish officers admitted they were lucky no one was killed. There was worse to come.

On 9 September, members of the 35th Battalion noted an increased operational tempo in the Katangan gendarmes. They also noted that there still appeared to be a lot of heavily armed white mercenaries around Elisabethville. Later that day, roadblocks sprang up around the city in a clear attempt to disrupt UN movement and communication. The Verfailles Garage – a facility in Elisabethville that was contracted to do service work on UN vehicles – was attacked, and the mob burned the building as well as a UN Landrover and a supply truck.

The most alarming news came on 10 September. The previous day, a radio communication from Cmdt Quinlan and his men at Jadotville confirmed that they had effectively been surrounded by a large force of Katangan gendarmes who had erected fortified roadblocks on all major access routes into Jadotville. The town – which is now known as Likasi – was about 160 kilometres north of Elisabethville on the road to Kolwezi. Jadotville was a typical mining outpost – quiet, with very few attractions in the town beyond farms and the local mine. About ten kilometres to the east of Jadotville was Lake Tshangalele, where there was good fishing but vicious mosquitoes. In ordinary times, a Jadotville assignment represented a quiet tour of duty. But now, with large Katangan paramilitary forces surrounding the town, the UN detachment suddenly began to appear extremely isolated. Cmdt Quinlan and his men were now entirely dependent on the single road supply line south to Elisabethville.

The 35th Battalion realised it had to resupply and reinforce the Jadotville unit without delay. However, on 10 September, a platoon sent to Jadotville reported that a strong Katangan gendarme force had established a roadblock at the strategic Lufira Bridge that they were unable to pass.

The UN – worried at the escalating tensions – gave the 35th Battalion six specific targets. They were:

* Seize the St Francois de Sales Radio College.
* Seize the 'Tunnel' crossing at Chaussee de Kasenga.
* Leave one infantry section to guard the Italian hospital.
* Arrest Tshombe's ally, Mr Jean Kibwe, at his residence at Avenue Drogmans or his ministerial office at Avenue Kambove.
* Retain one platoon in Albert Park to take into custody Mr Patrice Kimba, Katangan Minister for Foreign Affairs.
* Secure the refugee camp near 'The Factory' and arrange for the local security of Verfailles Garage.

Operation Morthor was officially ordered at 10 p.m. on 12 September and launched at 2 a.m. on 13 September, after Cruise O'Brien and his senior military commander, Brigadier-General Kas Raja, received clearance directly from the senior UN commander in Leopoldville, the Tunisian diplomat, Mahmoud Khiary. But controversy still rages to this day over whether Dag Hammarskjöld was aware in precise detail of what was now going to happen in Elisabethville.

Cruise O'Brien later described Hammarskjöld as 'convoluted and Machiavellian' in character. The Irish diplomat was adamant that Hammarskjöld knew precisely what was happening, but feigned ignorance when things went wrong. Writing in David O'Donoghue's *Far Battalions*, Cruise O'Brien insisted: 'He [Hammarskjöld] began by backing Khiary and myself in preparing the overthrow of the Katanga government by force. Then, when that began to go wrong militarily on the ground, he pretended that no such effort had ever been made and he issued a ridiculous document, which I deal with in my book *To Katanga and Back* in the chapter entitled "The Fire in the Garage". He had an imperious use of language so that words would mean whatever he chose that they should mean.'

The military operation was entrusted to three UN battalions – one Irish (35th), one Swedish and one Indian. The Indian battalion largely comprised Dogra units, later supplemented by one large detachment of Gurkhas. These troops – drawn from the foothills of the Himalayas – boasted a ferocious military reputation and ranked as amongst the toughest soldiers on earth. Such was the reputation of the Gurkhas that they were the only colonial regiment maintained by the British army after the end of the empire. Only the top graduates from Sandhurst, Britain's renowned military academy, are allowed the honour of leading a Gurkha unit. But, crucially, the attitude of the Indian Dogra troops during Operation Morthor proved significantly different to that of the Swedish and Irish troops. Whereas the European troops tended only to fire their weapons in self-defence, the Indians regarded any failure to comply with orders as a direct military threat and acted accordingly.

Back in their bases, the Irish troops knew that tensions were mounting and suspected that conflict was now inevitable. Pat Mullins had been listening to the rumours and stories that swirled around, but remained stoic in the face of it all. 'I think Pat was born to be a soldier,' Des Keegan recalled. 'Nothing seemed to faze him, nothing ever seemed to bother him. He was as cool as a cucumber. I remember him as a very quiet lad – and he always seemed happy just to get on with his job.'

For John, it was a period of enormous frustration as his injured hand limited his ability to participate in the dramatic events unfolding around him. 'I could only watch as the lads undertook patrols in the armoured cars. I was restricted to light duties which meant I was usually on security patrol around our base. I hated the cast and used a penknife and the barrel sight of a Carl Gustav to whittle off a piece of the plaster near my thumb so that it was easier to hold and fire my weapon. But the hand was still awkward to use.'

Pat and the Armoured Car Group of the 35th Battalion knew they would be critical to the success of any impending UN operations. They would escort UN troop movements around Elisabethville and would most likely be tasked with ensuring that supplies and reinforcements reached isolated outposts including Jadotville where Irish troops had gone to secure the area for the UN and protect local white settlers.

In Jadotville, Cmdt Pat Quinlan began to feel increasingly uneasy. The Irish commander ordered his men to dig in and prepare defensive positions in preparation for a possible attack. Those defensive preparations would soon be tested to the limit.

Many of the Irish personnel attached to the Armoured Car

Group had private concerns about any forthcoming action, largely in relation to the standard of their equipment. The main weapon fielded by the 35th Irish Battalion was the Ford Armoured Fighting Vehicle (AFV). The vehicle looked the part – big, rugged and with the legendary reliability of the old Ford V8 petrol engine. Col J.V. Lawless, founder of Ireland's Cavalry Corps, was determined that the army secure some type of suitable armoured fighting vehicle and he maintained a determined one-man campaign for the design until the government finally, and reluctantly, released funds for the fleet of Fords.

However, the Ford was a design inspired as much by the materials available to the poorly funded Defence Forces as by Ireland's need for an armoured fighting vehicle. 'They had some Landsverks up in the Curragh. I think Ireland had bought about eight of them from the Swedes. The Landsverk was a big, heavy car with a Scania truck engine and was armed with a 20mm Madsen cannon. Few people knew that it was actually designed by the Germans, who were prevented from making such vehicles because of the Versailles Treaty. What was remarkable about it was that it had two steering columns – one in the front and one in the rear. If the car had to be reversed in a hurry, the radio operator was sitting facing backwards and he could take over the driving,' Des Keegan explained. In the turret of the Landsverk, alongside the 20mm Madsen cannon, there was a .303 Madsen machine gun. There was another .303 machine gun in the front of the hull that could be fired by the relief driver.

Irish military chiefs had ordered the Landsverk to be copied using a Leyland truck engine. But the resultant cars were so big and awkward they were deemed totally unsuitable for operations in the Congo. Ireland had little else to offer in terms of armoured support. The Defence Forces did have a number of Second World

War vintage Churchill tanks obtained from Britain, but while a fine tank and equipped with a 75mm gun, the Churchills were painfully slow and heavy on fuel. Ireland's most modern tank – the Comet – had a 77mm gun and had been purchased from Britain following the Suez debacle. But, like the Churchill, it was totally unsuited to conditions in the Congo and so the Ford was designed as a more suitable replacement.

The Irish troops feared that their home-built Ford was hopelessly outclassed by the Katangan armour they were likely to face. The American-built Staghound – the Katangans' main armoured weapon – had a 37mm gun and 8mm of frontal armour. That armour comprised specially hardened steel shaped to try and deflect bullets and shells. Supplementing its main armament were three 7.62mm machine guns – all of which made the Staghound an effective reconnaissance vehicle and a formidable opponent. The Ford, in contrast, shared more in common with an industrial van or tractor than a true weapon of war. It was notoriously top-heavy, with its steel shell built on top of an old truck chassis. The result was that the Ford had a high centre of gravity and its cross-country performance suffered as a direct result. To make matters worse the vehicle only had rear-wheel drive and was susceptible to getting stuck in the African mud once it left the surfaced roads.

Of even greater concern was the fact the Irish vehicle had been manufactured from plate steel salvaged from old industrial boilers. At one point it was even proposed that plate steel from a ship which had run aground on rocks off Donegal, might be used. But the designers – the Defence Forces and Thompson's of Carlow – finally settled on heavy boilerplate from the Liffey Dockyard as they felt it would offer sufficient protection from small arms fire. Thompson's undertook construction at their Carlow works to army specifications. The armoured structure was placed on top of a three-tonne Ford truck chassis. It was built with plates that were not hardened steel and therefore offered no anti-penetrative resistance to heavy rounds.

The problem was graphically underlined when Irish troops discovered that if you fired a Lee-Enfield .303 round directly at the Ford AFV from a distance of fifty to sixty yards, rather than being properly deflected, the bullet gouged a lump from the steel plate. Bullet impacts could also result in lumps of metal flaking off from inside the armoured car – with obvious risks for the crew. The question then arose, what would happen if the Ford was hit with something bigger than a standard infantry rifle round? Worst of all, what damage would a direct hit from the Staghound's 37mm gun inflict?

Most of the armoured cars were equipped with turrets armed with the venerable Vickers machine gun, the design of which was already half a century old. The turrets themselves were circular and based on the design of the Lancia armoured car turrets left in Ireland by the British on their withdrawal in the 1920s. The turret could turn through 360 degrees – but it had to be moved with two large handles mounted to the left and right of the gunner. It was impossible to move the turret and maintain fire with the Vickers. Worse still, the turret was designed in such a way that anyone under six foot tall had to stand on a box just to be able to properly aim the machine gun.

A few armoured cars were left open-topped and were instead fitted with Browning machine guns. Part of the reason for this was to allow extra room so that infantry troops could be carried if required. The turreted Ford was cramped for five cavalry troops and it would have been absolutely impossible to carry infantry as well. The ejection of used rounds from the Browning was a relatively clean procedure and the Browning also boasted a higher rate of fire than the ageing Vickers. In the case of the Vickers in the turreted cars, there was no basket to catch the used shells on ejection. This resulted in the hot metal casings falling down onto the heads of the crewmen below. The Ford driver learned to wear a scarf or high collar to protect the back of his head and neck from the hot bullet casings cascading down on top of him. The casings also rattled around the floor of the armoured car, posing a further threat to the footing of anyone moving around the vehicle.

The Vickers had forged a formidable reputation for reliability and lethality in the First World War and was still as rugged, reliable and potent as ever. Properly maintained, the Vickers machine gun could maintain a devastating rate of fire for literally hours on end. But the Vickers was heavy, required cooling in the Congo heat and, because of its design, could not be turned upwards in the armoured car turret to engage aircraft. Its cooling system was a water-filled jacket – if that was punctured by shrapnel or incoming shells, the gun was rendered useless within a matter of minutes. In contrast, the Browning had no such cooling problems. Worse still, the Vickers was equipped with a condenser – meaning that, after long bursts of fire, the heated water in the cooling jacket would boil off into a special cup. Once cooled, it could be used to top up the cooling reservoir. But it was physically impossible to adapt such a system to an armoured car turret. So the Ford gunner had to try to fire in short, spaced bursts, otherwise he risked overheating and disabling the gun.

'The Vickers was one of the finest machine guns ever built. Properly used, it was one of the best squad weapons you could have. But it was getting old and the water-cooled version wasn't really suited for use in the armoured cars. The biggest advantage the gun had was that virtually every Irish soldier knew it inside-out. For instance, the lock on the Vickers comprised fifteen separate pieces making up a unit about the size of your hand and about a half-inch thick. We could assemble the lock blindfolded in a matter of seconds. That's how well trained we were on the Vickers,' Des Keegan explained.

The realisation that the Katangans had Staghound armoured cars and Magister jets came as a nasty surprise to the UN military commanders. The Irish troops knew that if their Ford armoured cars came into battle against the Katangans with their Staghounds, they would be entirely dependent on hand-held infantry weapons like the Carl Gustav 84mm recoilless rifle for primary defence. On its own, the Ford simply could not hope to face a Staghound with any success if the Katangan crew properly used their 37mm gun.

As reveille sounded at 2 a.m. on 13 September, Irish troops raced to their positions and launched Operation Morthor. The soldiers who prayed that Morthor would be a repeat of Operation Rampunch were about to be sorely disappointed. This time the Katangans were ready for the UN battalions, and, in some areas, were already spoiling for a fight.

Less than three weeks before, UN troops had secured key Katangan positions without having to fire a shot. Now all hell broke loose, particularly around the Radio Katanga building, where gendarmes, led by mercenaries, refused to surrender without a fight. Luckily for the Irish, that target had been assigned to the Indian battalion. The Irish units had secured their positions in other parts of Elisabethville by 4.30 a.m. and held their posts while listening warily to the sounds of heavy fighting around the Post Office and Radio Katanga buildings which echoed around the city.

One of these Irish-occupied positions was the Radio College (not to be confused with the Radio Katanga building). The Radio College was seized by a detachment of 'C' Company led by Lt

Thomas 'Tommy' Ryan. The building had a powerful short-wave radio transmitter and the UN was determined that once Radio Katanga was off the air, the Radio College should not be available to Tshombe's forces as an alternative rallying point. The building was located on Avenue Wangermee and was adjacent to a mission run by the White Fathers. Avenue Wangermee had numerous road intersections – one of which was Avenue Drogmans. A right-hand turn led back towards the new Irish base at Prince Leopold Farm on Rue Savonnier. But a left turn led to a T-junction on Boulevard Elisabeth – dangerously close to one of the Katangan gendarmes main barracks.

At Radio Katanga, the Indians moved steadily into position for an all-out assault. The mercenaries – realising they were outnumbered – ordered their black troops to hold their positions and then vanished into the warren of nearby houses. The Katangan gendarmes fought desperately until the Indians managed to fight their way into the building. In the fighting, an Indian sergeant was apparently killed by sniper fire. What happened next is still a matter of controversy. The Katangans claimed that every gendarme and security person left in the building was killed. A total of twenty-five gendarme bodies were eventually removed from the shell-pocked and bloodied Radio Katanga building and buried in a mass grave to the rear of the building. Katangans claimed the soldiers had been butchered and immediately accused the UN of a war crime. Initial reports indicated that the Katangan prisoners were herded into a small room and then hand-grenades were thrown in. The prisoners who survived the hand-grenades were then shot in the head by an Indian soldier delegated to the task. The Irish and Swedish soldiers attached as armoured support to the Indian battalion looked on horrified, but were utterly powerless to intervene. One Irish soldier formally complained to an Indian officer, but was quietly taken aside by one of the Swedes and reminded that the Europeans were outnumbered and, if they threatened to make a big deal about the executions at the scene, who knew how the Indian troops would react?

Following the horrific incident, one Irish soldier returned to base and became physically sick. Irish officers eventually heard rumours about what had happened at Radio Katanga and ordered statements to be taken. Yet, interestingly, there is no mention whatsoever of the incident in the official history of the 35th Battalion. In September 2005, one of the Irish eyewitnesses – who had been haunted for decades by the atrocity he had witnessed and been powerless to prevent – made a statement about precisely what he had seen.

'I kept my mouth shut. We all did. But we could hardly talk at the time because of what we had seen. It was murder – pure murder. I couldn't believe it. We were a peacekeeping force. But [after what happened] you would think we were a nation at war,' he said. The man suffered for years afterwards from nightmares about Radio Katanga. The nightmare was always the same – visibly terrified black soldiers, some of whom had their knees knocking in fear, being herded into a room before hand-grenades were thrown in after them.

More than anything else, the Radio Katanga incident transformed the entire mood in Elisabethville. Irish and Swedish UN troops became deeply wary of operating alongside their Indian colleagues. As word spread about the events in the Radio Katanga building throughout the city, the secessionists suddenly had a potent rallying cry. UN personnel found they were openly shunned by most of the European population in Elisabethville, while the African population in the city regarded the UN as occupiers rather than peacekeepers.

The Dogras didn't do much to dispel the rumours of a massacre.

One horrified Irish officer later watched as a Dogra soldier shot and killed an elderly black man as he crossed the street some 100 metres away from a building occupied by the UN. The man was unarmed and clearly a non-combatant, but was shot because he was in the wrong place at the wrong time. News correspondents later described stomach-churning scenes of Katangan soldiers being repeatedly bayoneted.

In Leopoldville, there was a swift celebration of the strong-arm UN tactics. The Congolese government praised the UN military intervention and claimed: 'The secession of Katanga is now over.' Conor Cruise O'Brien himself went on radio in Katanga and confirmed that the secession was now finished. But it was merely the calm before the storm. The Katangan mercenaries had simply withdrawn to regroup – unwilling to tackle battalion-strength UN units head-on, they now decided on an alternative strategy to hit isolated UN posts and patrols. They would also use their superior equipment to deny the UN access to specific areas including the Lufira Bridge, which was a vital nexus on the UN supply line. Worse still, the UN had failed to detain Tshombe due to some confusion in orders over what troops were supposed to do at the presidential palace.

The first signs of trouble came with repeated sniper attacks on UN positions. The Irish had decided – with admirable foresight – to abandon their tactical base near Albert Park in Elisabethville because of its exposure to both mortar and rifle fire. The Irish commanders chose Prince Leopold Farm as their main operations base and even this came under sniper fire. But, unlike Albert Park, their new base offered clear zones for defensive fire should the Katangans decide to make a direct assault.

# CHAPTER SIX

*6 p.m., 14 September 1961*

THE 35TH BATTALION's intelligence officers were the first to realise that something was wrong – badly wrong. Garbled radio signals had been received from the north over the previous four days that Cmdt Quinlan and his force at Jadotville were now under siege. The Katangans had mounted roadblocks to isolate the UN detachment, and it was now believed they had commenced an assault on the Irish lines. Without taking back the Lufira Bridge, the UN could not resupply or relieve Cmdt Quinlan given the lack of air cover and heavy transport helicopters. The Lufira River was too wide and swift flowing to be forded – and the UN didn't have the bridging equipment to bypass the Katangan position and create their own river crossing.

Even more worryingly, there were now confused reports from local sources that the Radio College building which had been seized the day before by Irish troops, had been assaulted and the troops under the command of Lt Tommy Ryan had been overrun.

UN intelligence slowly began to grasp that the number of mercenaries in Katanga had been badly underestimated and that the Katangan gendarmes were now being led by freshly recruited French, German, Belgian and South African soldiers who were Algerian veterans almost to a man. They weren't likely to run from a fight and, worst of all, they were well versed in the hit-and-run ambush conflict that now seemed to be erupting all over the province and crippling UN operations.

The Armoured Car Group now became central to the 35th Battalion's response. The Ford armoured cars could check on the status of the Irish, Indian and Swedish positions and offer fire-support if necessary. If the situation became untenable, the armoured cars would then help evacuate Irish troops back to more defensible positions.

The Swedes – who possessed one of the most potent air forces in Europe thanks to their home-designed Saab aircraft – were now being urgently pressed to send fighters to the Congo. This would allow the UN to counter the Katangese Magisters, which were causing chaos and severely restricting UN helicopter operations. But, even if the Swedes agreed to dispatch their Saab 29 Tunnan fighters, which were armed with four Hispano 20mm cannons, the planes – of a design fondly nicknamed 'The Flying Barrel' because of its thick fuselage – couldn't be operational in Elisabethville for at least a month. Operation Morthor would have to be fought with the skies effectively in Katangan hands.

The mission was quickly spiralling into the worst crisis of the UN's Congo involvement. As word of the escalating fighting spread beyond Elisabethville, the UN in New York followed events with mounting concern. UN Secretary-General Dag Hammarskjöld decided to fly to the Congo as soon as possible to launch ceasefire talks with Tshombe and his forces. Hammarskjöld – who was making his fourth trip to the Congo – arranged to fly to Katanga to personally direct the peace talks. His aircraft, for security reasons, would not file a flight plan as it skirted northern Rhodesia en route to Elisabethville. It would also undertake the journey with another aircraft flying ahead as a decoy in case anyone tried to attack the UN team. It would prove to be the last journey of Hammarskjöld's life.

At Prince Leopold Farm on the outskirts of Elisabethville, senior Irish officers knew their immediate priority was to obtain information about precisely what was happening to the detachments of the 35th Battalion now scattered around Elisabethville. They needed information and they needed it fast. The Armoured Car Group was the reconnaissance asset they now turned to.

A patrol was ordered and Sgt Dan Carroll immediately set about organising personnel at Prince Leopold Farm. The Irish now had a total of eleven armoured cars in Katanga. Two were already in Jadotville with Cmdt Quinlan, two were assisting the Swedish and Indian UN troops at the Elisabethville Post Office and Dr Munongo's home, three were with the Indian Dogra unit and two were assigned to the Radio Katanga seizure. Dr Godefroid Munongo was the Interior Minister for Katanga and one of Moise Tshombe's closest allies. The Katangan police and gendarmes – the more potent paramilitary force – both answered to him. That left two armoured cars as a 'floating' reserve for emergency support and relief duties. One was a turreted armoured car with a Vickers machine gun and the other was an open-topped 'Scout' car equipped with a Browning gun.

It had already been an extremely demanding day for the armoured car section. They had supported all the major initial actions of Operation Morthor while trying to evade the attentions of the Katangan Staghound armoured cars whose whereabouts were now a cause of major concern. To complicate matters further, the Katangans had deployed wheeled 37mm anti-tank guns near some of their key installations and the guns were being operated by mercenaries. A single well-aimed hit from that 37mm gun would transform the Ford AFV into a wheeled coffin for its crew. The Swedes and Indians both wanted the Irish armoured cars to attract fire so as to open up Katangan positions to allow them to return infantry fire. But the Irish NCOs were wary because they knew the limitations of the home-built Ford AFV and its vulnerability to armour-piercing fire.

'I was assigned that day to the turreted Ford with Captain Seán Hennessy, Sgt Tim Carey and Cpl John Joe O'Connor,' Des Keegan recalled. Sgt Tim Carey was one of the Armoured Car Group's most experienced men. A native of Skibbereen in west Cork, he was respected as one of the best sergeants in the entire army and his experience of the Ford armoured car was second to none. Journalist Raymond Smith later described Carey as 'one of the coolest soldiers I have ever met'. The sergeant had just returned from a series of patrols and, by rights, should have been allowed go off duty, but instead was sent back out again.

'We were first sent up to the mansion of Dr Munongo, the Katangan Minister of the Interior, to act as fire-support for the Swedish battalion who were occupying the place and looking for documents. Munongo was in charge of both the mercenaries and the Katangan gendarmes so his home was a very important target. He was one of Tshombe's key lieutenants. We took up position and then spotted Munongo's personal guard assembling by a building across the road. They were all heavily armed and were clearly getting ready for action. And that's when the firing started. I know some people say that the first shots that day were fired at Radio Katanga or the Elisabethville Post Office, but I reckon they were fired at Munongo's house,' Des continued.

What was most remarkable about the mission undertaken by Captain Hennessy and his men was that their Ford armoured car rumbled through 'The Tunnel' – a key link on the Elisabethville road network – en route to Dr Munongo's house without a single shot being fired. 'The Tunnel' was effectively abandoned with no military forces dug-in by the bridges that had given 'The Tunnel' its nickname. Over the next few weeks, 'The Tunnel' became one of the most fiercely contested sites in the entire city between the Katangan gendarmes and the UN forces. The bitterness of the fighting ultimately made it one of the most notorious battle sites of the entire Katanga operation. 'It was totally unoccupied when we drove through it. There wasn't a soul in uniform to be seen. You'd never believe at that point that "The Tunnel" would become one of the major battlegrounds in Elisabethville,' Des explained.

The troops eventually secured Munongo's house – though, crucially, without any trace of the Minister himself – and the Irish car was then tasked with escorting a Swedish casualty to an Elisabethville hospital. The young Swede had apparently been the victim of a friendly fire incident between two UN detachments and had suffered serious gunshot wounds. Despite being rushed to hospital, the young man died a short time later. It was an inauspicious start to the day.

Having left the hospital, the armoured car was then re-assigned to the Indian battalion that was now attempting to seize Tshombe's palace in the face of fierce resistance by Katangan gendarmes and French mercenaries. Captain Hennessy had been transferred to other duties, so the Ford now came under the command of Sgt Carey. The Indian commander, who was unaware of the lack of hardened steel on the Irish armoured cars, was particularly keen to put the Ford AFV in a position of maximum exposure to draw Katangan fire so as to identify their main defensive positions.

'The Indian officer looked at us and said: "Put your armoured car in the middle of the road. You will draw their fire and we will then kill them all." But Tim Carey, fair dues to him, was having none of it. He knew the Katangans had an anti-tank gun up there and he told the Indian so,' Des added.

Sgt Carey knew that exposing the Ford to such fire was tantamount to suicide. 'I knew what the Indian wanted – he wanted us to take all the fire so his men could move into position and establish where the Katangans were. But the armour on the Ford was so brittle that even the impact of a rifle round would have chips flying off inside the car. If an armour piercing shell hit that Ford it would go in one side and come right out the other and make mincemeat of anyone inside. There was no way we were going to be sitting ducks for the Indians,' Tim Carey recalled.

The Irish crew had also formulated a plan should they be confronted by a Staghound armoured car and its dreaded 37mm gun. Cpl John Joe O'Connor was driving the Ford and was under orders to instantly speed down any road to the flank of the Staghound. The trusty Ford V8 engine made the armoured car surprisingly sprightly, even though its brakes meant it had to be handled carefully. The hope was that, by using the flanks, the Irish armoured car could attack the Staghound from the rear, wrecking its engine with fire from the Vickers before the 37mm gun could be brought to bear. Failing that, the Irish crew were left with their 'nuclear' option – attacking the Staghound with a box of grenades stored in the armoured car.

'Our fear was that the Vickers wouldn't be much good against the armour on the Staghound from the front or sides. So, as a last resort, we planned to speed up to the Staghound so fast that its crew couldn't aim the 37mm and try to use the grenades to disable it. It wasn't much of a plan but it was the only bloody plan we had,' Des explained. Luckily, the Ford was untroubled that day by the Staghounds though the Irish had not heard the last of the Katangan armour.

The crew of the Ford – who had now been on duty since the early hours of the morning – eventually returned to Prince Leopold Farm in the late afternoon to refuel the armoured car, get extra ammunition for the Vickers and, if possible, catch a few hours precious sleep before the next round of missions. The Ford V8 – because of the weight of the chassis – delivered roughly 8.5 miles

(14 kilometres) to the gallon. With a fuel tank capacity of fourteen gallons the Ford AFV had a maximum possible range of 122 miles (210 kilometres), which meant it needed regular refuelling during peak mission activity. Des Keegan and John Joe O'Connor – having refuelled and rearmed the Ford – went straight to their billets to try and sleep. But, less than an hour later and much to their annoyance, Sgt Carroll assigned them to an impending Radio College patrol to be led by Cmdt Cahalane.

'John Joe pointed out to the sergeant that we had already been on duty all day and asked whether the relief crew could be sent out with the armoured car instead. He told Dan that we had just lain down to get some sleep, having been in the armoured car all day. We had already undertaken four or so missions and we felt we had done our bit for the day. John Joe wasn't being cheeky – he was basically pointing out that we had put in a long day. In fairness to the sergeant, he listened to us and immediately told us to go back to sleep. He would assign the relief crew, which were Tpr Pat Mullins and Cpl Michael Nolan. The car was already prepared and they took the turreted Ford, which we had been using all day. They took our place on the patrol that night,' Des said.

Sgt Carey was also going to be excused patrol duty but conscientiously insisted to Sgt Carroll that he wanted to accompany Cmdt Cahalane and was okay for the mission. Sgt Carey had an intimate knowledge of the local roads and felt he was best placed to guide the patrol to exactly where it needed to go. Privately, he also wanted to ensure that the patrol did not get lost on the dark Elisabethville roads and end up blundering its way into a heavily armed Katangan gendarme force.

Shortly before 6 p.m., Sgt Carey was ordered to stand by for the patrol, which would be led by Cmdt Pat Cahalane, the commander of the Armoured Car Group. Cahalane was a native of Dundrum in

Dublin and was extremely popular amongst his men because of the concern he always displayed for their welfare and their operating conditions. It was hoped that the patrol could now ease a lot of the worries about the Irish positions at 'The Factory' and the Radio College.

The patrol would feature the two 'floating' armoured cars – the open-topped Scout and the Ford. The armoured cars would be the primary weapons and would protect a Landrover jeep equipped with hand-held Carl Gustav anti-tank projectiles. Personnel not assigned to the two armoured cars and the jeep would be transported in a bus, which had been commandeered by the UN from a local Elisabethville coach company. The bus contained a full rifle section comprising two NCOs and eight soldiers. The soldiers were all equipped with the standard FN assault rifle, which, ironically enough, was the same Belgian-made weapon now wielded by most of the Katangan gendarmes.

The initial destination for the patrol was supposed to be an Elisabethville factory where a detachment of Irish soldiers had been stationed the previous day. The detachment occupying the sprawling industrial building nicknamed 'The Factory' was under the command of Sgt Sam Shannon from Kilrush, County Clare. Sgt Shannon had fifteen soldiers under his command – but the building now housed more than 600 refugees. These included both political prisoners who had been fleeing persecution in Katanga over the previous eighteen months, as well as soldiers from the Congolese army who had deserted and feared what would happen if they were captured by the Katangan gendarmes.

One of the few things known for certain in Battalion HQ was that 'The Factory' had already been surrounded and attacked by a large and heavily armed Katangan force. But, as far as battalion knew, Sgt Shannon had managed to hold his lines. The initial purpose of the patrol was to see if Sgt Shannon needed reinforcement – or whether he needed to evacuate his position under covering fire from the armoured cars.

However, as the patrol prepared to depart, one of the 35th Battalion's intelligence officers, Captain James 'Jimmy' Parker, approached Cmdt Cahalane and Sgt Carey and shared some private concerns. Captain Parker – a native of Mitchelstown who would later become Defence Forces chief of staff – spoke of growing fears about the safety of Lt Tommy Ryan's small Irish detachment at the Radio College. They had been assigned to garrison the facility as part of Operation Morthor, but it had been impossible to establish contact with the outpost over the past four hours and HQ now wanted the patrol to investigate local rumours that a large force of Katangan gendarmes had overrun the position and captured the entire Irish detachment.

The patrol's primary mission now was to establish precisely what had happened to Ryan and his men. If they weren't found at the Radio College, the patrol was ordered to occupy and hold the premises until UN reinforcements arrived.

Part of the problem now facing the 35th Battalion was logistical. The Irish units were equipped with C-12 radios that were valve-based and did not work properly when used inside a moving armoured car because of the heavy vibrations. Due to atmospheric conditions in the Congo, after nightfall the radios tended to suffer from extreme static, sometimes so bad that communication was totally impossible. Tim Carey recalled that you needed 'an aerial stretching almost to the moon' to get any kind of reception while on the move. Operation Morthor had landed the UN in a dangerous firefight, but confused UN commanders were now increasingly unable to keep track of either their troop positions or their combat status. That did not explain why the Irish troops at the Radio College – with access to a powerful radio transmitter – had not been able to report back on their situation. Unless, of course, the Katangans had overwhelmed them before they could raise the alarm.

Sgt Carey knew the maze of roads around Elisabethville like the back of his hand. He was the only man on the patrol familiar with Avenue Wangermee and Rue de Cuivre, the roads on which the sprawling Radio College was located. Sgt Carey's familiarity with the road network was a crucial advantage given the Radio College's proximity to a major Katangan gendarme base. The last thing the Irish troopers wanted was an unexpected nocturnal meeting with a large Katangan force. Cmdt Cahalane would lead the patrol, in command of the armoured car driven by Carey, with the jeep and bus following close behind. The open-topped armoured car commanded by Capt. Frank Whyte together with Sgt Peter Dignam and Cpl Paddy Holbrook would take up the rear position.

As the patrol slowly pulled out of camp, Tpr John O'Mahony watched anxiously from beside one of the base guard posts. Ordinary troopers were not consulted by senior officers about developments, but the soldiers knew full well from rumours on the base grapevine that things weren't looking good around Elisabethville. John knew there was a good chance the patrol leaving base wouldn't return without shots having been exchanged with the Katangans and their mercenary allies.

Other Irish soldiers not assigned to the patrol also watched as the small convoy prepared to set off. 'I think everyone was smoking – even people who didn't smoke at home ended up smoking in the Congo because we were issued with these awful "Belges" cigarettes as a form of payment in Elisabethville. To be honest, smoking was a way to bleed off the tension. I remember standing there smoking a cigarette with a few other lads as Pat, Mick and the others ran through their checklist with the armoured cars. A few of the lads in the bus waved to us as they prepared to depart,' John said.

Conditions in the Irish camp had deteriorated over the past week with businesses in Elisabethville now refusing to supply the UN forces with food because of fears of retaliation by Katangan gendarmes. Over the previous three months, the Irish troops at least had access to freshly cooked food like chicken and beef, as well as local vegetables. Now, they had to resort to living off pack rations such as 'dog biscuits' and tinned bully beef, which was heated in a pan. The only consolation was that the Irish troops vastly preferred their own pack rations to the US rations. Many of the American meals bore absolutely no resemblance to what was specified on the tin – and some Irish soldiers grumbled that it was probably dog food repackaged. Many soldiers simply refused to eat the US rations, or tried to swap them for either Irish or Swedish rations that seemed more appealing.

'I was cursing the fact that my hand was still in a cast and that I wasn't allowed to undertake duty in the armoured cars. I had wanted to volunteer for the patrol but I knew Sgt Carroll wouldn't allow me because, with one hand in a cast, I simply couldn't operate the turret. It was just too heavy to move it one-handed. I waved to Pat and he smiled back at me and raised his hand in salute. At that point Pat was in the open-topped Scout car that was bringing up the rear of the patrol. He was manning the Browning machine gun and would be protecting the patrol's rear. My abiding memory is of Pat waving from the open-topped armoured car as dusk fell and the patrol rumbled out the gate. I can close my eyes and still picture him waving to me,' John added.

The patrol had only travelled a short distance down the road when Cmdt Cahalane ordered a halt for a re-arrangement of personnel between the various vehicles. Cmdt Laurence 'Larry' O'Toole, an officer of the Medical Corps, had initially been travelling in the first armoured car alongside Cmdt Cahalane, Sgt Carey and Cpl Michael Nolan. However, Cmdt Cahalane decided that, as the lead Ford was the most likely to see action first, a dedicated gunner for the Vickers was an absolute necessity. With Cpl Nolan assigned to radio communications and Sgt Carey driving, another trooper was clearly required. Tpr Mullins was ordered to transfer to the lead armoured car – and, with five personnel making the car too crowded to operate effectively, Cmdt O'Toole was sent back to the rear. 'He was one lucky doctor,' Captain Art Magennis later acknowledged.

The Ford AFV now revved up again and led the small patrol directly towards the Radio College, some five kilómetres from the Irish base. The initial route took them out of the base, along Rue Savonnier, through the soon-to-be-infamous Tunnel, past the Hotel de Ville, and then, at the junction of Avenue Royale and the Cathedral, through a hard right onto Avenue Wangermee.

The patrol, moving slowly and carefully – paying attention to any signs of Katangan gendarme movements – wound its way around the western suburbs of Elisabethville. But the armoured cars were unchallenged. Approaching Avenue Wangermee, Sgt Carey brought the patrol's speed down to a cautious crawl. Cmdt Cahalane repeatedly scanned the surrounding buildings for any sign of trouble while Tpr Mullins manned the Vickers ready to respond to fire at a moment's notice. But there was no sign of trouble as they approached the college.

The college, founded by the Belgians in 1912, was one of the biggest and most modern facilities in Elisabethville. The building, with its brick, concrete and glass exterior, could easily be mistaken for a European or North American high school or college. The college not only boasted a powerful radio transmitter, it also housed a large bookshop and library on the first floor and a small student print shop in the basement. The building was approached through a tall arched gateway made up of steel and timber, and topped with a sign proudly boasting of the college's fiftieth anniversary year. At either end of the college were large block structures, each of which had twenty-eight large glass windows showing the staircase inside. The building was two storeys high with a flat roof and numerous windows. The college was fronted by a rather worn lawn, which had receded in parts to show the iconic rich-red soil of the Congo. Across the road from the college was some open parkland with a few hardy African trees offering shelter from the sun for students and pedestrians.

That night there was an eerie stillness all along Avenue Wangermee. There was not a single soul in sight, despite the fact that this was traditionally a popular time for locals, free of the sticky daytime heat, to savour the cool evening air.

On either side of the Radio College were residential properties. The families that lived there were either wealthy, European, or part of Elisabethville's fledgling native middle class. Most of the buildings were of traditional colonial design – single or two-storey, all with ample porches looking out onto the street. Most usually had European saloon cars such as Renaults, Citroens, Opels or Mercedes parked in the wide driveways. Avenue Wangermee itself was more of a boulevard than an ordinary road – wide enough for four vehicles to drive abreast. Unlike other parts of Elisabethville where road surfaces were compacted earth, Avenue Wangermee boasted a well-maintained tarmac surface.

The Irish patrol approached, keeping the Radio College on its left-hand side. 'As we approached the college the complete patrol was together and everything seemed to be quiet. There was an ambulance on the side of the road, on our left, and I pulled into the left-hand side,' Sgt Carey later recalled in an official army report. When the patrol halted and gazed around they saw no obvious sign of trouble. There wasn't a single indication of fighting – there were no rifle or machine gun cartridges scattered about and the college itself seemed to be completely undamaged. There were no windows broken and no sign of any bullet impacts on the brick and concrete exterior. There was nothing whatsoever to hint at a threat to the normal colonial tranquillity of this residential area. Similarly, there didn't appear to be any sign of Katangan forces or their vehicles. The Irish soldiers scanned the nearby buildings and avenues for any sign of Katangan armour, but saw nothing.

Yet, the absence of local residents made the Irish troopers nervous. This was a residential area – so where were the people who lived here? Elisabethville had suffered from power cuts as the Katangan crisis escalated and the entire street was now shrouded in darkness. The lack of streetlights and house lights along Avenue Wangermee made it very difficult for the patrol to see anything beyond what was immediately in front of them – not that there was anything to see, nor any sound of movement.

Of more immediate importance to the patrol was the location of Lt Ryan and his men. There was no disguising the throaty rumble of their Ford engines, which could be heard from hundreds of metres away, so the Irish detachment at the college should have heard their approach. But why didn't they signal or acknowledge the presence of the Irish patrol? And where were Lt Ryan's sentries posted outside the Radio College? Even if they were having problems with their radios, Lt Ryan's men should easily be able to contact the armoured cars on the battalion's bandwidth because of their sheer proximity.

The turreted Ford armoured car held its position in front of the jeep and bus and waited patiently for a signal from the Irish detachment. But still no signal came. The patrol would give Lt Ryan and his men a few more minutes before an armed inspection party would be dispatched into the Radio College to determine what the hell was going on. The Vickers and Browning machine guns could cover the inspection party as they approached the front door to look for any trace of Lt Ryan and his men. Several members of the patrol gazed at the silent and dark Radio College and held their breath.

Then, without warning, the darkness of the night was shattered by a meteor-like fire trail erupting from the left of the Ford AFV. The fire trail dazzled the eyes of every Irish trooper whose sight was magnetically attracted to the searing light. Less than a second later, the eardrums of every Irish soldier reeled from the concussion of a huge explosion. Then all hell broke loose along Avenue Wanger-mee.

# CHAPTER SEVEN

A BLINDING FLASH of light and a deafening roar was the only warning the patrol got of the incoming anti-tank round. But for Cmdt Cahalane and the three men inside the Ford AFV there was no warning at all. The armoured visor plate in front of the driver was raised and everyone in the car was studying the front door of the Radio College. The crew didn't see the flash of the anti-tank round being fired behind them and their world instantly dissolved in a thunderclap of heat, noise and smoke.

The anti-armour shell covered the distance from the carefully hidden Katangan positions to the stationary armoured car in just over a second – faster than the human brain could even process the threat. The darkness had aided the concealment of the Katangans in their ambush site, which had been carefully chosen and prepared by the gendarmes' French mercenary commander, Bob Denard. Having captured Lt Ryan and his small detachment, Denard knew the UN would send a patrol to discover what had happened – and any armoured escort would be vulnerable on its flank as it drew up outside the Radio College.

Denard had ordered the attack at precisely the moment the UN patrol was at its most vulnerable and he had carried out a textbook ambush. His Katangan gendarmes had shown admirable discipline in holding their positions until he personally ordered the anti-tank round to be fired. It helped that the Katangan troops were terrified of the French mercenary. Denard's biggest fear was that if the ambush was launched prematurely, his men would be exposed to the withering fire of the Vickers and Browning machine guns from the armoured cars.

The round struck the lead Ford armoured car just below the turret – and the Irish troops in the jeep and bus immediately behind could only close their eyes and cringe in horror at the ball of smoke and flame that consumed the armoured car. Miraculously, the warhead struck at such an acute angle that it glanced upwards before exploding. Had the weapon – a recoilless rifle – struck dead-on and true, it would have instantly incinerated the entire four-man Irish crew.

The huge explosion of the warhead still managed to lift the entire Ford car onto its two side wheels for a few brief seconds before it finally crashed back down onto the ground. What no one realised at the time was that the sheer force of the huge explosion had fused the turret to the sides of the hull and wrecked its turning bearings.

The patrol instantly descended into chaos as the Katangans trained heavy fire on the remaining vehicles. Denard had warned his men that they had to disable all the UN vehicles – they could not afford to allow any armoured cars or jeeps to escape the killing zone for fear they would then circle around and attack the Katangans from the flank or rear.

Two squad machine guns opened up on the Irish vehicles – and the rear armoured Irish car suddenly stalled and could not be restarted. At a stroke, the Irish patrol had been stripped of its two main defensive weapons. With the two armoured cars disabled – and the crucial firepower of their Vickers and Browning machine guns lost – the Irish patrol was suddenly little more than target practice for every Katangan with a gun.

Most vulnerable were the Irish troops in the commandeered bus. Staying in the coach was tantamount to suicide because even

9mm handguns could slice through the thin metal sides of the vehicle. 'Get out, get out, get out,' an NCO screamed at the shocked troopers. The driver threw open the front and rear doors and in seconds the soldiers were scrambling out to reach the shelter of the nearby buildings. If they could reach the buildings, a defensive perimeter could at least be established and supporting fire laid down for the lads in the armoured cars.

The crew of the jeep faced the same stark choice. They could either speed away and leave their comrades to their fate or dismount and try to provide some kind of covering fire. Because the jeep was not armoured, staying inside the stationary vehicle meant death. They had a stark choice: flee or stay and fight. The crew had to move before the Katangan anti-tank team had a chance to re-load – and they had to move fast.

Inside the stricken armoured car, amid a blinding cloud of smoke and flame, Sgt Carey struggled to make sense of what had just happened. It was hard to draw breath inside the armoured car, which stank of cordite fumes. 'The armoured car seemed to light up – that's all I can remember,' he said. 'We were obviously hit with an anti-tank round, there were choking gasses – clothing and other items seemed to be alight.'

Struggling to clear his head, the sergeant desperately scrambled around in the armoured car to check on his three comrades. Cmdt Cahalane – who appeared to have been standing up gazing out the turret visor when the anti-tank round hit – was badly concussed and only semi-conscious. To his horror, Sgt Carey realised he was crawling over the prone bodies of Tpr Mullins and Cpl Nolan on the metal floor of the vehicle. Tpr Mullins was lying on the floor just below the turret, with Cpl Nolan motionless and spread-eagled across his body.

'I went to go for the door and I know I went over Cpl Nolan's body. Tpr Mullins was blocking the door – I had to get my hands around him just to open the door and, when the door opened, he gave a sigh,' Sgt Carey said. Opening the door immediately helped clear the interior of the Ford of its noxious gases and the sergeant slowly helped his dazed commander towards fresh air.

But as soon as the main access hatch on the armoured car opened, there was a burst of well-aimed machine gun fire from concealed Katangan positions around the Radio College. The gendarmes had been trained to hit the armoured car with the recoilless rifle round – and then wait for the crew to try to scramble clear. Until the crew managed to get behind the right flank of the Ford, they were in full sight of the concealed Katangan positions. The gendarmes opened up with machine guns and assault rifles determined to settle scores with the UN.

Bullets clanged off the armoured car as Sgt Carey and Cmdt Cahalane emerged, some gouging lumps of paint and metal from the Ford's soft armoured hide. Seconds later, Sgt Carey reeled backwards as if he had just been kicked by a horse in the leg. He gasped as he realised a round had just hit him in the upper left thigh. Grimacing in pain, he desperately reached back and tried to help the two soldiers lying inside the armoured car. A second round of machine gun fire erupted and this time the Katangans used tracer rounds to better aim their fire in the growing darkness. The sergeant knew he had only seconds left to reach a defensible position and get his commander to safety before the machine guns cut them to pieces.

'The ammo was hitting the armoured car and everything around me seemed to be confused. Cmdt Cahalane seemed to be dazed and shocked. It looked like his eardrums had been shattered and he seemed out on his feet. I caught Tpr Mullins and tried to pull him. I don't think I was standing at the time.' The sergeant realised that he had to try and get his commanding officer to safety before his left leg collapsed underneath him. Courageously ignoring the waves of pain from his jagged wound and the blood now pouring down his leg, the sergeant half-pulled and half-dragged his concussed commander towards the shelter of a nearby building.

'Cmdt Cahalane and myself made a break for the building on our left. Then a shell hit the building just over us and masonry and glass came shattering down on top of us. We managed to get through the building and into a yard out back. There were some gendarmes coming over a wall towards our position and [then someone] fired an "84" and this seemed to stop the advance,' he said.

Cpl Dan Sullivan – a native of Cork city whose brother, Walter 'Wally' Sullivan, was the drum major of the battalion pipe band – had been travelling in the jeep when the lead armoured car in the patrol took a direct hit. He was responsible for the 84mm recoilless Carl Gustav anti-tank rocket, which was the Irish patrol's equivalent to the Katangan anti-tank weapon. As the jeep's crew desperately scrambled to safety, Cpl Sullivan had the presence of mind to take the Carl Gustav and its projectiles with him.

Inside the building, Cpl Sullivan's colleague, Private Pat Crowley, decided Katangan efforts to overrun the patrol could best be frustrated by a warning round from the 84mm rifle. While designed for anti-armour work, the projectile's exhaust plume and the spectacular detonation of its warhead was more than sufficient to persuade any infantrymen in its vicinity to keep their heads firmly down. One round was enough to persuade the Katangan gendarmes to abandon their assault on the rear of the building and resume their original ambush positions. Unfortunately, the back-blast from the weapon caught Sgt Carey, knocking him down as he struggled to keep his footing.

Other members of the patrol – realising the desperate plight of their commander and the sergeant – tried to offer covering fire and help the duo reach safety without further injury. But the descending darkness made it difficult to tell where the various elements of the patrol had scattered to, and it was increasingly impossible to tell friend from foe. Power cuts had left Avenue Wangermee darker than Hades and the Irish troops didn't want to fire flares for fear of attracting further fire from the Katangan forces. The patrol's two best weapons were mobility and the firepower of the two Ford AFVs – and they had just lost them both.

'We managed to get into the back of another house where Captain Whyte broke a glass door and we got in. At this stage, defensive positions were taken up. I was bleeding and had by now lost a lot of blood. Captain Whyte assisted me in applying a first aid bandage. I was passing out, but I had a bottle of water and that seemed to revive me. Captain Whyte and Sgt Dignam decided they would make a break to get back to camp to raise the alarm,' Sgt Carey recalled.

'I placed a tourniquet on my leg to try and staunch the flow of blood. It was pouring down my leg and almost filling my boot. It was so thick that when it dried and crusted I could hardly bend my knee. I knew I had to keep releasing the tourniquet and then tightening it up again or I would be in right trouble with blood loss,' he added.

In a bizarre coincidence, the Irish troops had just sought shelter in the villa of Gerard Soerte – the Belgian policeman who had supervised the exhumation and disposal of Patrice Lumumba's body the previous January. Soerte was at home with his wife, his two children and his brother, Michel, who was also a policeman. Their main concern was that the presence of the UN troops would trigger a gunfight in which they or their children could be injured.

Without the armoured cars, Captain Whyte knew the Irish

patrol desperately needed reinforcement or evacuation by the remaining elements of the 35th Battalion. Someone had to let battalion know that the two Irish units were now heavily engaged by the gendarmes. Having informed a semi-dazed Cmdt Cahalane what they intended, Whyte and Dignam wasted no time in setting off to try to get help. Just minutes later the Katangan gendarmes, shrewdly directed by the French mercenaries, closed the ring around the Irish troops. The patrol was now trapped. They would either have to fight their way out, or UN reinforcements would have to fight their way in to help them. The Katangans fired the odd volley of shots towards the buildings now sheltering the Irish patrol as if to discourage any idea of movement and to persuade the now trapped UN troops to keep their heads down.

Captain Whyte, in his report to Battalion HQ, confirmed that the attack on the patrol had achieved total surprise. 'I was observing to the rear [of the scout car] with a Bren [Browning] gun when the leading car was immobilised by an anti-tank gun. I ordered the driver to reverse and swing the gun around but could see no target to engage. The rest of the column had dismounted and taken cover beside Radio College. As I had seen no one leave the immobilised armoured car beside Radio College I thought all were dead. I had the men search for the enemy gunner and told the corporal driver to turn the near armoured car. In the meantime, I discovered that Cmdt Cahalane and Sgt Carey had escaped,' he said.

'I subsequently discovered that Sgt Carey was wounded in the left thigh. Cmdt Cahalane appeared deafened by the explosion. While the search was proceeding I was joined by Cpl Holbrook and the civilian interpreter. The armoured car stalled in turning. We moved into the grounds of the flats adjoining Radio College. I succeeded in gaining entry to a flat on the ground floor and Cmdt Cahalane disposed the men covering the front and rear. The men were still shocked but were recovering. I dressed Sgt Carey's wound. Cmdt Cahalane decided that since no radio message had been sent back somebody would have to go back for assistance and inform battalion of our position.

'The flat was occupied by a man, his wife and family and his brother-in-law. The buildings surrounding Radio College were occupied by the gendarmerie. During the original search an enemy soldier was captured, but he subsequently escaped in the dark. Cmdt Cahalane decided to stay put until daylight and asked for volunteers to make a break for it. Sgt Dignam and myself volunteered. I ordered the two Belgians to hand over the key of the civilian car in the rear. I was going to make a break for it in the car but decided against that as the anti-tank gunner was still outside. I ordered the civilians to hand over their coats and we put them on. We were covered from the back door and made a dash across the back garden, over the wall and into the grounds of a house in the rear. Keeping to the back gardens, generally, we made our way slowly in the general direction of our own lines,' he said. Sgt Dignam and Captain Whyte, after a slow and painstaking journey, finally managed to reach an Indian supply depot near the city centre and raise the alarm.

While they couldn't have known it, the relief patrol had walked into a trap carefully laid by the Katangan gendarmes in the hours after Lt Tommy Ryan and his unit had been overwhelmed earlier that day. When Lt Ryan and his men first deployed to the Radio College in the initial phase of Operation Morthor, everything seemed to be going well. At 2.30 p.m. a local woman called to the college and asked if the Irish troops were okay. Lt Ryan told her they were fine but would appreciate any boiling water she might be able to provide for tea. The woman's husband brought the boiling water to the Irish troops at 3 p.m. – and returned to collect the empty water container at 4 p.m. But this time the husband arrived at the college

The Galtee Mountains on the Cork-Limerick-Tipperary border make a dramatic backdrop to the Mullins family home at Boher, outside Kilbehenny. The farmhouse is marked with a red 'X'. *(Photo: Paudie McGrath)*

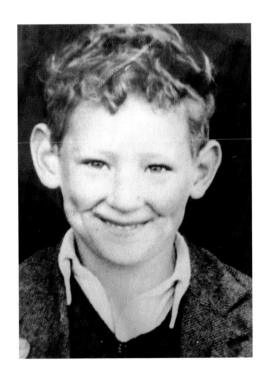

Pat Mullins shows a ready smile as a young schoolboy attending Kilbehenny national school. *(Photo: Mullins family)*

Mary Mullins married Tom Kent in October 1959 and the happy couple are serenaded by an accordion player. Pat Mullins is pictured, flower in his lapel, standing third from right. *(Photo: Mullins family)*

The Second Armoured Car Group of the 35th Irish (UN) Battalion poses for a photo in Fermoy in June 1961 before travelling to Dublin for their USAF flight to the Congo. John O'Mahony is far left, back row. Pat Mullins is beside him (second left, back row), Sgt Tim Carey is second from left in the front row. The officer in the centre of the front row is Captain Seán Hennessy. Tpr Des Keegan is third from right in the back row. *(Photo: John O'Mahony)*

Newly promoted to a three star Trooper, Pat Mullins poses proudly in May 1961 at the 1st Motor Squadron's base at Fitzgerald Camp in Fermoy. *(Photo: John O'Mahony)*

A 'handy hurler' in Munster GAA parlance, Pat Mullins was drafted straight into the 1st Motor Squadron team. Pat is pictured, third from left, in the back row. *(Photo: Mullins family)*

Members of the 35th Irish (UN) Battalion form up on parade outside Prince Leopold Farm. Note the blue helmets and the Carl Gustav sub-machine guns arming the troops. *(Photo: Art Magennis)*

Sgt Dan Carroll and Tpr Ned Regan on armed guard as a queue of Baluba refugees seek admission to a UN camp at Elisabethville. *(Photo: Art Magennis)*

The bush on the far outskirts of Elisabethville. The Lubumbashi River is in the left background while the sprawl of the city is just visible in the right background. *(Photo: Art Magennis)*

A young Tpr John O'Mahony poses for the camera while on duty at Elisabethville Airport in August 1961. Note the Magister jet to the left rear. In the centre is a ubiquitous Douglas DC-3 of Second World War vintage, while to the right is a Douglas DC-4. *(Photo: John O'Mahony)*

A group of a curious Katangese children crowd around a Ford AFV and its three-man Irish crew. Note the Vickers machine gun in the turret and the rear access hatch. *(Photo: Art Magennis)*

An Irish soldier indicates the impact point on the left side of Pat Mullins' Ford AFV where the Katangan anti-tank weapon struck. Captain Art Magennis – who located and recovered the Ford – is pictured third from left. *(Photo: Art Magennis)*

The scorched interior of the Ford AFV indicates attempts by the Katangan gendarmes to destroy the armoured car after its final battle. *(Photo: Art Magennis)*

Pat Mullins' Ford AFV pictured with its front wheels stuck in a drainage ditch. This photo was taken minutes after the armoured car was first located. *(Photo: Art Magennis)*

A graphic image of how the soft-steel hull plates of the Ford were unable to stand up to heavy fire. Katangan shells gouged holes in the 'armour' of both the hull and turret of Pat Mullins' car. Note the impact of the round on the Vickers machine gun cooling jacket. *(Photo: Art Magennis)*

The charred remains of a UN bus after the ambush launched against Pat Mullins and the Irish patrol by mercenary-led Katangan forces. *(Photo: Art Magennis)*

A UN truck lies burned out where it was attacked by Katangan gendarmes. The Katangans viewed the UN as favouring Lumumba's Communist-leaning political party, hence the hammer-and-sickle graffiti. This was the truck in which Trooper Edward Gaffney of the 35th Battalion was shot and killed on 13 September 1961 after the vehicle was caught in cross-fire. *(Photo: Art Magennis)*

An Irish UN patrol winds its way through a suburb of Elisabethville watched by curious Katangan residents. Note how high a silhouette the Ford AFVs have. *(Photo: Art Magennis)*

Pat Mullins' armoured car minutes after it was towed back to the Irish battalion's Prince Leopold Farm base following the ambush. *(Photo: Art Magennis)*

'It's a very long way from Fermoy.' Two Irish patrols take a break in the sizzling heat of August in Elisabethville. Four Ford AFVs are surrounded by five Willys jeeps. *(Photo: Art Magennis)*

Irish troops marvel at modern armoured weaponry. Note the shamrock armbands worn by the soldiers. The Swedish armoured car boasts proper hardened steel plate, four-wheel drive, wide visibility for the driver and, most intimidating of all, twin box-fed Madsen machine guns which could fire 1,100 rounds per minute. *(Photo: Art Magennis)*

An Irish trooper poses with a Katangan M8 Greyhound armoured car. The vehicle had proper hardened steel plate, six-wheel drive and a 37mm cannon. Sgt Tim Carey warned that if an Irish Ford was hit by a 37mm shell, it would go through one side of the hull, out the other and mince the entire crew. *(Photo: Art Magennis)*

The plight of refugees in any warzone is heartbreaking. Here, a group of Congolese refugees flee their homes amid safety fears following inter-tribal violence. *(Photo: Art Magennis)*

Congolese families gather at a UN-controlled refugee camp in Elisabethville. Such was the scale of the refugee problem that UN-run camps struggled to cope with the staggering influx of Congolese. *(Photo: Art Magennis)*

The cavernous hold of a USAF Globemaster is readily visible at Wheelus Field in Libya. This shot was taken when the 35th Battalion was en route back home in December 1961. *(Photo: John O'Mahony)*

The rains transformed the Congo in a matter of hours, with everything covered in a lush blanket of greenery. Captain Art Magennis (centre) is pictured at a temporary camp in the bush. Note the FN rifle propped against a tree. *(Photo: Art Magennis)*

In November 1998, just a few weeks before her death, Pat Mullins' mother, Catherine, had the satisfaction of seeing her son posthumously awarded the Military Star. *(Photo: Paudie McGrath)*

John O'Mahony photographed with his Irish United Nations Veterans Association (IUNVA) beret and blazer. *(Photo: John O'Mahony)*

Pat Mullins was eventually awarded three medals for his UN service in the Congo in 1961. Pictured left to right are the Military Star, the UN Peace Medal and the Congo Service Medal. *(Photo: Paudie McGrath)*

The Memorial Wall unveiled at the former Fitzgerald Camp in Fermoy, County Cork, in October 2009. Pat Mullins' name features twice on the monument. The old barracks' chapel is now Fermoy's Queen of Peace Church. *(Photo: John O'Mahony)*

Des Keegan reads the headstone inscription on the Mullins family grave behind Kilbehenny Church. Pat's parents, Catherine and Ned, are interred here. Pat's name is on the headstone but his body remains unrecovered in the Congo. *(Photo: Paudie McGrath)*

The Mullins family photographed at a family celebration in the 1990s. Front row, left to right, are Mary Kent, Catherine Mullins (Pat's mother) and Theresa Healy. Back row, left to right, are Dinny Mullins, Peggy Dwane, Tom Mullins and Nelly Kelly. *(Photo: Mullins family)*

Mary Kent, Dinny Mullins, Peggy Dwane and Tom Mullins pictured at the Curragh Camp in 2009 at the dedication of a special memorial in the name of Tpr Pat Mullins. To the left is Brig-Gen. Seán McCann, General Officer Commanding-Curragh and to the right is (now rtd) Lt Col Eamon Cullagh, Director of the Cavalry School (Curragh). *(Photo: Paudie McGrath)*

with a second man dressed in civilian clothing. The Irish troops discovered within minutes that it was a French mercenary serving with the Katangan gendarmes, Lt San Paul, who was detailed to try to persuade the Irish unit to surrender and avoid a battle.

'They told me that for the past twelve hours I was completely surrounded by Katangese troops. I denied this and said they were bluffing and what was their interest in this as civilians,' Lt Ryan declared in his official post-ambush report. 'The newcomer … said he was here to save our lives. He had no fears as we stood no chance.' A short time later a phone rang in the college and it turned out to be a missionary priest who was translating for another more senior Katangan officer. This man – a captain (Bob Denard) – confirmed much of what Lt Paul had just said.

'The priest assured me that what he had said was true and that I was outnumbered. The captain then asked that the two of us meet on Avenue Wangermee without arms to talk. I agreed to this and stated that I was leaving Lt Paul in the college as a hostage. I met the captain and the priest on the avenue and he repeated the fact that I was completely surrounded. He then told me how many men I had and what weapons I had. He also said that I had no communication with my unit,' Lt Ryan explained.

'This information I strongly suspected had been given to him by the priest who had visited the college the previous night with M. Tomberlaine to make a [radio] broadcast. He then told me he had men in every house around the college and that the priest's residence across the road was also occupied. He said he had an armoured car at one [corner] and an anti-tank weapon on a jeep on another. At a signal from him, a jeep appeared with a weapon mounted on it – an armoured car appeared at Avenue Ruwe and at every door and window of every villa black and white soldiers, not in uniform, appeared. I also noticed from ten to fifteen whites in civilian clothing on Avenue Wangermee, who at first I thought were civilians but who were now taking a more than curious interest in the proceedings,' he wrote.

'The captain then gave me five minutes to decide between surrender and being blasted out of it. I left him and then returned to the college and I released Lt Paul and the other civilian. I went around to my men and explained the situation. They all said they would be guided by my decision. In view of the lack of communication and the fact that I only had one Bren gun I decided we could not hold the position against the odds without my men being slaughtered and I decided to surrender. On notifying the captain of this, he asked us to leave all our weapons in the building and to come out on the road. We were then surrounded by forty to fifty paratroopers and gendarmes who threatened us and pushed us around and manhandled us. The intervention of a priest, the two white officers [Captain Denard and Lt Paul] and a journalist saved us,' Lt Ryan reported.

The Irish officer and his men were immediately placed under armed guard and transported away from the Radio College. Back on Avenue Wangermee, the French mercenary now laid his plans to deal with the expected UN relief force and its armour. Cmdt Cahalane and his men then stumbled right into the trap.

INSIDE THE RADIO College building, the soldiers who had taken shelter there and were manning the defensive perimeter wondered what the hell was going to happen next? If the Katangans brought up their Staghounds and started to shell the building around them, the patrol would be finished. The Radio College was too big, too open and had too many windows to properly defend against an all-out assault by a superior enemy force. If the Katangans used the Staghounds and their 37mm guns to shell the building, it would most likely collapse around their heads.

For several hours, Cmdt Cahalane and his men held their defensive positions in the various buildings they had taken shelter in and simply waited. It was now a race between UN reinforcements reaching them and the Katangans deciding to mount an all-out assault along their entire perimeter.

Then, without warning, came the distinctive sound of a Ford engine firing up. Cpl Sullivan – who was trapped in the building with the patrol – later recalled that nothing could be confused with the smooth, throaty roar of the Ford engine firing into life. 'I knew it was the Ford all right – you couldn't mistake it for anything else. At the time we thought it was probably the Katangans taking away one of our armoured cars. But it was so dark we could hardly see our hands in front of our faces. We couldn't see the armoured cars even though they were parked out on the road in front of us,' he said. The soldier later estimated the time at around 2 a.m. After a few minutes, the sound of the rumbling Ford engine faded into the distance.

Inside the building, the patrol was now getting desperate. They had no radio contact with Battalion HQ, their commander was badly concussed, their senior sergeant was barely conscious from severe loss of blood from his leg wound and they had little or no water. The Irish soldiers had no idea what was happening in the rest of Elisabethville and no inkling of whether Captain Whyte and Sgt Dignam had made it through Katangan lines to reach battalion and request reinforcements.

'In the morning we were completely surrounded and [the Katangans] called on us to surrender. We were approached by two white men, a priest and a nurse, and they told us that if we did not surrender they [the gendarmes] were going to blow up Soerte's house with Cmdt Cahalane inside. The nurse attended me and I was taken in the back of a car, covered over, to the Gendarme Hospital,' Sgt Carey explained.

The White Father missionary, Fr Paul Verfaille, and the medical sister initially thought the badly wounded Irish sergeant would die – but they bravely decided to try and help him. The missionary didn't tell the Irish platoon of his fears that if the wounded man was found inside the building after the surrender, he might he shot by the gendarmes because of the difficulty in moving and treating him. The courageous cleric decided it was his Christian duty to get the sergeant out of the building before that could happen.

As they helped Sgt Carey away, the remaining Irish troops debated what to do next. Dawn was likely to bring a full assault by the Katangan gendarmes and their heavy weaponry meant there was a distinct possibility they would blow up the building where the Irish were sheltering. The Irish troops' only heavy weapon was the Carl Gustav 84mm and there were only a few rounds for it. The patrol had a few hand grenades but was otherwise totally dependent on Carl Gustav 9mm sub-machine guns and FN assault rifles. The patrol had very little water and only emergency rations, so a lengthy siege was out of the question. Surrender – however unpalatable – suddenly seemed the only option available.

Cmdt Cahalane was still badly dazed from the concussion of the Energa warhead. He was also almost totally deaf from the explosion. But with Captain Whyte and Sgt Dignam gone to get help, and Sgt Carey en route to hospital with a jagged hole in his thigh, should Cmdt Cahalane be unable to continue in command, his deputy would now be a mere corporal.

The patrol re-checked their defensive perimeter and carefully weighed up their options. The Landrover and bus had been repeatedly hit by Katangan fire and were now *hors de combat*. The bus had caught fire and was burning with increasing ferocity. The flames from the blazing bus cast dancing shadows along the roadway and the Irish soldiers peered into the darkness in the hope that the fire might illuminate the Katangan positions. A short time after the bus caught fire, there was a sudden 'whoosh' as the fuel tank exploded and a jet of flame soared ten metres into the sky.

The lead armoured car had taken the anti-tank hit and, everyone presumed, had been wrecked. But someone – somehow – had got it started and it had rumbled away from the ambush site. The rear armoured car was still there by the roadside, but to reach it the Irish troops would have to cross an area of open lawn in full view of the Katangan machine gun positions. And even if they reached it, there was no guarantee it would start.

For Sgt Carey, the intervention of the priest and nurse initially seemed to cast him from the frying pan and into the fire. The journey with the priest from the Radio College to the hospital had been conducted in a haze of pain. By now, the entire leg of Sgt Carey's uniform pants was soaked red with blood. The little group eventually made it to the Gendarme Hospital and Carey was carried in and immediately treated by a female Belgian doctor. The doctor gently treated the Irish sergeant but was visibly furious at the consequences of the fighting going on around Elisabethville. However, Katangan soldiers, when they realised a wounded UN trooper had arrived in the building, reacted with outrage sparked by memories of what the Indian troops had done to their comrades in the Radio Katanga building.

'While I was in the operating theatre there, I was assaulted and punched by some [Katangans]. One guy came into the room as I was lying on a bed and came towards me with a knife. I looked up, saw him coming towards me and I thought my end had come. The doctor shouted "no" and the guy was hustled into a corner by a few of the nurses. I was immediately rushed from there into the back of a jeep lying down and brought to the White Father's Mission. There I was put into a laundry room – they then provided me with a blue suit, a shirt, socks but no shoes. A few hours later a little man came in to give me some coffee, an apple and a slice of apple cake. He never spoke a word and then left. They took any possessions I had and the following day they took me by ambulance to Sabina Villas on the Elisabethville Airport Road, which was occupied by Indian troops. They put me on the road, roughly 500 yards [away] and I had to make my way, as good as possible, to the barrier. The ambulance crew told me they could not drive me any closer as the Indians used to fire on civilian ambulances. I had to crawl and drag myself on one leg the last 500 yards to the UN checkpoint and no one came out to help me. Thank God when I got there, there was an Irish UN officer attached to the Indians from a signal company,' Sgt Carey said.

'After this I was attended by an Irish doctor, Cmdt O'Shea, and I had a letter in my pocket from the Congolese hospital to give to him. I think it was in connection with morphine. From Sabina Villas I was taken to Elisabethville Airport. While there, with others on stretchers in the lobby, a Katangese jet strafed the airport. It set fire to three aircraft and all the glass was blown into the lobby. Some more were again injured and I was [later] flown to Leopoldville to the UN Hospital. As I was in civilian clothes they put a guard on me thinking I was a mercenary. It took a further twenty-four hours to get the problem solved.'

Sgt Carey had survived a wound that might easily have killed him. The bullet had torn a hole in his upper thigh – and had slightly nicked his femoral artery. Had the tear in the artery been just a fraction bigger, the Irish sergeant would have bled to death in a matter of minutes. Even more incredibly, Sgt Carey had defied his wound to heroically help drag his commanding officer to safety – a feat impossible for a lesser man. 'They eventually flew me out of Elisabethville to Leopoldville on a DC-3 for medical treatment.

I discovered that it was a chartered flight and, when the co-pilot came back to check on us during an electrical storm on the way there, I realised he was from Ennis in County Clare. The next thing I knew he brought me back a drop of Canadian Club whiskey to help deaden the pain in my leg,' Tim Carey recalled.

Remarkably, a few months after he returned to Ireland, Sgt Carey was astounded when a carefully wrapped parcel arrived at his Fermoy home. The postmark on the parcel indicated it had come from Belgium. When he opened the package, the west Cork soldier was astonished to discover all the personal belongings that had been taken from him in the White Friar's Mission. Included was a note from Fr Verfaille who explained that he had travelled to Belgium and now wanted to return Sgt Carey's possessions. He wished the Irish soldier a full recovery. His note sparked a close correspondence between the two men for many years.

'I couldn't believe it to be honest. I never thought I would ever get my stuff back. They were very good to me in the mission and, if it wasn't for that White Father and the Belgian doctor, I don't think I would have made it out alive from Elisabethville. In fact, I kept the blue suit they put me in to smuggle me to the Indian checkpoint for years afterwards,' Tim Carey recalled.

BACK AT THE Radio College, the Irish patrol knew they were running out of time. Sentries had reported that the Katangans – again under mercenary supervision – had established several new firing points for their machine guns, which controlled all the main exits from the Soerte's villa, where the Irish forces were now gathered. The Irish soldiers could stage a break-out and run for it – but it was almost certain such an effort would result in heavy casualties. Even if a few soldiers made it to the second armoured car and reached the Browning machine gun, they would then have to re-cross the same lawn to reach Irish positions. A break-out into the surrounding neighbourhood was equally unattractive. Being on foot and unfamiliar with the terrain, they would likely be hunted down by the Katangans before they could even make it halfway back to Battalion HQ.

The last surrender demand had been almost surreal. Cmdt Cahalane could barely hear such was the damage to his eardrums from the anti-tank round impact and explosion. The Katangan demand had been levelled by a Belgian-born officer, Major Paul Janssens, who had now taken control of the Radio College scene on behalf of Tshombe's forces. Wearing thick black sunglasses, Major Janssens realised the injured condition of the Irish officer and was forced to bellow his surrender demands at the top of his voice despite the fact he had been allowed approach to within a few metres of Cmdt Cahalane. The Irish were left in no doubt that they faced an imminent all-out assault because the native Katangan troops were convinced the UN would try to send a rescue column to the Radio College.

Reluctantly, Cmdt Cahalane and his men realised they had little option but to surrender. An all-out assault by the Katangans on the Radio College could result in a massacre – and Major Janssens had promised that the UN troops would be treated properly and in accordance with the Geneva Convention if they laid down their weapons and surrendered on terms. The patrol, which had been sent out to discover the status of Lt Ryan and his detachment, was now about to share their fate.

Back at Prince Leopold Farm, concern was rapidly turning to alarm within Irish Battalion HQ. It had been confirmed that the Irish detachment at Jadotville was now under heavy and sustained assault. Without immediate reinforcements and resupply it was not clear how long they could hold out. In Elisabethville itself, there was no trace of Lt Ryan and his detachment at the Radio College. Worse still, the heavily armed patrol sent to check on Lt Ryan's status had also failed to return and was no longer responding to radio checks on their location.

The sniping attacks on the Irish base had suddenly increased in intensity – and virtually every man available to the battalion was now thrown into front-line duties. John O'Mahony prised open his cast in a desperate bid to be allowed to operate a machine gun while on guard duty. The Irish HQ at Prince Leopold Farm now echoed to the sounds of explosions and small arms fire from all over the Katangan capital. Then, just before darkness fell, came the sound all UN soldiers dreaded – the distinctive whine of the turbojet engines of a Katangan Magister jet. If the UN helicopters took to the air, they now ran the very real risk of being destroyed.

# CHAPTER EIGHT

PAT MULLINS DESPERATELY wiped the sweat from his eyes and muttered a swift prayer before he hit the 'start' button on the armoured car's metal dash panel. 'Please start, please Lord let it start,' he said. The V8 engine noisily turned over but agonisingly failed to catch. The Irish mechanics had exchanged the traditional ignition key for a simple push-button starter when the Ford was shipped to the Congo – but troopers were leery of the new-fangled start button. The interior of the armoured car still stank of sweat and smoke but Pat was oblivious to it all. He held his breath, struggled to clear the ringing sound in his ears and waited for the expected anti-tank missile to strike. But none came.

'Jesus, Mary and Joseph – please let it start,' he said as he desperately pushed the button a second time, this time with greater urgency. The Ford engine again noisily turned over, coughed and, a split second later, roared into life. Its distinctive rumble was like music to the young soldier's battered ears. 'You beauty,' Pat sighed as he looked out the driver's armoured slit and prepared to ease the lumbering car forward. He had secured the armoured slit open with its winged bolting nut because visibility was now more important than protection. The Ford AFV may have been battered and splintered but it was still resilient enough to move.

Pat knew he had to move fast. One more hit from an anti-tank round would rip the Ford apart so he had to clear the area around the Radio College fast. 'Don't give them an easy target', he recalled from the Fitzgerald Camp course he had started, but not completed, with John O'Mahony. He was fully qualified to ride the BSA and Triumph motorbikes used by dispatch riders but, despite being able to handle the Ford AFV, he still wasn't officially ranked as 'a driver' and instead – like John O'Mahony – was referred to as 'a gunner-driver'. But Pat reckoned he could still drive the Ford as well as anyone in uniform.

He tried to concentrate on the road ahead. The Vickers gun behind him was now angled towards the stars. If trouble erupted, he couldn't drive the Ford and man the Vickers at the same time. Before swinging himself into the driver's seat, Pat had tried to swivel the turret wielding the machine gun. But despite straining with all his strength on the two manual turning handles, the turret stubbornly refused to budge. Pat did not know it, but the sheer force of the anti-tank warhead explosion had literally fused the turret to its turning ring and wrecked the three turning ball bearings. With the ball turret weighing almost one tonne, it was impossible for it now to be moved by hand. The brake handle for the turret – essential for bracing it when the gunner was firing the Vickers – was now rendered equally redundant.

His friend, Mick Nolan, lay silent on the floor behind him and Pat knew he had to reach a hospital fast. He knew Mick was badly hurt and that every minute mattered. The Italian hospital in Elisabethville was reportedly the best in Katanga and it treated all the UN wounded. Best of all, there were Irish troops stationed near it, so if he could only make it there, he and Mick would have a chance.

Pat had made it barely 100 metres from the ambush site when, to his horror, he realised the darkness was all consuming. He could barely see three metres in front of the Ford. There was no street lighting and every roadside house, building and factory was shrouded in blackness. He would have to find his way by memory and dead reckoning.

Pat eased back on the throttle to give himself extra time to judge the road direction in the pitch-black void. He had no option but to hit the button for the headlights. It would advertise his position but he had to see where he was going – and if he kept the Ford moving he would present a very difficult target.

There was a spotlight fitted to the Ford, primarily used to benefit the Vickers gunner, but Pat was loath to switch it on because, difficult target or not, he didn't want to advertise his presence that blatantly to every Katangan soldier within a square mile. Despite the dim light offered by the small headlights on the Ford, he still did not recognise any landmarks to guide him onto a route he knew.

'How do I get back to battalion?' Pat wondered. He wasn't familiar with this road. He could retrace his steps back to battalion along the patrol route they had already used this night – but that would mean lumbering past the ambush site where the Katangan soldiers had their anti-tank position. Retracing his steps back along Avenue Wangermee was only asking for trouble. He had no idea how many Katangans were there and if he turned around and stumbled upon a Katangan roadblock, he'd be finished.

'Keep going, keep going,' Pat desperately thought. He strained his eyes through the armoured slit and willed himself to see a road, a building, a bridge, anything, that he could recognise. But the darkness beyond the flickering beam of the headlights was like a shroud. An icy knot formed in the pit of his stomach as he realised that, whatever happened, he simply could not afford to crash.

Suddenly, a road junction loomed out of the gloom in front of the Ford. There were two major routes to the left and the right but no signposts that Pat could see. Avenue Wangermee continued straight on – but he knew this would only take him further away from the Irish base and out of the city. Which way to go? He was terrified of bringing the Ford to a halt in case the engine stalled.

If the trusty V8 stopped he might not be able to restart it. After a moment's hesitation, Pat carefully swung the Ford to the left. He judged that this might bring him back towards the city centre where he could find a road he recognised leading to either the Italian hospital or Battalion HQ.

The armoured car rumbled on and Pat was careful not to gain too much momentum. The Ford, which utilised a non-synchromesh gearbox, had four forward speeds. Changing gears was an art form that took drivers repeated practice to fully master. You had to double de-clutch when going either up or down a gear, and if you didn't do it right, the Ford would threaten to shear its gears, not to mention jerking giddily in protest. Any sudden movement and the cabin rattled with the violent shaking of Vickers ammunition belts stored in the metal brackets welded onto the floor and hull sides.

Pat leaned forward and searched desperately to the left and right. There had to be something here that he could recognise. The armoured car rumbled past several smaller road junctions. After the fourth junction Pat began to panic. 'Where the hell am I?' he wondered. There were buildings to the left and the right but the darkness made it difficult to discern precisely what they were. The road surface was good, smooth tarmac, so this road must lead somewhere significant. The seconds passed like hours as the car rumbled away from the junction.

Without warning, the Ford arrived at another T-junction. The road to the left and right was much bigger than the route he had just travelled over. Maybe this was the road to the airport? Pat paused for a second, wondering whether to swing left or right. Finally, he eased the steering column to the left. He guessed that this would result in the armoured car doubling back on itself, which would bring him back towards either the Hotel de Ville or the Cathedral. Once there, he could find his way back to base.

Pat had travelled almost 100 metres when he got the first clue to his location. The road swung to the left before straightening out. As he looked right, he realised that he was driving past the Parc Zoologique with the River Lubumbashi flowing directly behind it. Pat was confused. If the Zoo was on his right, then wasn't he now driving away from the city centre instead of towards it?

Out of the darkness, a building loomed. It was a major structure, maybe three storeys tall with lots of glass and concrete. Out of the haze of his memory, Pat struggled to identify the building. 'What the hell is it?' he thought. Barely two seconds passed before Pat felt the icy ball in the pit of his stomach expand and spread its cold tentacles up to his heart. 'Oh Jesus, this must be the road into the African city,' Pat realised. In an instant he understood that by twice turning left at the crossroads, he was now heading into the African section of Elisabethville – where the staunchest bedrock of support for the Katangan secession was based. Virtually all the Katangan gendarmes either lived or had families in the African city, which was established alongside the vast Union Minière complex. The native city surrounded the vast mine complex and also the western side of the river. UN patrols were under strict instructions never to cross the river and to stay on the Elisabethville or eastern side of the Lubumbashi. The last place a damaged UN vehicle needed to be tonight was heading into the African city.

Pat slowed the Ford to a crawl as he slid the transmission into the lowest gear he dared without running the risk of stalling. In desperation he realised that he had no alternative but to turn around and head back to the junction. 'I should have turned right,' he thought bitterly to himself, 'I should have turned right.' He could have tried to turn left now but he reckoned he was too far south of the city centre for a simple turn to bring him back to his destination. It was safer to retrace his steps.

Staring grimly out the driver's slit, Pat tried to gauge a wide section of roadway where he could turn the armoured car. The Ford – despite its 4.5-tonne weight – was a relatively nimble vehicle. Its thirty-two horsepower V8 engine was its single greatest asset: rugged, reliable and capable of sustaining significant damage and still operating. The engine design dated back to the 1930s and variants of the V8 had powered everything from the Sherman tank to the Chevrolet C60 truck in the Second World War. If the engine had one problem it was that it was petrol rather than diesel fuelled.

Irish troops were fond of the Ford AFV but had learned that it needed to be treated with caution and respect. Ultimately, the chassis was still that of a three-tonne Ford truck. In fact, the chassis had been sourced by the Defence Forces from Ford's Cork plant and stripped down was identical to the Ford trucks that now plied the Irish roads carrying everything from coal to flour and milk to newspapers. The reality was that the chassis wasn't specifically designed for this kind of body weight, nor was it designed to offer anything like cross-country mobility. If you ignored the 'soft' armour, the Ford AFV's greatest weaknesses were its brakes and its turning circle.

The Ford lacked any form of power-assisted steering, so the driver guided the armoured car through sheer brawn and the force of his arms. That meant that its turning circle was nothing less than woeful. The wheels had tyres with a 7.5-inch width on a 20-inch diameter rim, which further worsened handling. But, without power steering, wider and heavier tyres simply couldn't be countenanced. Making matters even trickier was the fact the Ford had drum brakes that could barely cope with the 4.5-tonne body weight. Drivers who had to brake suddenly when the Ford was close to its top speed found they almost had to stand on the brake pedal, using their entire body weight to maximise the available braking power. Put bluntly, the Ford wasn't designed for doing three-point turns on narrow roads. But Pat had no other choice. And he had to move fast before the Katangans realised what was on their doorstep.

Choosing his moment, Pat settled on what appeared to be the widest stretch of the road in sight. If he swung hard into the turn, he would gain precious inches for the difficult reversing manoeuvre. Steering the Ford while reversing was an exercise in luck as much as judgement as the rearward vision was virtually non-existent. Worse still, Pat didn't have a gunner to shout reversing directions and distances to him at the steering wheel. He knew there were steep drainage ditches on either side of the roadway, so he had to judge the turn to perfection. Pat mouthed a silent prayer as he swung the wheel to the right.

The Ford turned precisely as Pat had planned. The sharp angle of the turn meant that he achieved the sweep he had intended so as to make the reversing manoeuvre easier. The nose of the Ford was exactly where Pat intended and he hit the brakes. But then disaster struck.

The front wheels inched over the tarmac road surface and suddenly came onto compacted earth. The brakes bit hard but the heavy Ford just kept edging forward. The wheels fought for grip but, instead of biting hard tarmac, they slid on the compacted earth. The weight of the armoured body inexorably pushed the Ford into the turn – and, with maximum brakes now applied, the 7.5-inch wheels struggled to halt the car's forward momentum. With a crunching sound, the Ford's front wheels skidded off the elevated road into the steep drainage ditch beyond. The underside of the chassis scraped and scratched along the road surface – finally grinding to a halt and achieving what the brakes had failed to. The Ford was now lying on its belly on the edge of the roadway, its front wheels sunk deep in the drainage ditch. Its rear wheels were still on the road surface but the Ford was now pitched forward at a thirty-degree angle into the ditch. The Vickers machine gun was pointed down into the drain – a danger now only to Congolese frogs and rats. The force of the sudden stop had jolted some of the Vickers ammunition belts free from their storage brackets and they now rolled noisily across the metal floor.

The sudden drop of the Ford's nose had propelled Pat out of the driver's seat. The jolt as the Ford then settled onto its belly slammed him hard back down into the seat and, for a few seconds, he sat dazed. Then, with growing horror, he realised that the Ford had skidded too far forward and the vehicle was now stuck. The engine had stalled and the silence left Pat with nothing but a ringing in his ears and a sick feeling in the pit of his stomach.

His hand reached for the ignition start. The venerable Ford engine, still hot, caught at the first turn as Pat kept the transmission in neutral. But, as he slid the car into gear and gingerly eased out the clutch in an attempt to reverse, his worst fears were realised. The rear wheels spun and tyres squealed as the rubber desperately tried to get a grip. The car stayed stubbornly still. Too much of the car's heavy nose was now wedged into the ditch – there just wasn't enough grip for the double rear wheels to drag the car back up onto the road.

The Ford only had rear-wheel drive. Pat realised that even if it had four-wheel drive it would still have been touch-and-go whether it could pull the 4.5-tonne chassis weight clear of the ditch. With a sinking feeling, he realised that a winch would probably be required to get the armoured car free of the ditch, and the Ford had no winch fitted as standard.

Pat's head dropped for a second with the stark realisation of what had just happened. The armoured car was their best chance of reaching safety and now it was gone. What were they supposed to do now? A quick glance into the back made up Pat's mind. Mick was badly hurt and he needed to get medical attention. If they had to get away over the fields and walk to a hospital then that is what they would do. If he had to carry his friend, so be it.

Pat slid awkwardly out of the driver's seat and onto the floor beside Mick Nolan in the rear. He reached over and opened the side access hatch and, when it only creaked open a few inches, he used his boot to kick it open further. Pausing for only a second, he jumped out into the Katangan night. Pat gazed around warily but there was only silence along the road. He reached back into the Ford and, after scrambling around for a few seconds, finally found the Carl Gustav sub-machine gun he was looking for. He slung it over his shoulder and reached back in to try and get a grip on Mick's unconscious form.

'Come on, Mick – it's time to go. We'll get you to a doctor straight away,' he whispered. The angle of the car and his friend's limp position made getting him out of the vehicle all the more difficult. But, after a minute, Pat had finally eased Mick out of the Ford and propped him up alongside the armoured car. All he had to do now was get his arm around Mick and try to walk and drag him away from the stranded UN vehicle. Maybe they could move along the drainage ditch for extra cover, he thought. But the idea vanished as, out of the darkness, came a sudden guttural shout.

Pat cringed at the realisation that they had just been discovered. He knew instantly from the tone of the shout that it was not a local resident curious at what had just happened on the road. The shout had the tone of soldier or policeman stamped all over it – it was a challenge not a simple question. Then, from the darkness, came the distinctive metallic 'click' of a weapon having its safety catch released.

Pat's training took over. He turned to ease Mick back against the armoured car for shelter, and in one smooth motion, swung the Carl Gustav off his shoulder and brought it to bear on the area where the shout had come from. 'Damn it but we weren't even able to get clear of the armoured car,' Pat thought. 'But, then again, if there's going to be a fight, better that it is by the car for some kind of cover.'

From the darkness came a second shout. Pat couldn't make out what was said – he was not even sure if the language was French or Katangese – but he knew it was not the accent of a friend. He crouched down in the ditch, careful not to offer any outline of himself or Mick against the armoured car. He reached back to check that Mick was okay, but his friend was slumped motionless against the Ford. Pat hadn't even time to bring his hand back onto the Carl Gustav when the first volley of shots shattered the stillness of the night.

One hundred metres from the Ford, a patrol of Katangan gendarmes knelt by the side of the roadway. They had been on duty near the perimeter of a nearby gendarme barracks when, in the distance, they heard the distant approach of a vehicle. The engine revs were being kept low as if the vehicle was being driven very carefully and cautiously. The noise of the engine sounded louder as the vehicle came closer. Then, suddenly, there was a slight 'crunch' and the engine noise stopped. It started up again a few seconds later only to be cut off a second time.

The gendarmes initially thought it was a UN patrol but realised that the Irish, the Indians or the Swedes wouldn't send just a single vehicle into this neighbourhood. The base on Boulevard Elisabeth was the major camp for the Katangan gendarmes in Elisabethville and everyone had been on high alert since the fighting broke out over the past twenty-four hours. And it was clear that the noise was that of a single vehicle. The senior gendarme ordered one of his privates back to HQ to report what had just happened to his Belgian mercenary commander. 'Les Afreus' would know precisely what to do, the corporal decided. In the meantime, he ordered his men to follow him up the road to determine what was going on.

The Katangan patrol had travelled barely 100 metres when, in the darkness, they made out the distinctive shape of a vehicle across the road. 'Mon Dieu,' the corporal whispered, 'it is a tank.' He frantically waved to his patrol and the gendarmes spread out along the road, trying not to offer a single target to the tank's guns. 'What the hell is a single tank doing here?' the corporal thought. 'And where are its infantry?' The corporal decided to hold position until his mercenary commander arrived at the scene with reinforcements. Suddenly and without warning, one of his men issued a shouted challenge to the tank. Emotions had been running high over the past twenty-four hours because of all the UN operations around Elisabethville, but the corporal was appalled that the man should so readily have given away their position.

Before he could hiss a reprimand at the man, one of his comrades – emboldened by his friend's challenge – shouted a warning of his own. The corporal – now furious at his men – decided safety was now the best policy and he slipped the safety catch off his FN rifle, which he now brought to bear on the tank shadowed in the gloom. He was peering at the vehicle for any sign of a threat when, in the darkness, he thought he spotted a shadowy movement. 'Merde,' he whispered to himself as he squeezed the trigger without a second's hesitation.

The volley was well aimed and noisily 'clanged' off the armoured hide of the tank in the darkness. The corporal heard the sound of footsteps behind him as his Belgian officer brought gendarme reinforcements racing to the scene. That sound was instantly obliterated by the roar of gunfire to his left and right as the other members of the patrol followed his lead and opened fire on the tank. Ignoring his own training, the corporal glanced sideways straight into the muzzle-flash of an assault rifle – instantly losing what little night vision he had.

In the drainage ditch, Pat Mullins pressed himself into the damp earth as the bullets whistled around him. Mick was in the shelter of the armoured car but Pat knew he had to try and keep from being flanked. He realised that the soldiers were to his front and right. There was no sound of movement or gunfire coming from behind him or back up the road on which he had just travelled. 'Protect your flanks, fire aimed bursts and watch your ammunition,' he thought as he levelled the Carl Gustav.

The Swedish sub-machine gun roared into life as Pat fired a short burst. He eased the muzzle to the left and fired a second short burst. The Carl Gustav fired a 9mm shell, which was fine for close and medium quarter work, but pretty useless for long-distance fire. 'Don't be gung-ho and empty a whole magazine,' Pat recalled his training sergeant warning. 'Short, aimed bursts,' the NCO had chanted as a mantra. The young trooper was uncertain if he heard a shout of pain in the darkness, but he scrambled over to the armoured car to get whatever 9mm magazines were available for the Gustav. Above his head, the Vickers machine gun aimed limply and uselessly into the bottom of the ditch.

Out on the roadway, the Katangan gendarmes had scattered looking for shelter as the bursts of 9mm fire whistled around them. One gendarme fell, screaming that he had been shot in the leg. Several jumped into the drainage ditch on the opposite side of the road from the tank and emptied their entire magazines in its general direction. The corporal waved at his men to fire and move as they had been taught, but they were oblivious to him.

'Idiots,' roared a voice in French from behind the corporal. The corporal's mercenary commander had arrived on the scene and immediately took charge. 'Allez-vite, allez-vite,' he shouted, indicating that he wanted the gendarmes to fan out and manoeuvre around the tank. As the initial excited bursts of gunfire eased, the gendarmes heard the furious demands of their officer. Slowly, the Katangan soldiers heeded his orders and began to use the drainage ditch to move up on the flanks of the tank. In a few minutes, the tank would be taking enfilading fire from two different directions.

On the roadway the Belgian mercenary crouched and peered at the hulking vehicle in the darkness. It was clearly a UN vehicle. He knew instantly that the Katangans had nothing remotely like this. 'Why does it not fire?' he wondered. And then he realised, from the angle of the vehicle's hull, that it must have crashed into the ditch. 'Maybe it was damaged at the Radio College engagement earlier?' he thought. Another burst of gunfire came from beside the vehicle, and the mercenary guessed that it was 9mm fire, which meant a sub-machine gun. After listening to several short bursts, he realised that it all came from the same location. 'One man, maybe two. Definitely not three,' he smiled. He also realised that the enemy was armed only with a sub-machine gun, which his men would out-range with their new FNs. 'Move around and finish this,' the Belgian snarled to the corporal.

In the ditch, Pat was now desperate. Mick had slid down from his position by the side of the armoured car and was now lying motionless in the bottom of the ditch. Pat wasn't sure if he had been shot or had finally succumbed to his wounds, but he realised with horror that his friend was most likely dead. Seconds earlier a volley of shots had drilled into the hull of the Ford just inches from where he had taken up position. 'God help me, what do I do now?' Pat thought as he swept the Carl Gustav across the roadway, looking for a target to engage. He had already used three magazines for the sub-machine gun and now had only two left. That meant a total of seventy-two rounds. There were hundreds of rounds of .303 ammunition inside the armoured car for the Vickers, but the old British gun was useless to him. 'What a joke,' he thought, 'stuck in a battle with loads of ammunition for the wrong gun.'

As he cradled the Carl Gustav in his hands, Pat noted that the pressed-metal stock was now sweaty to the touch. Some of the lads thought the Carl Gustav was an ugly weapon, but he had always appreciated the gun for its firepower and convenience and found the polished wooden butt behind the trigger comfortable. He just wished someone had thought to throw a few extra magazines into the Ford for the sub-machine gun. The Gustav could fire 600 rounds a minute, but there was no selector switch for single-round fire. That meant the Gustav ripped through magazines if your finger lingered on the trigger for half a second too long. The Swedish gun weighed 3.9 kilos, but tonight it felt like an extension of Pat's own hand.

Pat gazed up at the mute Vickers to see that incoming fire had torn several jagged holes in its cooling jacket. If only he could have brought the old British gun to bear tonight he might have held these characters off for hours.

From behind him, Pat heard a muffled sound like a twig snapping. Reacting instantly, he swung around, held the Carl Gustav rock-steady to his body and fired an extended burst into the darkness. There was a shout, the sound of a crash and then silence. The incoming fire stopped momentarily and the returning silence of the night now seemed eerie.

Pat knew he had only minutes left to make a move. The Katangans were slowly working their way around his position and he simply couldn't cover all three flanks at the same time. He had been forced to stay by the armoured car and the Katangans knew exactly where he was. Once they moved around behind him, he would either be caught in a lethal crossfire or overwhelmed in a sudden assault.

He realised his only option was to drop into the ditch, combat-crawl on his hands and knees through the tangled undergrowth on the far bank and disappear into the fields in the darkness behind. If he was lucky, he would find a UN patrol or a protected base before the Katangans hunted him down. At least out there in the open fields he would have a fighting chance. But he just couldn't leave Mick – not here in a ditch like this. With a shake of his head, Pat ruled out that option. No, he would not leave his friend behind. His hand tightened on the Carl Gustav as he decided to make his final stand here by his fallen friend's side.

Pat slid the magazine out of the sub-machine gun's mounting slot just ahead of the trigger guard and squinted in the darkness to check it. The last burst had emptied it so Pat clicked in a full thirty-six round replacement and threw the old magazine into the mud of the ditch bottom. It was his last magazine so he would have to make it count. His only hope now was for a UN rescue column to reach him. But why would they come this far towards the African city, he thought? Maybe, just maybe, a relief column had reached the Radio College and they had heard the gunfight, which had been going on now for almost thirty minutes. 'It's in God's hands now,' Pat smiled grimly.

On his three flanks, the Katangan gendarmes worked their way slowly and carefully into their final positions. They had finally achieved the flanking manoeuvre the mercenary had demanded – and done so despite the ferocious defence mounted by the UN soldier. Initially, the gendarmes had been convinced they were up against a whole UN patrol. But the firing against their positions always seemed to be from the same location and from the same kind of weapon. Most of the gendarmes now guessed that they were up against a single man – a brave enemy who had chosen not to flee.

From the safety of a position some 100 metres away, the mercenary silently ordered the Katangans to finish the fight. He'd been a brave one, this UN soldier, the man admitted to himself. The soldier hadn't panicked and had kept the Katangans under accurate, short bursts of fire, which made their flanking manoeuvre all the more painstaking. Luckily for them, the mercenary realised, the heavy machine gun had not been brought into action. It was time to end this fight before dawn broke and brought with it the risk of another UN patrol. 'Move now,' the mercenary said.

A few minutes later, the end came. From three sides of the armoured car the Katangan gendarmes rose as one and fired heavy bursts towards the suspected position of the UN soldier. While some Katangans maintained covering fire, others raced forward to storm the position. The 'clang' of rounds striking the hull of the armoured car was now even audible over the firing. Then, to the Katangans' immense relief, an intense burst of gunfire from the ditch was suddenly cut short. As they moved forward, there was silence.

There was nothing Pat Mullins could do. When the gunfire erupted around him from three sides he realised the Katangans were storming his position. Pat swung to engage the point of heaviest fire. The short, stubby Carl Gustav shuddered in his hands from the extended burst of fire. But he couldn't cover all three flanks at once. He never heard the volley of shots that caught him in the upper body. Suddenly, he found himself twisting in midair as if he had been kicked full in the chest by a horse, and then he landed hard on his back, but strangely felt no pain. He lay in the ditch conscious that it had gone strangely quiet.

Pat found himself staring up at the African sky as darkness cast an enveloping shroud around him. Pat had never realised there were quite so many stars. As he finally closed his eyes, the darkness on the eastern horizon seemed to falter and then recoil from the first tentative rays of sunlight. A new day was dawning in the Congo.

The first Katangans cautiously approached the armoured car, each gendarme careful to cover the movements of their comrade. Each soldier scanned the scene with their FN rifles. Despite the silence, they were wary of walking into a trap. But after a few seconds it was clear that the battle was over. The first soldiers to creep around the flanks of the armoured car spotted the bodies lying in the ditch and instantly waved the other gendarmes forward.

They were amazed to discover that there were just two bodies in the ditch. One soldier lay on his back, his face staring up at the sky – a sub-machine gun still gripped in his hands. His friend lay crumpled on his side beside the armoured car. One gendarme kicked out at what he spotted were cartridge cases lying on the ground. The Katangan corporal looked down and realised they were 9mm shells – all from the sub-machine gun. A quick look revealed that the other soldier had clearly been badly injured before he'd been shot – there were old, dark bloodstains on his uniform blouse. Had a single man held off an entire platoon for thirty minutes just to protect his wounded friend, the corporal wondered?

After a moment of silence, the younger Katangan soldiers suddenly erupted into cheers and whoops of delight at their victory. Several danced around the armoured car, jabbing their rifles in the air. They had shown the UN that they too could fight. The younger men were also proud that they had shown the Belgian mercenary that they wouldn't run away from bullets. They were warriors too. Several of the younger soldiers jumped down into the ditch.

Down the road, the mercenary visibly relaxed and warily got to his feet. His corporal grinned and waved him towards the armoured car, which had been the focus of the firefight for the past half an hour. The Belgian simply shrugged and turned away, walking slowly and stiffly back towards the gendarme barracks. The armoured car and the UN patrol would no longer threaten the Katangan gendarme base. He had done his job. He cast a final look back at the armoured car, which was now surrounded by a rapidly thickening throng of jubilant Katangan soldiers jostling to get into the ditch, and turned away in disgust. He wanted no part of whatever else would happen this night.

# CHAPTER NINE

IN THE HOURS after the surrender of Cmdt Cahalane and the Radio College patrol, senior UN commanders struggled to cope with the flood of bad news. Several UN detachments around Elisabethville had been overrun and UN soldiers seized by Katangan forces. Cmdt Quinlan and 155 Irish UN troops were trapped in Jadotville with hopes of rescue fading fast. Then, senior UN officers received the news they had been dreading. The Katangan gendarmes intended to execute the Irish officer captured at the Radio College unless the UN withdrew from all seized positions and immediately returned all captured Katangan personnel, both military and political. The Katangans also demanded assurances on the treatment of their personnel who had been seized by the UN.

The situation now facing both the UN and the 35th Battalion was rapidly spiralling out of control. The detachment in 'The Factory' was under fire and effectively trapped. The Radio College detachment and the patrol sent to their relief had been attacked and overcome. A Katangan Magister was strafing all suspected UN targets and had destroyed several transport aircraft at the airport. Roadblocks made moving around the city extremely difficult for UN units. The UN knew the Irish battalion had already suffered one fatality – Trooper Edward Gaffney – in a sniper incident on 13 September and there were now unconfirmed reports that at least two more Irish troopers had been killed or were missing at the Radio College.

Worst of all was the news filtering down from Jadotville. UN commanders realised that without immediate reinforcement and resupply 'A' Company under Cmdt Quinlan would have no option but to negotiate a surrender. The Irish detachment – comprising 155 men, mostly drawn from the Western Command – had been sent to Jadotville on the express instructions of UN headquarters in New York as a direct response to claims that Belgian settlers had been attacked by rampaging Congolese national troops. European and American newspapers were full of reports of out-of-control Force Publique troops overrunning plantations, shooting Belgian farmers and raping women. Cmdt Quinlan and his men were to set up base in Jadotville and offer vital protection for the local settlers.

However, the UN high command failed to take into account the fact the settlers were virulently opposed to the UN presence in the Congo and were staunch supporters of the Katangan secession. The UN also ignored intelligence reports of a build-up of Katangan forces in the area. When the 4,000-strong Katangan force – led by French and Belgian mercenaries – finally began the assault on the small mining town, the Irish troops were too isolated for the battalions in Elisabethville to offer proper support.

But Cmdt Quinlan was a resourceful, wily commander held in high regard by his men. He would not surrender without a fight – and if the UN could fulfil their promise to support him, he would hold his position. On arrival in Jadotville, Cmdt Quinlan quickly realised the weakness of his company's position and ordered his men to begin digging defensive positions. It was only later that the Irish troops realised a Swedish unit had earlier been assigned to Jadotville but had withdrawn after declaring the position indefensible given the hostility of the population and the resupply distance from Elisabethville. Cmdt Quinlan knew he needed defensive positions and needed them fast. It was the crucial and timely preparation that allowed the Irish to hold their positions when the first assault poured in. For over five days the fighting proved ferocious as 'A' Company refused to yield their position to an enemy that outnumbered them twenty-six to one.

It is believed 'A' Company inflicted more than 300 casualties on the Katangans for the price of just seven wounded Irish soldiers. But lack of ammunition, food and water – not to mention being surrounded by a hostile populace – made the Irish position untenable in the medium- to long-term. UN promises of air support proved illusory, while Katangan roadblocks and enfilading fire on the strategic Lufira Bridge meant the UN could not get ground reinforcements and resupply convoys in. Even the crack Gurkhas could not breach the Katangan defences around the Lufira Bridge to reach the beleaguered Irish garrison.

With ammunition supplies virtually exhausted, Cmdt Quinlan put his men's interests above UN politics and agreed to surrender on the promise his troops would be well treated. A refusal to surrender on terms could provoke a massacre. 'A' Company had staged one of the most heroic and defiant defences in Irish military history – yet their courage was for decades effectively ignored back home.

The grim reality for the 35th Battalion back in Elisabethville was that they simply didn't have sufficient troops for all the critical tasks now rapidly unfolding around them.

In the midst of the confusion, came one of the most dramatic and courageous incidents of Ireland's entire four-year involvement in the Congo – an incident that saved the lives of several captured Irish officers, if not all Irish detainees. It involved an officer, Captain Art Magennis, who had been placed under the command of the Dogra Battalion of the Indian UN troops. He had been present with an Irish armoured car unit when the Indians had captured the Elisabethville Post Office. Despite UN loud hailers pleading in French, Swahili and English for the Katangan gendarmes to surrender, the Post Office had turned into a bloody battle. After the facility had been captured, Captain Magennis was shocked to see Indian soldiers nonchalantly bayoneting the body of a dead Katangan soldier as they walked passed it. Mercifully, it was the only corpse the captain would see that day as he stayed out of the interior of the building.

Captain Magennis' younger brother, Tim, worked as a journalist in Nyasaland (now Malawi) far to the south-east of the Congo. He was a correspondent for *The Globe*, a South African-based newspaper, and his primary job was reporting on the fledgling nationalist leader, Hastings Banda. With nationalism raging like a bushfire across Africa, Hastings Banda was being looked to for inspiration by many aspiring African leaders. South Africa, acutely mindful of its white minority rule, was following developments in detail.

'Tim had arrived out in South Africa and his news editor called him into his office. He said: "Look, there is no point you sticking around here – it will take you ages to come up to speed." The news editor then said that as Tim was from Northern Ireland he should know all about British colonialism. "The place for you is up in Nyasaland with the British and Dr Banda," he said. So they sent him up there to cover what was going on,' Art Magennis explained.

Tim Magennis was good at his job and, as the years passed, word spread that if foreign news crews were ever visiting Nyasaland, Tim was the crucial local contact. For the price of a few beers or a meal, they could be brought up to speed on whatever background they needed for their current story. That reputation would prove crucial when a German reporter, Hans Gomani, flew into Nyasaland en route to Katanga to cover the escalating crisis. Coincidentally, the German crew arrived in Nyasaland at the very time the Irish Armoured Car Group was being ambushed on Avenue Wangermee.

Gomani, who worked for a German TV station, was an intriguing character. At that time in his early forties, he had served in the army during the Second World War and boasted a deep understanding of the military. He was also an experienced observer of African politics and, increasingly, African conflicts. Best of all, Gomani didn't panic in war zones because he had spent enough time in uniform to know precisely how to react. That September, he was en route to Katanga to report on what now threatened to become a bloodbath, with the UN at its epicentre. He met up with Tim Magennis in Nyasaland to get a first-hand briefing on what was happening. Tim advised him to seek out his older brother, Art, who was serving as a captain in the Irish 35th Battalion with the UN in Katanga.

'Tim said to him: "Look, there is no point talking to me about Katanga. I have a brother with the Irish army in Elisabethville. Contact him and he will tell you what is really going on." That is how Gomani came to seek me out in Katanga,' Art added.

Gomani then travelled through northern Rhodesia and presented himself at the Katangan border in order to secure a pass to travel onwards to Elisabethville. However, the German was stopped by Katangan soldiers and, in the presence of a white mercenary officer, was arrested and ordered into their command post. He was then told he had to carry a message to the UN in Elisabethville from Dr Godefroid Munongo, the Katangan Minister of the Interior. It was to Dr Munongo that both the gendarmes and the mercenaries answered – and it was known that he had the complete trust of President Tshombe. Munongo's power was further cemented by the fact that he was a direct descendent of King Msiri of the Nyamwezi, one of the major tribal kingdoms of the Congo in the mid-nineteenth century.

The UN already knew that Dr Munongo was not a man to be trifled with. He was one of those responsible for Prime Minister Patrice Lumumba's execution. Dr Munongo – unlike others who later tried to distance themselves from the killing – was quite frank when later questioned about his role in the affair. In one report he wrote: 'I will speak frankly. If people accuse us of killing Lumumba, I will reply: Prove it.' Hans Gomani also knew of Dr Munongo's reputation and readily agreed to carry the message.

The message was a blunt threat from the Katangans that Cmdt Cahalane would be shot unless the UN complied with specific demands. They warned that other Irish and UN soldiers would also be shot as a direct response to a UN order that they claimed implied a shoot-on-sight policy for all those spotted carrying arms in Katanga. The gendarme commander said that if the UN's special representative, Conor Cruise O'Brien, wished to reply to Dr Munongo's message and negotiate new terms, Gomani would be acceptable as a go-between. The German realised he now had an opportunity both to help save lives and potentially secure a priceless exclusive for himself. Gomani – who was told he would be immediately released and escorted to Elisabethville if he agreed to carry the message – nodded his acceptance.

He was then escorted to Elisabethville. But in the chaotic aftermath of the UN's Operation Morthor, how was the German to safely contact a senior UN official? Word had spread of the fighting and he knew that if he approached the Indian lines in a civilian vehicle he risked being shot on sight. Gomani then recalled his conversation with his journalist colleague in Nyasaland and decided to seek out Captain Magennis in Elisabethville. Thus, Captain Art Magennis suddenly found himself drawn into a remarkable diplomatic manoeuvre to avoid the execution of prisoners.

Eventually, despite the chaotic communications, a meeting was arranged between Captain Art Magennis and Hans Gomani in the Leopold Hotel in the city centre. The Leopold was a favourite colonial-era haunt of soldiers, plantation owners, mining engineers and journalists who visited Elisabethville. Its wood-panelled rooms were festooned with old sofas, armchairs and wooden stools where customers escaped the steamy heat and savoured chilled bottles of the local brew, Simba Beer. Over recent weeks the Leopold had become a sanctuary from the madness spreading in the streets. Such was the scale of that madness, Magennis had to travel to the Leopold in an armoured car for fear of snipers.

After brief introductions, Gomani relayed Dr Munongo's message and Captain Magennis visibly paled at its import. 'He said that the Katangans were going to court-martial Cmdt Pat Cahalane in the morning, they would find him guilty and they would shoot him. Unless, of course, the UN released the Katangan propaganda officer who had been arrested a few days before,' Art Magennis explained. 'Surely the Katangans wouldn't shoot unarmed prisoners?' the Irish officer thought. But, as he gazed out the window at the carnage in Elisabethville, he knew that anything was now possible in Katanga.

The Irish captain knew the message had to be relayed to Conor Cruise O'Brien instantly. But first, Captain Magennis had to brief his immediate superior, the Dogra Battalion commander, on what he had just learned. The Indian listened carefully but immediately stressed that the only person who could now act was Conor Cruise O'Brien. He agreed to release Captain Magennis from his battalion duties to make contact with the UN special representative. That was easier said than done given the damage sustained by Elisabethville's phone system. Following Operation Morthor, the Post Office and Telephone Exchange were left virtually as shell-scarred ruins. The exchange itself was a mass of wire and conductors spliced and knotted together like spaghetti.

Miraculously, a UN communications team had managed to re-establish a single line from the exchange – and that ran directly to Cruise O'Brien's headquarters. The Irish diplomat was shocked when he heard of the Katangan warning and dismayed that an earlier UN order had been so misinterpreted. Cruise O'Brien stressed to Magennis that the UN was fighting according to the rules of conflict as set out in the Geneva Convention and Katangan prisoners would be treated with dignity and respect. But the Irish diplomat bluntly warned that if the Katangans executed Cmdt Cahalane – or harmed any other unarmed UN prisoners – there would be dire consequences.

Cruise O'Brien then further shocked Captain Magennis by asking if he was willing to take the message back to Dr Munongo with Hans Gomani personally and return with his reply? The Irish diplomat had ordered that his reply be translated into French, typed out on official UN paper and then copied. Two copies were handed to Captain Magennis for Dr Munongo and his Katangan commanders.

'He [O'Brien] said he was going to write a letter to Munongo but he asked whether I would volunteer to deliver the letter? Now I am not in the habit of volunteering for anything, but I said "I am here now and I cannot volunteer for anything without the authority of my commander." Dr O'Brien said he would get in contact with Lt Col McNamee and tell him about the situation. He rang me back after about 10 or 15 minutes and said "Lt Col McNamee has no objections to you volunteering yourself." So I said that Cmdt Cahalane was my commander so of course I would go.'

The Irish officer now had to link up with Gomani to find out how to contact Dr Munongo and the Katangans. Captain Magennis raced back to the Leopold Hotel to discover what to do next. 'He [Gomani] said "you have to be blindfolded from when you leave the hotel. You must be unarmed and I have been tasked with disarming you and seeing that you have no weapons of any nature." He also said that he had to drive me there. He knew the route to the location but he couldn't tell me where we were going. What the hell other option had I? I had to go along with what he was saying,' Art explained.

'I handed over my pistol and sub-machine gun, which were locked into a hotel safe in front of me. We set off in his car. It was a fabric-roofed Citroen 2CV which had just two seats. Off we went, but we were only gone about a kilometre out of the city when a smell of burning started coming from the bloody car. I said that the clutch was burning and Gomani turned to me and asked, how did I know? I looked at him and said, "What the hell do you think the smell is?" The next thing the clutch burned through and the car stopped,' Art explained.

The 2CV car – Citroen's famous 'Deux Chevaux Vapeur' or 'two steam horses' – was renowned for its reliability, but the Congo's heat, humidity, appalling roads and chronic lack of proper servicing took its toll. The problem the duo now faced was that, with conflict raging across the city, pedestrians ran a high risk of being shot.

'Gomani looked at me and said, "What are we going to do now?" I shrugged and said, "You're the man in charge – don't ask me. I don't even know where we're supposed to be going." I had to laugh when the German looked at me and asked where we were. I was sitting in the car wearing a blindfold so we could have been on the Moon for all I knew.'

The Irish officer took off the blindfold and realised that they had broken down directly outside Parc Albert. The local hospital was less than 200 metres away. 'I said to him, "Look, if you can go over there and explain what is going on, maybe they can give you a car." He agreed and I said there was no way I was staying waiting for him in the car. There was a big drainage ditch by the side of the road so I said I would wait for him there.'

After a thirty-minute explanation and negotiation, the German reporter finally arrived back with a car, which the hospital authorities had agreed to loan him. The duo jumped in and motored off – leaving the 2CV stranded by the roadside. They had gone less than ten kilometres when they came upon a roadblock mounted by the Katangan gendarmes. Gomani produced the documentation he had been given on Dr Munongo's behalf and received clearance to proceed. Sitting in the passenger seat with his blindfold in place, Captain Magennis wondered what was going to happen next. Without warning, he felt himself being roughly pulled from the car and searched by the sentries before, satisfied the UN officer was unarmed, both the captain and the reporter were ordered into a second vehicle driven by the Katangan officer controlling the roadblock.

'We drove off to some kind of house a short distance away. I had the blindfold firmly in place so I'm not even sure what sort of house it was. I was led out of the car and, when I was inside, the blindfold was taken off. I discovered the building was the home of an Italian family who were farming in Katanga. I immediately realised that there were two white officers present as well as a number of black junior officers. I explained that I had a letter from Conor Cruise O'Brien of the UN to be delivered personally to Dr Munongo. They said they would not be able to get me to him at that time.

'I thought they were only pulling my leg. So I said, "I'm sorry but my instructions are to deliver the letter personally – I can only deliver it to Dr Munongo, no one else is to get it." There was a bit of an argument but, fortunately, Gomani had very good English and French and he was able to talk with the officers. Gomani was a very intelligent guy and he obviously understood my position.

Finally, one of the French officers – a mercenary – said, "Look, if you cannot see your way to give this letter to Munongo's aide-de-camp," who I had now been introduced to, "we will just have to go ahead with [Cmdt Cahalane's] court martial." I was in a quandary because that was the last thing I wanted to see happen.'

Captain Magennis agreed to hand the letter to the ADC on the strict understanding he would personally deliver it to Dr Munongo. As an added precaution, he wrote directly across the letter's seal – so that the Katangan minister would know if the document had been tampered with. Seconds later the ADC left the farmhouse and sped off on a motorcycle waiting outside.

'They then sat me down and a short while later I was served a most outstanding meal. The Italian family were incredible cooks and the smell coming out of the kitchen reminded me of the home cooking we were all missing back in Ireland. We chatted very sociably because the French officers were all able to speak English. About an hour later, the French officer said I must be tired after the adventures of the day and he brought me to an upstairs bedroom. I had to promise not to look out the window to try and identify landmarks so the farmhouse could be located at a future date. But that was it.

'Shortly after dawn the next day, there was a knock on the bedroom door and I was informed that I was being taken back to Elisabethville because my mission was complete. But I said: "What about Cahalane? What about all the Irish prisoners? What are you going to do with them now?" The French officer turned to me and assured me that they would treat them as prisoners of war in accordance with the Geneva Convention. I asked whether I had his word as an officer on that and he looked me full in the face and said that I did indeed have his word. I thought that was about all I could do, so we got back into the car again and drove back to Elisabethville.

He [the French officer] pulled in at the White Father's mission near the site of the ambush at the Radio College. He got out of the car and there were three or four priests on the roadside. This French guy went up and the first thing I saw was them all smiling and shaking hands and kissing each other on the cheek.'

The sight appalled and enraged the Irish captain. What were these clerics doing embracing mercenaries when UN soldiers were fighting and dying to keep the peace, he thought? Did they not understand what they were doing? The realisation that his commander, Cmdt Cahalane, had very probably been threatened with an execution and that dozens of his comrades were now under armed guard by the Katangans made him seethe all the more.

'It was the first time in my life I ever felt such a rage. I was absolutely furious with these priests, one of whom I actually knew. His father had a garage that we [the UN] did business with. Here they all were kissing this mercenary on the cheek, laughing and joking with each other. Eventually, the French officer came back and said "I will drop you back at the hotel now". But I asked him to wait and give me just a minute. God forgive me but I was so bloody mad I walked up to the priests and said if anything happens to my commander or any of my soldiers I will come back and burn down this church of yours. I was so furious I could hardly believe these priests, the way they were behaving. And of course at this stage I knew that I had already lost two soldiers from my unit.'

The French mercenary – in a matter-of-fact manner – had earlier confirmed to Captain Magennis that two Irish soldiers had been killed in the course of the ambush. He did not know their names or their ranks, but he said that they had been in one of the armoured cars. The Irish officer realised that this French mercenary had actually commanded the Katangan unit that had mounted the ambush on the Radio College.

'After I had spoken to the priests I turned on my heels and the French officer dropped me back to the hotel. I collected my gear, including my weapons and walked back towards the Dogra Battalion. I realised that they would know me from my time with them so I should be fairly safe. From there I waited for the negotiations to produce a ceasefire so I could hopefully rejoin the 35th Battalion.'

Unknown to Captain Magennis, his courageous mission had already proved to be a success. The Katangans had now emphatically ruled out any form of action against the UN prisoners and, in particular, against Cmdt Cahalane, as they were mindful of the treatment of Katangan politicians and officers arrested by the UN. Cmdt Cahalane and his men had been taken to a remote farmhouse some sixty kilometres to the south-east of Elisabethville, not far off the main road to northern Rhodesia.

Cmdt Cahalane was initially kept with his captured men – all twenty-five of them – and they were instructed by the Katangan guards to remove their shoes, socks and personal items. The Katangan guards immediately pocketed all the watches taken off by the Irish troops. About an hour later, a French officer – one of the Katangans' senior mercenaries – arrived to question the prisoners and reacted with fury when told that they had been stripped of their personal possessions. Under the mercenary's baleful gaze, the abashed Katangan guards immediately handed back the watches.

The Frenchman, who was a veteran of the bitter Algerian conflict, ordered Cmdt Cahalane into a room on his own for questioning. But, before he could commence the interrogation, the Frenchman realised that Cahalane was not only partially deaf from the anti-tank rocket explosion but also showing signs of concussion. The mercenary ordered that Cahalane be given a jug of water and provided with a hot meal. He later insisted that Cahalane lie down on a bed in the farmhouse to recover his strength and promised that a doctor would be called to offer medical attention as soon as was possible.

But the mood in the plantation house began to change. An Italian prisoner was brought in to join the Irish detainees but was brutally beaten by the Katangan gendarmes in the mistaken belief that he was Indian and one of those soldiers responsible for the Radio Katanga killings. But for the intervention of a handful of Irish soldiers, who explained in broken French that the man was Italian and not Indian, he would most likely have been beaten to death or shot.

The next day, Cmdt Cahalane discovered to his horror that he was expected to write and sign a letter to the UN special representative, Conor Cruise O'Brien, which detailed a stream of alleged abuses against UN forces, in particular the Indian contingent. Cahalane was shocked to realise that he was now expected to endorse Katangan allegations that Indian troops had murdered unarmed prisoners and that UN forces were guilty of atrocities including firing on civilian ambulances, and to insist that a ceasefire was to be ordered within twenty-four hours with the phased withdrawal of all UN forces from Elisabethville.

Cahalane was bluntly warned that if he did not sign the letter within the allotted two-hour deadline, he would face potentially dire consequences. He was also warned that the safety of his men could no longer be guaranteed. When the two hours elapsed, the French mercenary returned and, when he realised that the letter had not been signed as requested, he responded with a typical Gallic shrug. 'You are making things very difficult for yourself,' he said. 'You are making things very difficult for yourself with the Katangan authorities. You are making things difficult for me to ensure your safety.'

Unperturbed, the Irish officer responded with remarkable sang-froid and steadfastly refused to sign the letter. Later that night, Cmdt Cahalane was ordered into a room where a group of Katangans sat around a table, at the head of which sat a white European. The stunned officer was informed that this was his 'interrogation trial' and that a guilty verdict could well earn a sentence of death by firing squad. Throughout the bizarre proceedings, the Irish officer was questioned in French, with a French mercenary translating. The unnamed white European was identified merely as a Katangan judge. The focus of the 'trial' proved to be the actions of the Indian UN detachment and what position the Irish officer adopted towards them. Throughout, Cmdt Cahalane repeated his request to be treated in accordance with the Geneva Convention. In one memorable exchange, as set out in Raymond Smith's book *The Fighting Irish*, the Dublin officer bluntly rejected any suggestion of tainting his honour with an inappropriate action. 'I will tell you nothing. I will not betray my honour as an officer and an Irishman. Not even if you torture me.'

The charade finally concluded about two hours later and the Irish officer, somewhat to his surprise, was later privately congratulated by one of the French mercenaries for his doggedness and his courage despite the intimidating surroundings. 'I congratulate you, captain, on your performance,' the Frenchman smiled as Cahalane was led back to his quarters. Captain Magennis' intervention had, in the meantime, ensured that no harm would come to the Irish prisoners and, a few days later, the Irish contingent were moved to another farmhouse closer to Elisabethville.

However, the Armoured Car Group commander remained a special prisoner and, unlike the other Irish prisoners, had his own security detail including a mercenary and six gendarmes. Eventually, the entire group were moved north to where Cmdt Quinlan and the soldiers captured at Jadotville were being held pending ceasefire talks to secure a release of prisoners on all sides.

# CHAPTER TEN

A CEASEFIRE WAS finally announced on 21 September, a week after the Radio College ambush and the assault on Jadotville. It suited both sides: the UN desperately needed to defuse the situation and negotiate the return of its captured peacekeepers, while Tshombe needed his regime to appear reasonable and killing more UN peacekeepers was not going to help him gain international recognition for his regime.

Captain Art Magennis breathed a sigh of relief when the ceasefire was announced and he was finally given permission to return to the 35th Battalion from his assignment with the Indian Dogra Battalion. He had already heard about the missing Irish patrol and knew that swift action was now vital if the missing personnel were to be tracked down. He immediately reported to the operations room at the Irish Battalion HQ for a debriefing.

It proved to be a crucial meeting because of Captain Magennis' experiences over the last couple of days. Most informative had been his meeting with the mercenary – a man he later discovered was Bob Denard. Over the next thirty years, 'Colonel' Denard carved out a reputation for himself as one of Africa's top mercenaries and was involved in military operations from Angola to Zimbabwe and from Gabon to the Comoros Islands. In 1961, Congo was Denard's third major conflict after his involvement in Algeria and Indo-China.

The Frenchman had been unfailingly polite and courteous to the Irish captain – and indicated he derived no pleasure from fighting UN soldiers, let alone Irish troopers. But Captain Magennis realised that this was not a man to be underestimated – the Frenchman was an experienced soldier and was clearly only in Katanga for the money. Denard had been in charge of the Katangese gendarme units at the Radio College and had apparently mounted the ambush there. The fact that the ambush had been so expertly set and so carefully concealed from the arriving Irish patrol indicated the involvement of an experienced soldier who knew the techniques of mounting an ambush. Details of what Denard had to say would prove crucial in later helping piece together precisely what happened on Avenue Wangermee.

Yet, in a baffling turn of events, a second Irish patrol, sent out to check on the status of the patrol led by Cmdt Cahalane after Captain Whyte and Sgt Dignam had raised the alarm, had reported back to base that there was absolutely nothing to been seen on the original patrol's route. They had found no trace whatsoever of the two armoured cars, no sign of any major fighting and no trace of Cmdt Cahalane and his men. It was nothing short of astonishing. The only explanation Captain Magennis could offer was that the second patrol had not been able to retrace the correct route and had simply not found Avenue Wangermee. Somehow, they had taken the wrong route. The captain was determined that the 35th needed to act now to try to find out exactly what had happened at the ambush scene and to confirm the fate of the two Irish soldiers Denard had mentioned. He obtained permission to lead a patrol out the next morning.

'I went back to the tent that was doubling up as an office and I called in Squadron Sgt Dan Carroll. I told Dan I wanted to go down and look at this ambush site immediately. I told him to get a few jeeps and we would take a team down there. I distinctly remember telling him that we would all go well armed. Quick as a flash, Dan was back and everything was ready. He was a great guy, Dan, and the kind of NCO you always wanted on your team. An absolutely magnificent soldier who knew his job and what the circumstances required,' Art said.

'After breakfast we set out in two cars. I led with Squadron Sgt Carroll, followed by Technical Officer Frank Lawless and two of his fitters in the second vehicle. We carefully followed the route of the Cahalane patrol, through 'C' Company's position in the Tunnel, we turned right at Saio heading north and on towards the Radio College on Avenue du Wangermee [*sic*].'

'As we approached the college and were still about 100 yards south of it, we saw the first of the missing patrol's vehicles. It was the turretless armoured car with its machine gun aligned towards us at maximum elevation. It was by the side of the road and what immediately struck me as very strange was that the Browning gun was aligned to the rear. An attempt had been made to burn it, but it had managed to survive with its wheels and tyres intact. It was driveable and all that had happened was that some of the paint had been scorched off the side of it. We collected the Browning machine gun and moved on. I asked Frank to check the barrel of the gun and he turned to me and said: "This gun wasn't fired." It was yet another baffling detail in a confusing situation,' he added.

As the team took up position outside the Radio College, they quickly realised that Cmdt Cahalane had been ambushed and that the patrol had found itself involved in a firefight. 'A little further ahead was a burned out Landrover and, still further ahead, was the chassis of a bus. It had been completely burned out and all that was left was the skeleton of the chassis. But there was no sign at all of the lead armoured car, which had apparently been the one hit by the anti-tank shell and immobilised. There were some spent cartridge cases from both 7.62mm and 9mm weapons, which had clearly been fired. But where could the lead car be? And what had become of the bodies of the two soldiers reported dead?' Art asked himself.

The Irish team – warily keeping their weapons close to hand – began a minute inspection of the scene in a bid to piece together precisely what had happened on 14/15 September. By the side of one of the buildings, Sgt Carroll spotted what he believed to be blood. All around the building was broken glass, fragments of masonry and obvious evidence of gunfire. 'There were ammunition shells all around us but not as many as you might have thought. Not so many to indicate a prolonged firefight.'

Captain Magennis – in his previous conversation with Denard – knew that an anti-tank round had been used and that two Irish soldiers had allegedly been killed, though at what point in time in the ambush was unclear. The scene spread in front of the Irish team made no sense.

'Why would the Frenchman go to all the trouble of taking away a disabled armoured car and two dead bodies and yet leave a perfectly intact armoured car behind? Frank and I were chewing this over when Dan Carroll said, almost to himself: "Maybe the two boys weren't dead – maybe one or both of them was just knocked unconscious?" It was the first time anyone had considered that possibility but, the more I thought about it, the more sense it made,' Art said.

Studying the scene, Captain Magennis could only surmise that maybe his sergeant was right. 'But if so, where are they? And where is the armoured car? I knew we had best get back to camp and report everything that we had seen. So having taken photographs of the scene and checking to ensure we had all the recoverable weapons, we returned to base leaving the recovery of the vehicles to the afternoon. The operations section was as puzzled as we were about the failure of the second patrol to see the destroyed vehicles and we left it with them to make further inquiries … I remember thinking, after having come back from the ambush scene, how in the name of God could a patrol have followed the route of Cmdt Cahalane's patrol and come back to report that nothing had been seen? I still cannot understand that to this day. The only explanation I can offer is that they took the wrong route and mistook their directions,' he said.

Later in the afternoon, the damaged armoured car and incinerated jeep and bus were brought back to the base. But there was still no trace of the missing second armoured car. The Irish battalion now had to rely on local intelligence-gathering sources because, if the armoured car had been taken out into the bush, they simply didn't have the manpower or resources to mount such a search operation. With no air cover, they also could not fly reconnaissance missions in the hope of tracking the missing Ford AFV.

As luck would have it the 35th Battalion's intelligence section received an anonymous tip-off – believed to be from an Elisabethville-based European worker – that a UN armoured car had been spotted abandoned along Avenue Drogmans/Boulevard Elisabeth, a route which led directly into the African section of Elisabethville. The road ran alongside the Parc Zoologique and effectively parallel to the Lubumbashi River. A patrol was immediately ordered and Captain Magennis, with Technical Officer Lawless, again set off to take personal charge.

'In the end, we had no difficulty in locating the car. It was at an angle across the road and its entire front end was lodged in a roadside trench. These drainage trenches were about three feet deep and were on both sides of Boulevard Elisabeth to carry off surface water during the rainy season. An examination of the scene indicated that an attempt had been made to do a U-turn with the

armoured car and the driver had apparently misjudged the distance
to the trench.

'The trench on one side of the front wheels was absolutely littered
with spent 9mm cases which suggested to me that there had been
a prolonged period of combat. The angle of the car ruled out any
possibility of using the turret machine gun. When we checked the
inside of the car, all the equipment had been taken. It was totally
stripped down to its bare component parts. It was the same on the
outside – everything that could be taken had been taken. There was
nothing that could be associated with either of the missing soldiers
except possibly a set of keys found close to the car.'

The discovery of so many 9mm shell casings in the drainage ditch
was a crucial clue to what might have happened. The Carl Gustav
sub-machine gun, which armed the cavalry troopers – including
Tpr Mullins the night he went on the fateful patrol – used a 9mm
Parabellum shell. The Swedish weapon was capable of emptying
its entire thirty-six round magazine in a matter of seconds. But
while lethal at close range, it had limited use for aimed fire over
distances. The Carl Gustav was not a weapon to challenge an FN,
Kalashnikov or even the French MAS-49 assault rifle in a shooting
fight over distance.

Captain Magennis did not realise it at the time, but the recovered
keys belonged to Tpr Mullins. John O'Mahony felt his heart sink
when he was shown the keys later that evening and was asked to
identify them. Pat Mullins always carried his keys in the pocket of
his uniform tunic. John was certain his friend had the keys on him
when he went on patrol to the Radio College that fateful night.

'We photographed the car in situ; we finally managed to get
it out onto the road and then combed the area thoroughly. But
nothing else was found. On the level ground we found that the
turret had jammed and the [Vickers] gun looked as if it had not

been fired. The gun's water jacket had been perforated with small arms fire. It was clear that, even if the gun had been fired, it would have over-heated and seized up within minutes. But the big question remained – how did the car get there? The more we discussed it the more likely it seemed to me that Dan Carroll's solution seemed the likely one. One or both of the missing men may not have died when the car was hit.

'I think the evidence clearly suggests that while one of those boys may have been injured or even dead [at the Radio College], the other one was alive and had driven the armoured car. He had then protected his comrade [at the drainage ditch] and he kept firing until he was killed. Everything we discovered pointed to a second battle away from the Radio College,' Art explained.

But that still didn't answer the question as to where the bodies of the two missing Irish troopers were. 'If they had survived the ambush and had driven the car to this location and had subsequently been killed in a firefight – as evidenced by all the spent 9mm cases – where were the bodies now?' Reluctantly, Captain Magennis and his team realised there was nothing more they could do at the scene. They carefully hitched a tow onto the recovered armoured car and slowly escorted it back to the Irish base for more detailed analysis and repairs.

The captain and Lawless were immediately ushered into the operations section for a briefing on their findings. Such was the concern over the incident that the Battalion Commander, Lt Col McNamee, joined the briefing. Having sifted through all the evidence, the group reached a single unavoidable conclusion – one of the troopers must have survived the missile hit on the armoured car and desperately tried to save his injured comrade.

'There was general agreement that the Katangan gendarmerie were most unlikely to have been responsible for moving the Ford

AFV away from the Radio College. It just made no sense. Why would a gendarme – or even a mercenary for that matter – drive away in an Irish armoured car only to have a change of heart near their base and attempt to do a U-turn at speed? And if a gendarme or mercenary was driving the car, then what is the explanation for all the 9mm casings found beside the armoured car and the multiple small arms fire hits on the car and its Vickers machine gun? The gendarmes were hardly likely to be shooting at each other.'

The battalion's intelligence section promised to make immediate inquiries amongst local sources about the fate of the bodies. The officers now hoped that the individual who had passed on the information about the armoured car's location would know something about the whereabouts of the two bodies. Inquiries were discreetly made and members of the 35th Battalion hoped and prayed for a response. Within a week, those prayers had been answered.

'A few days later I was summoned to Battalion Headquarters and was told that information had been received from a city convent that a burial had taken place in a local cemetery of one or possibly two white UN soldiers. It was immediately agreed that our engineering section would carry out an exhumation. Captain Seán Donlon and the legal commandant, Tadhg O'Shea, would attend and, if I wished, I could also be present. I opted to go because I had been so involved in investigating the matter up to this point.

'We were told nothing about the source of the information, simply that if the bodies were buried in wooden coffins they were definitely Caucasians. We drove to an ethnic cemetery in the African section of the city. I had seen a few African funerals at close hand over the previous months and realised that the dead were always buried in a type of shroud, never a wooden coffin. We reached the cemetery, which was a desolate, lonely kind of place.

There was one fairly wide unpaved track running down the centre of the cemetery and there were footpaths running left and right of it. The rainy season had begun and the red clay underfoot was sticky and greasy.'

The task facing the Irish engineering detachment was not an easy one. Unlike in Irish or European cemeteries, there were no headstones here – the grave markers usually took the form of personal mementos or items of household goods left as offerings. That lent a shabby aura to the whole place. It was as depressing a place as the Irish soldiers could have imagined. The only guidance the Irish team had was that the burial was recent and so they focused on an area just off the centre track where recent burials had taken place.

'The engineers started digging straight away and it was very difficult work because the clay was already totally saturated. It was heavy and sticky, and every shovel seemed to be sucked into the red clay. Just when they would get the grave open, it would begin to fill with rainwater. Then came the sound the team had been hoping for and dreading in equal measure – the scrape of metal against wood,' Captain Magennis explained.

Without speaking, Irish soldiers and officers alike gazed at each other. No training manual dealt with the nightmare scenario they were now forced to deal with. This was the body of a comrade – a friend – and none of the soldiers knew precisely what they were likely to find in the grave. Finally, with a silent nod, they began the awful task at hand. The earth was carefully cleared away from the lid of the rough-hewn coffin. Seconds after the lid was prized off, the team staggered back under the smell of putrefaction.

'I had to withdraw from the scene and escape back to the cars. I am glad I did because it was about as terrible a job as you could ask any soldier to do. I felt violently ill and sick at heart for the two soldiers. These young lads deserved far better than this. When the team eventually came up to the trucks, I was told the body in the coffin was identified by the identity discs around the neck as being that of Cpl Nolan. The grave was searched deeper but there was nothing else there. There was no trace of Tpr Mullins and the team seemed satisfied that there hadn't been another burial nearby. Back in camp, the legal officer made the necessary reports. I went to my billet and stretched out on the bed and listened to the rain that was now cascading down. I just couldn't sleep and even the mere thought of food repulsed me.'

With Cpl Nolan's body now recovered, Captain Magennis was determined that everything possible be done to locate the remains of Tpr Mullins. He met up with Frank Lawless and Dan Carroll and talked over the best course of action now open to them. But what the three officers did not realise was that the battalion had already made a catastrophic omission, which would have far-reaching implications for the search.

The 35th Battalion – in line with standard UN procedure – had notified the Congo command of what had happened on Avenue Wangermee and Avenue Drogmans/Boulevard Elisabeth and that two Irish soldiers were missing, presumed dead. The UN command was then informed that the body of Cpl Nolan had been successfully located and recovered. They were also informed that the search for Tpr Mullins remained ongoing. However, no formal request for specialist assistance was ever issued – a critical omission given that the Swedish UN battalion already had a special dog-search team in place in Elisabethville.

The failure to make such a formal request for search assistance remains baffling to this day. The Swedish dog handling team were trained in tracking techniques. But the Swedes remained ignorant of the missing Irish soldier. The Irish only realised weeks later that the Swedes had such a vital resource available. Any of Tpr Mullins' personal belongings left at Battalion HQ would have provided the dogs with a vital scent from which to work. And Tpr Mullins' last known location by the drainage ditch on Avenue Drogmans/Boulevard Elisabeth was the perfect place to commence a dog search operation.

Meanwhile, the Irish officers staged informal briefings amongst themselves in a bid to pool information or ideas about how to search for Tpr Mullins. But, having located the armoured car so fast, the trail suddenly began to go cold. The officers only got scraps of information from local sources and none of it related to where Tpr Mullins' remains might be located.

One Katangan businessman, who befriended a few of the Irish UN officers, confidentially briefed them on what he had heard about the firefight on Avenue Drogmans/Boulevard Elisabeth. Captain Magennis and Company Sgt Carroll were correct in their painstaking reconstruction of what might have happened. The one crucial additional piece of information he supplied was that the Katangans were so impressed by the soldier's courage and loyalty to his comrade that his body was separated from that of the other trooper and taken away by the gendarmes. The businessman reckoned the body was most likely taken for use in some kind of tribal ritual. Congolese tribes had for generations believed that specific body parts carried human attributes such as courage, loyalty and intelligence. Some of the body parts of a brave enemy were believed to convey courage to those who took them and, as such, were prized. The shocked Irish officers realised that, more than likely, Tpr Mullins' body had been dismembered and used for tribal purposes.

The information galvanised the Irish officers to redouble their efforts to find Tpr Mullins' resting place, if such a grave existed.

Battalion intelligence was charged with the task while, given the deteriorating security situation in Katanga, the rest of the officers were relieved of the responsibility and assigned to other pressing UN duties. 'There was very little we could do except keep our eyes and ears open when meeting native people, particularly children. Children everywhere love to gather around soldiers and chat with them even through sign language. But ultimately the hard gathering of information on Tpr Mullins' burial place would rest on the battalion intelligence section,' said Art Magennis.

The search was badly hampered by circumstances. Despite the ceasefire, tensions were running high between Katangans and the UN. Tshombe's gendarmes did everything in their power to make the work of the UN difficult – setting up roadblocks along UN supply routes and shadowing any UN patrols sent out around the city. It was also routine for Katangan forces to cut electricity and water supplies to areas where the UN troops were based. Some local food stores, including bakers, were warned that supplying the UN carried dire consequences. A trade boycott inevitably erupted.

A further problem was that any Katangans – and some Europeans for that matter – who conversed or even socialised with UN personnel immediately came under suspicion of spying or providing intelligence. The Katangan Ministry of the Interior was by now genuinely feared in Elisabethville and locals were terrified that contacts with the UN, however innocent, would have serious consequences for them.

By early October, it began to look like another serious outbreak of fighting was likely. An Irish intelligence section officer was fired on as he drove near the battalion base. On another occasion, an Irish sergeant on a dispatch mission suddenly found his Landrover surrounded by a hostile crowd, which began to stone the vehicle. Katangan forces also increased their patrol tempo and Irish troops noticed that the number of mercenaries around Elisabethville seemed to be increasing by the day. Security concerns were so great that Irish troops were only allowed to move around in armed groups of four and social expeditions to the city centre were forbidden.

These circumstances meant that battalion intelligence's priorities had inevitably shifted away from the search for Tpr Mullins. Captain Magennis – acutely aware of the importance of a timely search – decided to take matters into his own hands and contacted a South African national he had befriended in Elisabethville. Bill Williams was a unique character. He had been born and raised in South Africa yet spoke with the soft lilt of the Welsh valleys. Few people knew Africa as well as Bill, and Art Magennis was now desperate for help in uncovering information about the missing eighteen-year-old soldier.

'I first met Bill and his wife shortly after the main body of the 35th Battalion arrived in Elisabethville. A bonfire had been lit in the area between the HQ building and the road. The troops gathered around the fire and an impromptu singsong started. Then the battalion pipe band arrived complete with dress uniforms and started into their concert repertoire. It was a masterstroke of public relations because, within an hour, a crowd had gathered – both whites and blacks – and joined in the event enthusiastically,' Art recalled.

'I happened to be near the entrance gate when I heard a pronounced Welsh voice say: "Captain, welcome to Katanga." That is how I first met Bill Williams. His father had emigrated to South Africa after surviving the First World War. Bill was born in South Africa but picked up his father's Welsh accent and kept it throughout his life. He was in Katanga for about ten years and had established a very successful quarrying business supplying road-making stone to the government and to Union Minière. We soon became good friends.'

With telecommunications now non-existent in Katanga, arranging a meeting with the quarry owner was easier said than done. Irish troops were under orders only to move around in groups of four and inviting Bill Williams into a group like that in public could pose personal security risks for him. Finally Captain Magennis hit on the idea of trying to contact Bill through an intermediary, a Polish neighbour, Stan Zurakovsky, who was easy for the Irish troops to contact as he lived near the base and troopers passed his home on a near daily basis and who could carry a message to the quarry owner.

'I made contact with Bill through Stan and we arranged a meeting for 24 October. He agreed to try to ferret out any information there might be amongst his Katangan employees about what had happened between Avenue Wangermee and Boulevard Elisabeth. The South African said he would make discreet inquiries but that it would take at least two or three weeks to discover anything. The date of that meeting with Bill always sticks out in my mind because, the very next day, the Katangan authorities released all the prisoners who had been captured by the gendarmes. They were released on the old airstrip by the main airport road. We were glad to see them all back safe and well.'

Pat Cahalane – who had been a prisoner with his patrol for a month – went back into command of the Armoured Car Group though his hearing was still badly affected by the recoilless rifle round explosion. The 35th Battalion's Armoured Car Group was now nearly back to full strength with the exception of Cpl Nolan, Tpr Mullins and Sgt Carey, who was receiving medical attention in Leopoldville.

However, the prisoner release failed to ease the tensions around Elisabethville and November proved to be a miserable month both in terms of the weather and the tightening economic blockade now being mounted against UN forces. The rains poured down and made patrols, guard duty and vehicle maintenance an exhausting ordeal for the Irish troops. Then, in mid November, Captain Magennis finally got a message that Bill Williams wanted to meet him. It was proposed that they meet up at Stan Zurakovsky's home.

'It was obvious from Bill's face the minute I walked into the room that the news he had was anything but good. He had learned that, early on the morning of the incident, shortly before daybreak, an armoured car had driven down Avenue Drogmans and turned left [onto Boulevard Elisabeth]. The car was travelling relatively slowly. A short while later, the car stopped and attempted to do a U-turn, but ended up sliding its front wheels into a roadside drainage trench. A soldier got out by the rear door and was helping another soldier. They both got into the trench.

'But some Katangan soldiers arrived on the scene and the shooting started. One of the UN soldiers was hit and fell into the trench. The other soldier continued to shoot until he apparently ran out of ammunition and he, too, was killed. The Katangan soldiers took all the kit out of the car and then they put the body of the second UN soldier to be killed into a truck and drove off towards the ethnic [African] city. They left the body of the other soldier in the trench. That body lay there for two days until it was taken away and buried in an ethnic cemetery.'

The Irish captain's face was ashen as he listened to his worst fears become a reality. He had hoped against hope that Tpr Mullins' body might be located in some part of the African cemetery. But he had clearly been taken elsewhere.

'Bill added that there was a long-standing practice to use the bodies of brave enemies for tribal purposes. It was most likely that this was what had happened. There was a rumour to this effect already within the African city. Further than that, Bill had no more information from his sources.'

Art Magennis and several other Irish officers had taken note of the fact that the River Lubumbashi ran directly behind the Parc Zoologique, which was where the bullet-chipped armoured car had been found nose-down in the drainage ditch. The river was also readily accessible from the native city, which is where Bill Williams clearly believed Pat Mullins' body had been taken after the final firefight. Was it possible that, after the tribal ritual, the remains might have been disposed of in the river rather than accorded a proper burial?

Given the deteriorating security situation between the UN and the Katangans/Belgians, it was obvious that further enquiries were currently impossible. Captain Magennis and Bill Williams thanked their Polish host for helping arrange the meeting, shook hands and parted company. It was the last time that the Irish captain and the South African businessman would meet. In 1962, fearful of the mounting chaos within the Congo, Bill Williams moved his family back to South Africa. Incredibly, Stan Zurakovsky was later arrested by the UN on suspicion of facilitating gun attacks on a UN base. It was a bizarre accusation to level against a man who had given such assistance to the Irish battalion. Crucially, it meant that, from 1962, the Irish had few, if any, local assets to investigate the location of Tpr Mullins' grave.

Operation Morthor – which had been hailed as the end to the Katangan insurrection – was effectively abandoned, leaving eleven UN personnel and, according to reports of the time, fifty Katangese dead (though the latter figure is now estimated to be vastly higher). It left a legacy of hatred and mistrust between the various parties in Katanga and the province was now more militarised than at any time in its history.

In the wake of Operation Morthor and the death of Dag Hammarskjöld in a plane crash, Conor Cruise O'Brien resigned from his post with the UN. Within the Irish army, the shock of Niemba was now followed by the hammer blow of the Jadotville surrender. Politicians and military chiefs alike effectively chose to ignore the courage and heroism displayed by the soldiers at the isolated outpost and, instead, chose to remember the fact that they had surrendered.

Captain Art Magennis finished his tour with the 35th Battalion and rotated back to Ireland in January 1962. The captain didn't return to the Congo until early 1963 when he was stationed at Kolwezi. By 1964, Ireland and the UN were winding down their operation in Katanga after a soon-to-be-breached peace deal had been signed between the various Congolese factions. Within twelve months of Ireland withdrawing from the Congo, the country entered the darkness of the US-backed Mobutu regime where corruption, incompetence and brutality left one of Africa's potentially wealthiest countries on the verge of collapse.

MEANWHILE, IN IRELAND in September 1961, a nightmare began for the Mullins family. Two ashen-faced army officers climbed the winding road to Boher to explain to Catherine and her children that her youngest son was missing and feared dead. Tom Kent heard the news and, fearful of his wife Mary hearing about the tragedy before he had a chance to bring her to her family, he disconnected one of the fuses in the radio so that no Radio Éireann broadcasts could be heard.

In early January 1962, Lt Col Hugh McNamee and Captain Art Magennis also travelled to Boher to explain to the family at first hand as much as they could about what happened to Pat. A short time later Sgt Tim Carey also made contact with the family to explain what had happened. Cmdt Pat Cahalane, who hailed Pat as a loyal and courageous soldier, also made contact.

But the family didn't hear the full details of what happened between Avenue Wangermee and Boulevard Elisabeth – in part because the army itself was not certain back in 1961/62 precisely what had happened. So Catherine Mullins simply knew that her youngest son had died in an ambush, that he had done his duty and that his body was now missing. It would be almost four decades before crucial details could be added to that summary.

# CHAPTER ELEVEN

As Irish troops prepared to pull out of the Congo and bring the curtain down on the country's first major UN peacekeeping mission, it didn't seem like much of a victory – at least not at the time. The secession of Katanga had successfully been prevented and the integrity of the Congo preserved, but, for the first time, UN troops had sustained significant losses and there were question marks over just how far 'peacekeeping' could go.

The uneasy ceasefire after Operation Morthor broke down on 5 December when heavy fighting again erupted. The UN launched Operation Unokat, which was aimed at clearing routes of Katangan gendarme roadblocks and getting mercenaries out of the country. The 35th Battalion's return to Ireland was delayed for a fortnight due to the heavy fighting. They ultimately left the Congo when the new 36th Battalion relieved them in the line under fire. On 10 December, John O'Mahony and other elements of the battalion were ordered to Rousseau Farm near Elisabethville Airport and they began to fly home on 18 December. John flew out on 20 December, but due to an engine failure on his USAF flight home, was forced to spend three days at Wheelus Field Air Base in Libya before finally arriving back to Baldonnel on Christmas morning.

Ireland ended its Congo mission and words like 'Niemba', 'Katanga' and 'Baluba' permanently entered the Irish lexicon. To this day, half a century on, the phrase 'Baluba' is still used in a derogatory sense in some rural areas of Ireland. The Irish had mixed emotions about the country's involvement in the Congo

– Niemba and Jadotville had been a massive shock to the system of an army relatively untouched by the Second World War and the military developments of the Cold War. Worst of all, soldiers from the Southern Command – and, in particular, the cavalry units – returned home in the knowledge that the body of a comrade lay in an undiscovered African grave.

The Congo was a bruising experience for the UN as well as Ireland. The UN had experienced the cataclysmic difference between peacekeeping and peace-enforcement – and the resultant political fallout. It also, for the first time, had the spectre of bloodshed to deal with due to rumours filtering out about how some blue-helmeted troops, most notably some of the Indian contingents, had dealt with Katangan soldiers in and around Elisabethville during Operation Morthor.

In his excellent history of the UN's first half century, *United Nations – The First Fifty Years,* Stanley Meisler pointed out that the Congo represented the steepest learning curve in the organisation's short history and became a conflict that would mark UN operations for decades to come. The Congo not only cost the UN the lives of some of its peacekeepers, and arguably its finest secretary-general, but also a substantial chunk of its innocence. 'The Congo had also jarred the mood of confidence about the emerging Africa. The UN had not mounted such a large and audacious military force before. At Suez, the troops were performing what would be known as the classic peacekeeping tasks – the impartial patrolling of ceasefire lines between belligerents who were content, for the time being, to avoid conflict. The blue helmets at Suez fired their weapons only to protect themselves. The Congo operation took the UN onto much more dangerous ground,' Meisler wrote.

'The Congo now appears a greater triumph for the UN in the microscope of history. When the UN (eventually) withdrew its troops after four years, an era of chaos and murderous suppression still lay ahead in the Congo. But, amid much bitter controversy, the UN had managed to suppress the secession of Moise Tshombe's Katanga province with his mercenary-led army. It was a grand victory of sorts.'

What is most noteworthy is that it would be another three decades before the UN was prepared to mount an operation in any way comparable to that undertaken in the Congo. The UN was deeply reluctant to endure the kind of headlines that marred some of its military operations in Katanga. For example, the shooting of a Swiss banker by an over-enthusiastic Ethiopian UN soldier armed with a bazooka provoked such outrage in Europe that Britain's Prime Minister Harold MacMillan was moved to comment that: 'Even Swiss bankers have rights.'

The Swedes and Irish left the Congo with a deep mutual respect for each other's peacekeeping skills. Both European nations were also deeply impressed by the fighting qualities of the Dogra and Gurkha solders with the Indian contingent, but regarded them more as fighting troops than peacekeepers. They took a similar view of the Ethiopian troops, who were considered to be trigger-happy by virtually everyone in the theatre. In contrast, the Irish were less than impressed with the Malaysian forces when they effectively refused to put their armoured units in harm's way in 1962–63.

The cause of UN peacekeeping was similarly not helped by the misguided bombing missions undertaken by UN jets in late 1961 and throughout 1962 and 1963, which hit the Catholic cathedral in Elisabethville, the crowded Prince Leopold hospital and a local mine among other things. UN mortars also missed assigned targets and hit a mission run by the Seventh Day Adventists. Worst of all were the rumours that continued to swirl around what precisely happened when Indian troops captured the Radio Katanga building. In official terms, the UN did little or nothing to quash the rumours and that, in turn, damaged the fledgling reputation of the blue beret. Not until the ethnic strife in Somalia and Bosnia would the UN be willing to run such a gauntlet again.

Congo and Katanga also – unlike Suez – underlined how difficult it was to match military realities with rapidly shifting political priorities. The US was the UN's primary driving force and every UN operation depended, to varying degrees, on US support and goodwill. It is worth remembering that Ireland could never have deployed its battalions to the Congo without US air support via the Globemaster II transport planes. Similarly, US bases like Wheelus Field became major staging posts for UN troops en route to and from the Congo.

With the removal of Patrice Lumumba and the emergence of a western-friendly Mobutu regime in Leopoldville, the US saw no reason to deepen the UN's involvement in the Congo. President Dwight Eisenhower had once famously commented that Africa should be left to the experts – Britain and France. The US was wary of a deepening UN commitment to Africa – which it would ultimately be asked to either fund or facilitate – when its forces were already committed in West Germany, South Korea, Japan, Cuba, central America and, increasingly as the 1960s wore on, in South Vietnam.

If the US showed a rekindled interest in African affairs with the election of President John F. Kennedy, his assassination and the nascent presidency of Lyndon Johnson ensured a swift cooling of that ardour. In areas where there were no strategic interests at play and no obvious threat of Soviet-Cuban involvement, the US was willing to accept the local pro-western strongman. With the US reluctant to deepen its involvement in African affairs given the mounting Vietnam crisis, the UN's commitment to the region was always going to be short-term.

Another disincentive for western countries to get involved in African affairs – particularly in southern Africa – was the status of the Republic of South Africa. Run on an apartheid basis, with its black majority effectively disenfranchised, South Africa was wealthy thanks to its vast gold and mineral reserves and, equally as important, was militarily independent. South Africa had the largest and best-equipped army south of the Sahara and was willing to use that power to destabilise bordering countries that it perceived as a threat to itself and its regime. South Africa did not appreciate excessive European interest in its African affairs and, in the 1960s and 1970s, still had the power to make those feelings known. The Congo was generally outside the South African sphere of influence, but neighbouring countries, particularly Nyasaland and southern Rhodesia, were hugely important to Pretoria and could not be destabilised.

For Ireland, the Congo represented a similarly steep learning curve. Politicians and military commanders realised that you couldn't send soldiers into harm's way in the 1960s and 1970s with equipment designed for combat in the 1920s and 1930s. The Vickers machine gun may have set firing records in the First World War, but was it really suited to the UN operation in the Congo? Communication was now also appreciated as a vital element of battalion co-ordination, as was proper logistical support for isolated units such as the one at Jadotville. The importance of air support, armoured support and operational co-ordination would never be underestimated again.

The reality was that the Congo was like a classroom for an army that, in its forty-year history, had only ever undertaken static defensive tasks. In the space of just two years, the Irish army went from using Lee-Enfield rifles and doing combat marches between major Irish towns, to deploying a modern assault rifle and dealing with firefights against more numerous and better-armed opponents.

After Niemba, Irish units never again made the same mistakes about clearing roadblocks. After Jadotville, troops were never again assigned to isolated locations unless they could be properly resupplied by air or by road. Within a few years of returning from the Congo, Ireland quietly replaced the old Ford AFVs with modern French-built Panhard armoured cars that offered vastly greater flexibility and potency in operations. It is worth noting that Ireland deemed the Fords of such low worth that most were simply left in the Congo despite the fact they were still fully operational. The Air Corps – until then reliant on British hand-me-downs such as the Supermarine Spitfire and De Havilland Vampire – moved to purchase helicopters that, as the US was to shortly prove in Vietnam, were a crucial weapon in modern warfare.

Having witnessed the havoc that even a humble jet-trainer armed with machine guns and rocket pods could cause against opponents with no air cover, the Air Corps also decided to acquire a new jet aircraft. The aircraft chosen was the Fouga Magister with its distinctive butterfly tail, which, until its retirement in the 1990s, remained Ireland's principle air defence weapon.

The Congo was so important because it gave the Irish army a chance of proving itself in a combat situation. For the first time since the War of Independence, Irish troops were thrown into a combat situation from which they emerged wiser and more skilled. Irish troops displayed admirable courage throughout the four-year Congo deployment and, as Tpr Pat Mullins personally demonstrated, were capable of the most incredible acts of bravery, loyalty and sacrifice. If the soldiers who served throughout 'The Emergency' were the core of the Defence Forces in the late 1940s and 1950s, the soldiers who returned from the Congo between 1960–64 formed the bedrock of the army which, in the 1970s and 1980s, emerged as one of the UN's most respected and skilled peacekeeping forces.

Irish troops who arrived in the Congo and Katanga 'green', went home as experienced operators who had witnessed the best – and the worst – elements of modern conflict. Some of the things that Irish soldiers witnessed in the Congo would remain with them for the rest of their lives. Most of the experiences helped make the young troops better soldiers by reminding them that warfare is a terrible thing and that simple mistakes can sometimes have catastrophic consequences.

'There is no substitute for having been under fire. You either have combat experience or you don't. And you never really know how a soldier is going to react under the pressure of combat,' Des Keegan explained. 'We were all pretty innocent when we went out there, but the Congo had a way of shocking you and showing you that it wasn't all stories like *Beau Geste*. I remember during the fighting of late 1961, after the ceasefire following Operation Morthor in September had broken down, a Katangan sniper started taking pot-shots at the Irish camp at Prince Leopold Farm. He only started shooting at night, usually as we were sitting down in the mess tent for something to eat. His shots all fell high which meant he wasn't in the best of firing positions. It was more of an annoyance than a threat I suppose. But we had an ex-Congolese army sergeant [working on the base] with us. He had no love for the Katangans and, one night after the sniper started shooting, he turned to us in the mess tent and said, "I will fix sniper." He borrowed a combat knife and slipped out of camp into the darkness. He was so black himself that he blended into the night like a shadow.

'To be honest, none of us took much notice. I think a few of us thought he only wanted an excuse to get out of camp and maybe go looking for a woman or a beer. But then, about an hour later, we noticed that the firing had stopped. Not long after that, the Congolese sergeant slipped quietly back into camp and walked proudly over to a group of us having a smoke outside our tents. He handed one of the lads a soggy newspaper, which had been wrapped in a ball. "Here is sniper," he grinned. The Irish lad opened up the package and almost vomited up his dinner. In the newspaper in his hand was a bloody penis and a pair of testicles. The sergeant had crept up on the sniper and cut his throat. He only cut off the guy's penis and testicles just to prove to us that he had done what he said he would.'

It wasn't just the military that discovered that the Congo could be a bruising classroom rife with conflicting interests and priorities. In December 1961, Conor Cruise O'Brien resigned as UN Special Representative in the Congo. *Irish Independent* reporter, Raymond Smith, writing in 1962, was prescient when he mused that, had Operation Morthor proved a success on 13 September, Dr O'Brien 'would probably have emerged as a world hero'. But the reality was that, far from being a success, Morthor had come close to wrecking the UN mission.

In announcing his resignation just three months after Operation Morthor, the Irish diplomat said that nothing should be left in place that might impact on settlement talks between the various Congolese parties. 'As most members of the [UN] Security Council have laid great stress on the necessity of conciliation in the Congo and as some powers have maintained that my contribution has been an obstacle to conciliation, I feel it would be better for me to go lest I should be thought to be frustrating the policy of conciliation. By its nature the UN must pursue such a policy by every means, setting aside any obstacle that there may be in the way,' Dr O'Brien explained.

However, the politician shortly to be famed as 'The Cruiser' was never shy of courting controversy and in 1962 he caused outrage when he accused Great Britain of playing a hidden agenda in the

Congo, supporting the UN Security Council position in relation to the Congo on the one hand, while doing everything possible to frustrate the implementation of UN policy on the ground in Katanga. It was a claim that provoked a storm of controversy not just in Britain and Westminster, but also in Rhodesia, where it was felt Dr O'Brien had effectively accused them of offering tacit support to Katanga, which, if true, could have had serious diplomatic and security consequences for this neighbouring state.

Britain has a long memory and Conor Cruise O'Brien's accusations were never forgotten. Thirteen years after the Congo crisis, when 'The Cruiser' was part of Liam Cosgrave's Fine Gael-Labour coalition government, a British diplomat threw Katanga back in his face. Dr Garret Fitzgerald, writing in his autobiography *All in a Life*, recalled that in the mid 1970s Katanga was used to try to discredit the coalition government's support for the Council of Ireland. 'Dublin political correspondents were invited to Belfast to meet the Secretary of State [Willie Whitelaw]. A very senior British civil servant referred to Conor Cruise O'Brien and myself in Whitelaw's presence as "third rate academics", one of whom had been in charge of a "second class" colonial area – a reference to Conor's role some thirteen years earlier as UN Administrator in Katanga. Whitelaw had looked at the journalist to whom these remarks were addressed, showing no inclination to demur at them,' he wrote.

The truth was that in the 1950s and 1960s Anglo-African politics were about as clear as mud. The British government was deeply concerned about the aftermath of independence in a host of its former colonies from Kenya to Uganda and from Rhodesia to Nyasaland, and their biggest fear was that chaos in Katanga could destabilise adjoining countries – most of which were former British colonies – in their race to independence.

The Congo mission drew to a close in 1964 when the UN,

having effectively disarmed Katanga, handed the country over to a government that promised to be inclusive of all provincial and tribal groups. Moise Tshombe – having returned to the Congo after fleeing at the start of Operation Morthor – was even given a ministerial role. Yet, within twelve months of UN troops leaving, the deal fell apart and Joseph Mobutu copper-fastened his iron grip on power by abolishing parliament. Mobutu – privately assured of US support for his promised pro-western policies and anti-Communist stance – had transformed the Force Publique into his personal army. He was now unassailable.

Tshombe fled for his life for the final time, and Mobutu imposed direct rule. The US was happy with the new status quo and saw no reason to take a stand for democracy in the Congo once Mobutu maintained his pro-western policies. The powerful mining interests were immediately promised stability and non-interference in their affairs by the new government and were equally quiescent. Once the mines paid a stipend to Mobutu and his cronies, all would be well – or so at least they hoped.

Between 20 July 1960 and 15 May 1964, more than 6,000 Irish soldiers served in the Congo. The involvement formally ended when Ireland's 2nd Infantry Group under General Redmond O'Sullivan formally stood down and returned home. In a fitting link, the armoured car unit of the 2nd Group was under the command of Captain Art Magennis. He formed a connection between the last Irish armoured unit in the Congo and the armoured unit that suffered the heaviest casualties in the African country two years earlier. The 1963 unit was again reliant on the Ford AFVs, but the decision had been taken that they simply weren't worth the trouble of bringing back to Ireland. The three vehicles that weren't *hors de combat* were formally handed over to the Congolese National Army at a special ceremony in Kolwezi. The cars were handed over by Lt Ken Kelly, and Captain Magennis took a special photograph of the ceremony. Showing how little things had changed, an African officer casually smoked a cigarette as he inspected the armoured cars – while a Belgian officer commanding the Katangan-born soldiers watched.

The UN formally ended Ireland's mission in the Congo in May 1964, although as the Irish troops departed Kolwezi on the first leg of their marathon journey home, an ironic sight greeted them. One of the Ford AFVs was left abandoned, effectively impaled on a steep roundabout where a Congolese crew had crashed it a few hours earlier. It was the last thing the Irish unit saw as they left Kolwezi.

The next month the UN formally ended its mission, although fighting would continue in the Congo through rebellions and coups for the next forty years. Irish troops had acquitted themselves with honour in the Congo. Furthermore, they had shown an empathy with the indigenous people who had suffered under colonialism that could only be offered by a nation that had endured similar suffering. That reputation earned Irish soldiers a unique kind of respect and made them extremely useful to the UN in the world's hotspots.

Perhaps the greatest proof of Ireland's new-found peacekeeping skill and respect comes from the case of the Baluba tribe itself. The Balubas had attacked and butchered Irish troops at Niemba and yet, within a matter of eighteen months it was Irish troops who were protecting the Balubas from persecution. Irish troops defended Baluba refugee camps in and around Elisabethville during the fighting of 1961 and 1962. At one point more than 35,000 refugees were in the care of Irish and Swedish troops in Elisabethville. Far from seeking revenge for Niemba, Irish troops had followed a noble course and left the Congo with a reputation for fairness and decency that would only be enhanced through deployments in Cyprus and Lebanon.

As it turned out, the Defence Forces didn't have long to wait for their next UN assignment – in fact Irish soldiers were dispatched on UN duties to Cyprus before all units had been withdrawn from the Congo. The Cypriot involvement – while always a smaller logistical deployment than Katanga – continued for years. Tortuous negotiations over the fate of the Turkish-speaking northern section of the island continue to this day.

But the major application of the hard-won experience in the Congo came in Lebanon, when Ireland was asked to deploy peacekeepers following the eruption of a ferocious civil war. The UN had mounted a small deployment in Beirut in 1958 and had helped successfully stave off civil war, but by 1978 tensions within Lebanon could no longer be contained. After an influx of hard-line Palestinian factions from Jordan over previous years, fighting erupted. The UN deployed troops under the UNIFIL (United Nations Interim Force in Lebanon) mission. The situation in 1978 was complex and violent as the various Lebanese factions allied themselves to outside influences including Israel, Syria and Iran, and at times Lebanon served as a proxy battleground for these countries.

Irish troops would ultimately remain in Lebanon for twenty-three years, until 2001, when a painstaking peace deal was finally agreed. Lebanon remains Ireland's biggest and longest-running UN mission – and ultimately cost twenty-seven lives.

The speed with which Ireland switched from peacekeeping duties in the Congo to those in Cyprus meant the Irish military had new priorities. The army suddenly had a major logistics operation on its hands; therefore, there was less time to focus on the lessons and tasks still remaining from the Congo. Amongst these was the fact that when the 2nd Infantry Group took down their tents, packed up their gear and stowed their rifles for the long flight back to Ireland in 1964, one Irish soldier was still unaccounted for in the Congo.

The search for Trooper Pat Mullins was about to dip below the radar for almost thirty years.

# CHAPTER TWELVE

It is hard to explain precisely why the case of Pat Mullins faded so quickly from the national consciousness. The Defence Forces maintain that his case file was always kept open and inquiries were repeatedly made about his fate. But it is curious to note that rather than being officially deemed 'Missing in Action', which is factually what happened to Pat Mullins, the young trooper was accorded a different official status. Instead of being recorded as 'MIA', he was regarded as being: 'Dead, presumed to have been killed'. The decision to omit the word 'missing' from his status has never been fully explained.

There was certainly no apparent political decision made to ignore the matter. Rather it seems that Ireland's first MIA fell victim to a combination of the traditional acceptance of the age, the geographic realities of where he died and the fact that Ireland was accelerating out of the de Valera era of economic deprivation into the heady world of 1960s expansion and growth overseen by Seán Lemass. For some strange reason, the Congo deployment was quickly associated with an old, fast disappearing Ireland, while Cyprus and Lebanon was part of the proud, new modernised nation.

Undoubtedly, another key factor is that within a decade of Pat Mullins' death and disappearance Ireland found itself dealing with 'The Troubles' and the increasingly vicious border battles between the resurgent IRA, Royal Ulster Constabulary and the British army. Faced with the threat of Northern Ireland tearing itself apart, the Defence Forces had more immediate priorities than the events of an African mission of a previous decade.

Twenty years after Tpr Mullins vanished in the Congo, Ireland added a second name to its list of MIAs. The second incident centred on Ireland's UN peacekeeping involvement in Lebanon. At the time, in the late 1970s, many wondered if the bloodshed in Lebanon would be as bad as it had been in the Congo. Lebanon, over the course of twenty-three years, proved to be far deadlier, with twenty-seven Irish soldiers killed in the country whose capital Beirut was once hailed as 'the Paris of the Mediterranean'. Yet many army veterans believe that, but for the experience hard-won in the Congo, Ireland's death toll in Lebanon could ultimately have been far higher.

On 27 April 1981, Private Kevin Joyce (20) was on guard duty at a UN observation post in south Lebanon when he was kidnapped. He was never seen again and is now officially regarded by the Defence Forces as: 'Missing in Action, Presumed Dead'. Despite hopes that the blossoming peace process in Lebanon might lead to information about where his remains are buried, no trace of the Inisheer-born soldier has been found to date.

Ireland's last UNIFIL battalion in Lebanon had made it one of their primary missions to obtain information about Pte Joyce's burial site before Ireland, like other UNIFIL countries, withdrew their troops in 2001. In May of that year, Henry McDonald, writing in *The Observer*, revealed that the battalion was working with the Christian Maronite Bishop of Tyre as well as the Lebanese Minister for Missing and Displaced Persons, Senator Mirwan Hamadi.

Crucially, for the first time Palestinians from refugee camps in south Lebanon agreed to discuss the possible location of Pte Joyce's burial site – the first time anyone had ever admitted any knowledge about the missing soldier or the precise events of that fateful April day. In perhaps the ultimate irony, Pte Joyce's kidnapper, Abu Amin Dayk, was himself condemned and executed by the Shia militia, Amal, for crimes against the Lebanese people. Dayk was hanged in May 1984.

Back in 1981, Dayk had emerged as the leader of a hard-line Palestinian faction in the south Tyre area. He was Lebanese by birth but was determined to 'earn his spurs' with his Palestinian allies. Amid the chaos in Lebanon between 1978 and 1990, factions fought the Israelis, the Lebanese army and very often each other. They fought over politics, religion, territory, access to weapons and, in one notable case, over running water supplies.

On 27 April 1981, Dayk and his militia decided to raid a UN position at Dyar Ntar, possibly in the hope of securing some heavy weaponry. But the raid quickly went wrong and one of Dayk's men shot one of the two Irish UN peacekeepers on duty at the post. Pte Hugh Doherty was just twenty years old and was shot three times in the back, dying instantly. Pte Joyce was disarmed and was dragged away by the gang before UN reinforcements could arrive.

Intelligence reports later revealed that he was taken to Tyre, ostensibly to facilitate negotiations over the price of his release. He was kept under armed guard in a house in a Palestinian refugee camp. Tragically for the Irish soldier, it was a time of escalating conflict between the various Lebanese-Palestinian factions and UN forces. A few weeks later a Palestinian militia ended up in a major gun battle with a unit of Fijian UN troops. The firefight erupted at Deir Amis and, as the Fijians bravely refused to withdraw from their positions, several Palestinian fighters were killed in a heavy exchange of rounds. Furious at having had men killed, the Palestinians demanded retaliation and Dayk's gang was ordered to execute the Irish soldier captured a few weeks earlier in a tit-for-tat punishment. Pte Joyce was shot and his remains buried at a secret location.

Initial Irish efforts to locate Pte Joyce were hampered by the chaos caused by Israeli Prime Minister Ariel Sharon's invasion of Lebanon a few months later in 1982. The UN – again caught like the meat in a sandwich – wouldn't be able to re-open useful local lines of intelligence until 1983/84.

Bizarrely, shortly before he was arrested by Amal, Dayk had a meeting with UN officials. The meeting was staged at Dayk's specific request and UN officers suspected that he was trying to cut a deal whereby he would be granted safe passage out of Lebanon in return for information. One Irish UN officer shrewdly suspected that Dayk's reign as a minor warlord was coming to an end and that his rivals and enemies were tightening the noose around him. Dayk clearly felt himself to be under threat. The Irish officer gave the following description of Dayk: 'Dayk was in his mid-thirties. He was of slight build. He had black hair and spoke in a very deep monosyllabic tone. I remember during that meeting he appeared to be very nervous. You could tell that he was aware that his enemies were closing in. It was quite weird being in the same room as the man we suspected had been behind the Dyar Ntar attack. He was very uneasy during the meeting and he kept looking out the window. When people like Dayk sought a meeting with UNIFIL you could be sure their power was waning,' the officer explained.

The UN was eventually able to determine that, contrary to black propaganda and local rumours, Pte Joyce had indeed been executed in the Palestinian refugee camp. One bizarre rumour had previously claimed that he had changed sides and agreed to fight for a Palestinian faction. Another rumour had it that he was accidentally killed during a massive Israeli air strike on Palestinian positions near a refugee camp and his body was buried under a collapsed building.

*The Times'* then-Beirut correspondent, Robert Fisk, correctly assessed that the attack on the Irish UN post was as much about getting weapons as embarrassing Yasser Arafat, who had been desperately trying to maintain good relations with the UN. Fisk, in his superlative history of modern Lebanon, *Pity the Nation,* tracked down details of the young Irish private's last lonely weeks before his death: 'The soldier had been imprisoned in an underground cell beneath the Ein Halweh Palestinian refugee camp at Sidon but had (it was then claimed) been killed there when an Israeli air raid destroyed the bunker. Later, the Irish army would be told that he was taken not to Sidon but to Beirut where, after months of lonely imprisonment underground, he was coldly executed just prior to the 1982 Israeli invasion,' Fisk wrote.

In May 2001, the Joyce family travelled to Lebanon to try and offer first-hand assistance in the campaign to locate Kevin's remains before the formal withdrawal of Irish troops as part of the UNIFIL mission. They were accompanied by the then-president of PDFORRA (Permanent Defence Force Other Ranks Representative Organisation), John Laffery. PDFORRA had taken a high-profile role in campaigning for every effort to be made to repatriate Pte Joyce's remains and escorting the family was a gesture of their support.

'This is a festering sore for the Defence Forces. Every soldier that has served in Lebanon over the past twenty-one years owes to Kevin Joyce that we do everything to find him. Talks are underway and we hope his remains can be found. All the Joyce family want is to take Kevin's remains back to Ireland so he can be given a Christian burial on Inisheer,' John Laffery told reporters in Lebanon. Tragically, as of 2010, Pte Joyce's remains are still unaccounted for.

It is interesting to note that between 1981 and 2000 the Irish media repeatedly focused on the case of Pte Joyce while inexplicably ignoring the fact that another Irish soldier had been 'Missing in

Action' for almost two decades longer. A simple Internet search will underline the difference, with 4,670 hits for 'Trooper Pat Mullins Congo' in contrast to 27,800 hits for 'Kevin Joyce Lebanon'. What is also noteworthy is that the overwhelming majority of posts in relation to Tpr Mullins have all occurred post-2005 when a determined campaign to highlight his case began to gain some interest within the Irish media.

It is perhaps understandable that so much focus should have been on the kidnapping of Kevin Joyce given that it occurred in Lebanon, which, for innumerable reasons, was never out of the news headlines in Ireland. Lebanon also represents Ireland's biggest and longest-running peacekeeping mission, which has contributed to making Joyce's case so high profile. Another factor was that, thanks to intelligence work and investigative reporting, so much eventually emerged about the circumstances of Pte Joyce's kidnapping and death. In Tpr Mullins' case, after he was shot and killed on Avenue Drogmans/Boulevard Elisabeth, the trail goes cold.

The contrast in the Irish media's handling of the two cases over the past twenty years has also been marked. There were news reports updating the search for Kevin Joyce's remains and an inquiry into precisely what had happened to him. RTÉ carried repeated reports in their main television news bulletin over a period of years. Sunday newspapers carried detailed analysis pieces on the factional fighting in Lebanon and who may have been responsible for the kidnapping. The decision to wind down the UNIFIL operation in Lebanon and the eventual withdrawal of Irish troops also spawned a series of articles on Ireland's missing soldier and efforts to locate his final resting place.

Yet, unwittingly, the reports ignored the plight of Ireland's other MIA, Tpr Mullins. Pat Mullins had by then fallen so far under the radar that one British newspaper, *The Observer*, even reported that Pte Joyce was the only Irish UN peacekeeper to remain MIA. Almost like the Congo, Pat Mullins seemed to have been forgotten by all except his family, close friends and former comrades.

For almost thirty years, the search for Pat Mullins remained in this strange kind of limbo – the army file was open but, from the family's perspective, there appeared to be little or nothing happening. Worse still, the family were confused over the precise details of Pat's final hours. At first they understood that he had been killed in the initial ambush, but then word began to filter to them from some Congo veterans that Pat's fate was not quite that simple. The family felt that, at the very least, they deserved more detailed answers about Pat's death, but most of all they wanted his memory and his sacrifice better honoured.

Pat's father, Ned, died on 30 November 1960 – just eight months before Pat flew out to the Congo with the 35th Battalion. The family was grateful that he wasn't alive to endure the nightmare of not knowing Pat's fate and the whereabouts of his youngest son's body. But it was a nightmare that Pat's mother, Catherine, poignantly had to live with for the last thirty-seven years of her life.

Catherine died on 10 December 1998. She was eighty-eight years old and had prayed for Pat every day of her life since September 1961. Catherine was a strong woman but her children suspected that she had never really gotten over the disappearance and death of Pat. His brothers and sisters knew the pain she felt over her missing youngest child – and, above all else, they didn't want to do anything that might add to her suffering. Part of the reason the family didn't launch a high-profile campaign in Pat's name in the 1970s and 1980s was concern over the hurt and pain it might cause their mother. As Catherine got older, Pat's siblings worried about the impact such a campaign might have on her. Pat's disappearance remained an unhealed wound with Catherine until she died. Her main instruction to her family before her death was that she wanted her youngest son commemorated on her gravestone in the cemetery located directly behind St Joseph's church in Kilbehenny.

One month before her death, Catherine got the greatest signal yet that Ireland had not totally forgotten the heroic sacrifice of her eighteen-year-old son. On 8 November 1998 a special ceremony was organised in Collins Barracks in Dublin to honour Ireland's UN dead. (A few years later the barracks itself fell victim to Ireland's military cost cutting and was transformed into an annex of the National Museum.) But, that November day, Defence Minister Michael Smith formally presented a total of thirty-six Military Star medals to the relatives of Defence Force personnel killed overseas on UN duties, including the Mullins family. The Military Star – one of the highest awards that can be bestowed by the Defence Forces – aims to recognise personnel killed overseas in the course of their duty. The award ribbon is made up of the Irish Tricolour framed by black-edged purple bands – the traditional colours of requiem. The central depiction on the eight-pointed bronze medal is that of Cú Chulainn, the fabled warrior of Ulster and core figure in Ireland's classic poem, *The Táin*. The depiction is that of Cú Chulainn bravely standing his ground against his enemies despite being mortally wounded. The bar on the ribbon carries a single word – 'Remembrance'. The reverse of the medal carries Pat Mullins' army number, his name, the date he fell in action and the UN mission he was supporting.

'I think that medal meant an awful lot to my mother,' Mary Kent said. 'It was as if they were saying that, despite all the years, what Pat did and the courage he showed had not been forgotten. It was something. We wanted Pat's body to be found and brought home. But at least this was something.'

The award meant that Pat's service record now included three medals – the Military Star, the Congo Medal, which was awarded to all Irish personnel who served in the UN mission, and the UN Peace Medal which, following the 1988 award of the Nobel Peace Prize to the United Nations, was awarded to all personnel who had worn the blue beret. The medals and ribbons were framed and now enjoy a place of honour on the wall of the Boher house where Pat Mullins grew up.

But medals couldn't hide the reality that Pat's body was still missing and unaccounted for in the Congo. Yet there appeared little the government could – or would – do about the matter. The government and Defence Forces faced a political and logistical headache in terms of getting anything done in Africa. Under President Mobutu, the era of UN involvement in the Congo was now ignored, as were all the issues arising from it. For Mobutu, the past held painful and potentially damaging truths – particularly about his involvement in the death of Patrice Lumumba who had emerged as one of the martyrs of African independence. Lumumba's murder was a political minefield the US, the UN and particularly the Belgians were deeply conscious of.

As the Congo slid deeper into the mire of corruption, stagnation and anarchy, powerful interests were determined that stability would be preserved at all costs for the vast mining wealth of Katanga. Humanitarian as a search for the missing Irish UN peacekeeper might seem, if it threatened to embarrass the Congolese or the Katangans, it was something the corporations could do without.

Back in Ireland, the Defence Forces' position was that the file on Tpr Mullins remained open and active. But, in truth, little of consequence was done. No investigative team was ever sent to Katanga after 1964 to search for clues to his whereabouts, despite the fact that the fighting was long since over in the southern province. What was most agonising about this delay was the fact that age, disease and emigration had inexorably whittled down the number of people potentially in a position to help with information about Tpr Mullins.

By 2000, a ten-year-old Katangan child who might have witnessed the Irish soldier's fate or burial back in 1961 was now forty-nine years old. Tragically, in a country wracked by disease, poverty, malnutrition, poor medical services and regular armed revolts, very few people live into their fifties. According to World Bank figures, the average life expectancy in the Democratic Republic of the Congo in 2004 was just 53.7 years. In contrast, the average life expectancy in Ireland in 2004 was 79.4 years.

It wasn't until the 1990s that momentum finally began to build to get something tangible done for the Mullins family. The key factor was that Pat's former comrades and friends began to retire – and, one by one, they suddenly had the time to devote to reviving and reinvigorating a search campaign. Crucially, a lot of his friends were no longer in the army and no longer worried about the potential implications of being seen to 'rock the boat' over the handling of the Pat Mullins case.

Foremost amongst those who helped kick-start the campaign was Art Magennis, who had retired with the rank of commandant. Art had never forgotten the information he had received from Bill Williams in Elisabethville or the scene at the mission cemetery where the remains of Mick Nolan were finally recovered. He felt honour-bound to do his best to reinvigorate the campaign to high-light Pat Mullins' case and, if possible, persuade the government to send a search team out to Elisabethville – now called Lubumbashi.

Similarly, John O'Mahony had never forgotten his best friend. He kept all his photos of Pat Mullins and their time together, both in Fitzgerald Camp and the Congo. Some of the only photos now in existence of Pat Mullins in the last weeks of his life survive thanks to John. Over time, Art and John began to correspond over precisely what to do. Other former Congo colleagues gradually joined them and they decided that, to begin with, they would work just to highlight Pat Mullins' status and the courage he showed in the Congo.

A major breakthrough came on 10 February 1990 when a new military representative organisation was set up following a meeting in Dublin of ex-soldiers. The Irish United Nations Veterans Association (IUNVA) was set up with the primary role of providing advice and counselling to members and their families who have been affected by their overseas service with the UN. The Association, which is endorsed by the Minister for Defence, is financed by membership fees, voluntary contributions and fundraising. It also organises social, cultural and sporting events for its members. But, crucially, IUNVA took up the cudgel on behalf of the Mullins and Joyce families, particularly through their Fermoy-based Post 25. With their help, the Mullins case began to re-emerge in the headlines.

'It was slow going at first. Initially, a lot of people simply hadn't heard about Pat Mullins, even in north Cork and south Limerick where Pat was from. A lot of people didn't even know the fact that the bodies of two Irish UN peacekeepers had not been brought home. A lot of younger people had heard about Ireland sending UN peacekeepers to Lebanon, but the only thing they seemed to know about the Congo was a vague recollection about the Niemba ambush and Balubas. I was shocked to meet a few Congo veterans who didn't even know that an Irish soldier's body hadn't been brought back,' John O'Mahony explained.

Efforts to generate publicity slowly began to bear fruit. Articles appeared in *The Avondhu*, a local newspaper based in Mitchelstown, and then in the *Irish Independent*. This coverage triggered a succession of other stories, and between 1998 and 2005 numerous stories were carried about Pat Mullins in *The Corkman, The Evening Echo*, the *Irish Examiner* and *The Irish Times*.

A further boost came from the renewed interest in what had actually happened during Ireland's UN mission in the Congo. A total reappraisal of Ireland's first major overseas UN mission was now underway, in part helped by books which aimed to set the record straight about events at Jadotville, one of the most disputed events in Irish military history.

Three excellent books were published on the Congo: two specifically about the siege at Jadotville, while another focused on recollections by politicians, journalists, peacekeepers and colonial administrators associated with the Congo and Katanga. The impact was in direct proportion to the general ignorance of the Irish public about the Congo. One Cork family only discovered in the wake of the coverage of the Jadotville books that their grandfather had not only served in Elisabethville at the time but, during Operation Morthor, had witnessed some of the most brutal fighting between Dogras and the Katangan gendarmes. The man had had nightmares for years afterwards about what he had seen but bluntly refused to discuss what had happened.

The debate about Jadotville inexorably spread from the book-shelves to national and provincial papers – and commentators began re-examining why Irish troops who had fought with such heroism at Jadotville, despite horrendous odds, came home only to find themselves treated like lepers by some elements of Irish society because they had surrendered. It is somewhat ironic that while most Irish people recognise the name Niemba, they had never heard of Jadotville, which represented one of the most defiant hours of the Defence Forces.

The national debate about Jadotville slowly became a key factor in helping generate further publicity for Pat Mullins' case. Stories about the Congo were suddenly of interest to Irish news editors. But what astonished the family most was the fact that even reporters familiar with covering military and UN matters were completely ignorant of the fact that an Irish trooper was MIA in the Congo.

One report in particular generated enormous feedback for the Mullins family. RTÉ reporter Jenny O'Sullivan broadcast a special feature on the Pat Mullins case as part of the *Nationwide* TV series in 2008 and the response was incredible. The family suddenly found themselves receiving cards and letters from Congo veterans who were absolutely appalled that more wasn't being done both to commemorate Pat's name and to locate his resting place. Veterans offered to support campaigns and to attend any events in remembrance of Pat Mullins.

The Congo also figured in the memoirs of Conor Cruise O'Brien. O'Brien wrote his biography, *Memoir – My Life and Themes* in 1999 and it was updated in 2004. The Katangan mission and Operation Morthor were discussed in forensic detail over thirty-three pages. O'Brien went to great pains to defend the operation and its goals. But, interestingly, the former UN special representative never once mentioned the fact that three Irish soldiers died before and during Operation Morthor. Pat Mullins' name does not feature in the book. One of O'Brien's final comments, relating to events after 15 September 1961 and the escape of Moise Tshombe across the border to Rhodesia, was: 'By this time, Morthor had definitely gone off the rails.'

Such omissions merely added fuel to the campaign for better recognition of Pat Mullins. IUNVA's Post 25 began to stage annual memorials to the young soldier's memory, including a special anniversary Mass in Kilbehenny in the same church in which Pat Mullins made his Holy Communion and Confirmation. Pat

Mullins also had a room in the Curragh Camp named after him in commemoration. The tribute was organised by the Cavalry Corps and Lieutenant-General Seán McCann GOC, and it was a gesture that thrilled both the Mullins family and Art Magennis.

The dedicated room is a lecture hall in the Cavalry School Combat Support College. There are three lecture halls in the school, each dedicated to a cavalry soldier who will be remembered as long as the corps survives. One room is dedicated to Col J.V. Lawless, veteran of the War of Independence, founder of the Cavalry Corps and designer of the Ford armoured cars which played such an important role in the Congo. The second room is dedicated to Paddy Lynch, also a veteran of the War of Independence and a retired squadron sergeant, who for many years was foreman of the Cavalry Workshops and a close associate of Col Lawless. The third and final dedicated room has Pat Mullins' name. The dedication citation aptly reads: 'The bravest of the brave of whom it can be said – greater love hath no man than he who laid down his life for his friend.'

Then, on 10 October 2009, IUNVA and Fermoy historian, Paudie McGrath, unveiled a special memorial plaque outside the old Fitzgerald Camp barrack chapel, now called the Queen of Peace church, dedicated to all those who died on UN peacekeeping duty. The dedication ceremony was performed by Lt General Pat Nash who had recently been given overall command of the peacekeeping mission in Chad. A native of Limerick, Pat Nash had commenced his career at Fitzgerald Camp and was also a former commanding officer of 85th Infantry Battalion/UNIFIL in Lebanon between April and November 1999. For his achievements in Chad he was awarded France's Legion d'Honneur medal by President Nicolas Sarkozy.

Pat Mullins' name was inscribed twice on the memorial – once as a UN peacekeeper who died on duty and, secondly, as a former Fitzgerald Camp member who died while in service. In a further fitting tribute, the memorial programme featured a two page outline of the eighteen-year-old's story and the circumstances of his disappearance in the Congo.

# CHAPTER THIRTEEN

THE MORNING DAWNED cold and bright with a hoar frost belying the fact that it was almost springtime. The upper slopes of the Galtees still had small traces of snow in the gullies after one of the coldest winters in living memory. But, with the promise of spring hanging in the air, the daffodils were now cautiously poking their heads out of the ground around St Joseph's church in Kilbehenny.

Few people in the tightknit village realised it that day, but Thursday 11 February 2010 was arguably the most significant time for the Mullins family since two pale and visibly nervous army officers had trudged up the laneway to Boher almost fifty years before to break the terrible news that Pat Mullins was missing in the Congo.

After half a century of questions, frustration and confusion, the family were finally hoping they would get some answers about the circumstances in which Pat died and, more importantly, what happened to his body. As the members of the Mullins family prepared for the special briefing with senior army personnel, they were privately praying that an Irish team would at last be sent to Katanga to search for Pat's final resting place.

Over the previous four years, the Defence Forces had been researching an updated report on the status of Pat Mullins. The research was launched in direct response to a letter sent by Mary Kent on 20 March 2006 to Defence Minister Willie O'Dea. Writing the letter wasn't easy for Pat's sister, but she felt the family now had no other option but to appeal directly to the cabinet level of the government.

In the letter, Mary wrote: 'From a family point of view, we have never been furnished with the details of his [Pat's] death or what efforts were made to recover his body. His body has never been recovered and we, the family, were never informed of what were the actual circumstances surrounding his death.

'We as a family feel very hurt that we have never had closure with regards to Pat's death. If we had his remains and he was buried properly, at least that would allow us to move on. Pat was forgotten – other names were mentioned but never Pat. We find the current state of affairs very upsetting. We as a family request that you set up a board of inquiry without delay to see what can be done to recover his body and clarify the circumstances of his death.'

What hurt the family most of all was they felt Pat and his sacrifice had somehow been forgotten. The family felt that he was only remembered within a rapidly decreasing circle of family, friends and now-ageing comrades. Pat had made the ultimate sacrifice on UN duty in Africa and the Mullins family were determined that his memory deserved better recognition. Yet, amongst the general public, the mention of 'Pat Mullins' and 'the Congo' was still more often than not greeted by a confused shrug of the shoulders, even in his native south Limerick and north Cork.

The impetus for the renewed interest in the young peacekeeper's status came from myriad different sources. But perhaps the most obvious source of fresh momentum was the fact that the then Minister for Defence was Willie O'Dea, a Limerick TD. One of the most dedicated constituency workers ever produced by the legendary Fianna Fáil organisation, O'Dea took an early and personal interest in the case. It certainly helped that Pat Mullins' address was in the same county that O'Dea considered his personal stomping ground.

The Limerick TD, once interested in a matter, was a tireless worker who expected the same levels of commitment from his staff. The minister was sympathetic to the Mullins family's plight and his concern was echoed by some of the Defence Forces' most senior officers, several of whom felt there was a duty of honour owed to the family. Having received Mary Kent's letter, Minister O'Dea agreed to a review of the matter with the Defence Forces' top brass.

Under the new review, Col Paul Pakenham was requested to re-examine Pat Mullins' file to determine if any new information had come to light. It was a task perfectly suited to Pakenham – a native of Dublin – who not only had a keen interest in the Pat Mullins case, but also brought to the review a forensic knowledge of military administration and UN bureaucracy. It also helped that he was one of the army's most respected senior officers and well versed in file studies. Every aspect of the Mullins file was now re-examined and analysed, and the colonel decided to interview the remaining survivors of the 35th Battalion to determine if anything had been omitted from the original inquiry. There was also the chance that the importance of some data may have been underestimated.

It was a mammoth undertaking because the veterans first had to be tracked down. Not all were involved with the ONE (Organisation of National Ex-Servicemen) or IUNVA, which made the task all the harder. Some were also in poor health. A further difficulty was that while the Defence Forces maintained a small mountain of files from the 1960–64 deployments to the Congo, a lot of relevant files were also overseas in New York.

With Minister O'Dea's permission, it was quickly decided to send two senior officers to UN headquarters in New York to re-examine any files on the Congo mission. Cmdt Victor Laing and Lt Col Peter Richardson were assigned to the task and travelled to New York in November 2006, just five months after the receipt of Mary Kent's letter. Their task was to comb through all remaining

UN documentation, files, orders and intelligence with regard to events in Katanga in 1961 and, in particular, the fallout of Operation Morthor.

The officers would also try to cross-reference files held back in Ireland with the UN files to determine if additional data may have been received by the UN from the Swedish or Indian battalions. The UN also had intelligence from various other sources including Europeans working in Elisabethville such as doctors, nurses, engineers and contractors.

Processing the UN data took time and it was decided to focus on this before launching the nationwide series of interviews with those Congo veterans still alive. It quickly became apparent that the clock was ticking. One Congo veteran who was interviewed by Col Pakenham and his team, died while on a Spanish holiday several months later.

Finally, three years after the review was launched, all the data was assembled and work began on preparing the final report, its conclusions and its recommendations. It was submitted for consideration to Minister O'Dea and the army chief of staff before a briefing was arranged with the Mullins family.

On 13 January 2010, Minister O'Dea wrote to Mary Kent and the Mullins family to say that the review report was now completed and would be available to them if they so wished. Minister O'Dea explained that the four years had been required because of the complexity of the review and the sheer volume of documentation. 'The review has been exhaustive, involving the review of thousands of files in UN headquarters in New York, Ireland's military and national archives, and files in the Department of Foreign Affairs. Interviews have also been conducted with a range of individuals including retired Defence Forces personnel and other persons connected to the events at the time,' he wrote.

Minister O'Dea stressed that, given the potential nature of some of the review material and the fact that it could be distressing for the family, it might be best for the Mullins family to be briefed on the details by a liaison and support officer from the Defence Forces. He stressed that, after that meeting, he would be available to meet the family himself if they had any concerns arising from the review report.

'May I take this opportunity to extend to you and your family, on behalf of the state, the government and the Defence Forces, my sincere and deepest sympathy and condolences on your terrible loss. I hope the report helps you and all of your family to bring some measure of closure to this tragedy. Patrick was taken at such a young age with his whole life ahead of him. We recognise and commend his bravery and his ultimate sacrifice in the cause of peace in a country far away. *Ar a dheis De go raibh a anam*,' he wrote.

By February 2010, Col Paul Pakenham had been promoted to brigadier-general and was now the general officer commanding (GOC) of the 1st Southern Brigade. Were Pat Mullins to join the Defence Forces of 2010 in Limerick or Cork, Brig-Gen. Pakenham would be his most senior commander.

Brig-Gen. Pakenham – as the officer who supervised the Mullins review – was asked to personally brief the family on the report and its findings. That day of 11 February 2010, Pakenham was accompanied to the Firgrove Hotel in Mitchelstown, just five kilometres from Pat's old Boher homestead, by the head chaplain to the Defence Forces, Monsignor Eoin Thynne, and the Defence Forces personnel support service officer, Cmdt Michael Rowan.

It was fitting that Pat Mullins' old friend and comrade, John O'Mahony, was also present. John – like the Mullins family and Art Magennis – had never stopped campaigning for answers and it was entirely appropriate that he was present to discover whether, after fifty long years, his friend might finally be coming home. John knew a lot of the data that would be included in the report, but was still hoping against hope that something critical might have been unearthed in the UN archive search in New York.

A private room had been set aside in the Firgrove for the family and the army team. The Defence Forces had requested that the briefing be restricted to Pat's immediate family members. Present were Pat's siblings Mary Kent, Dinny Mullins and Tommy Mullins. Also present were Pat's nephews, Ned Mullins, Patrick Mullins and Donie Dwane.

The meeting began at 2 p.m. and, over the course of the next four and a half hours, Brig-Gen. Pakenham took the family slowly and sensitively through what their review had found. It was a detailed report, which, for the first time, was able to hint to the family precisely what had happened to Pat and the circumstances of his final hours.

Pakenham explained that the Defence Forces would never forget Pat Mullins or his sacrifice and vowed that they would continue to support the Mullins family. He immediately tried to put the family at ease by stressing that there was no time limit on the briefing – and any questions they wanted to ask would be answered as honestly as possible.

Brig-Gen. Pakenham explained that the review had five specific objectives including: 1) to acknowledge that Tpr Mullins and Private Joyce were the only soldiers who died overseas and whose remains did not return home; 2) to modify the official Defence Forces position re Pat Mullins; 3) to offer the Mullins family a better understanding and insight into the circumstances of how Pat died; 4) to offer satisfaction to Pat's former comrades re the events of September 1961; and 5) to expand the army files in relation to documents assembled as part of the 2006 review.

However, Brig-Gen. Pakenham stressed that, given the extreme sensitivity of the report and its findings, it should only ever be accessed on a 'need to know' basis. The full report runs to sixty-one pages, though not all pages specifically relate to Pat Mullins.

According to Pat's former colleagues, back in 1962, the army decided that there was no need for a formal court of inquiry into the circumstances of Pat Mullins' death – and, under the regulations in force at the time, there was absolutely no legal requirement for such a formal hearing. As a result, the Mullins family was effectively left in the dark about many aspects of the case. It was explained to them that, back in the early 1960s, such information was deemed by the military authorities to be 'inappropriate and undesirable' to be made available to the family involved. In essence, the army wanted to spare families the pain and suffering of hearing precisely how their loved ones died. But, unwittingly, instead they sentenced families to years of doubt and confusion.

Crucially, the review ended with a forty-eight-year-old letter which was written in June 1962, following an investigation by a legal officer, which stated that the body of Tpr Mullins was no longer in existence. It was a startling revelation for the Mullins family.

In November 1963, the Defence Forces issued a death certificate for Pat Mullins giving his cause of death as: 'Killed in Action – presumed to have died of bullet wounds on September 15 1962 in Elisabethville, Democratic Republic of Congo'. While this certificate was more than likely passed to the family in the 1960s, Pat's brothers and sisters have no recollection of it. Crucially, the reference to 'bullet wounds' suggested that Pat Mullins may not, in fact, have died in the initial ambush. Because he was inside the armoured car, he could not have been struck by bullets fired from around the Radio College. Had Pat died at the Radio College, he would have had to have been hit by fragments from the anti-tank rocket.

During the course of the February meeting, Brig-Gen. Pakenham advised the family that, given the evidence available and the lack of documentary proof, it cannot be said for certain what precisely happened to Pat Mullins. However, the available evidence hinted at certain things – and now allows a possible outline of the last hours of Pat Mullins' life to be drawn. The general advised the family that, on the balance of probabilities, Pat died on September 15 following a hostile engagement with Katangan gendarme forces.

Based on discussions with his colleagues and the meeting in Mitchelstown, some possible conclusions could be suggested. Foremost amongst these is that Pat Mullins was not killed outside the Radio College in the initial ambush. Secondly, the evidence also suggests that either Pat or Mick Nolan drove the armoured car away from the initial ambush site. Finally, and perhaps most importantly for the Mullins family, the available evidence hints that both men died in a gun battle with Katangan gendarmes not far from one of their major barracks after the armoured car somehow got stranded on the roadside in Elisabethville.

One account, in particular, is of huge significance to Pat's family and friends. In September 1961, Professor Daniel Despas was just a teenager. He was in Elisabethville and heard, at first hand, reports of the ambush outside the Radio College. Several of the Irish soldiers took shelter in the home of a Belgian man living nearby, Gerard Soerte, before surrendering to the Katangan gendarmes. Soerte had been extremely kind to the Irish soldiers in the hours before they were taken into custody.

In an account subsequently recounted to one of Pat's colleagues, Despas heard that during a lull in the fighting efforts were made by two men to help the men inside an Irish Ford armoured car. Dr

Defru and Fr Verfaille approached the armoured car and tried to offer the men help. Dr Defru apparently knocked on the car door while Fr Verfaille shouted out 'I'm a missionary'. But, a few seconds later, there was a burst of machine gun fire into the air and both men fled to the safety of a nearby building. Despas recounted a story that several of Pat's colleagues would later hear in different versions. It involved a simple misunderstanding – that Pat Mullins or Mick Nolan inside the armoured car might have misheard a shouted call of 'missionary' as 'mercenary'. The immediate burst of fire into the air from the Ford armoured car was proof that those inside thought there was a problem. The missionary and the doctor scrambled for cover and watched the armoured car drive off, ultimately in the direction of a Katangan gendarme strongpoint. It is crucial testimony because it clearly indicates that one or both of the Irish troopers was still alive after the ambush and that they, and not Katangan gendarmes, drove the armoured car away from the Radio College.

The army now accepts that it is quite likely the Ford was driven away from the Radio College ambush site by one of its remaining crew members, Pat Mullins or Michael Nolan. Former comrades now believe it was likely that Pat was the driver, because Michael Nolan died from a combination of a serious shell injury and bullet wounds. It was only possible for Mick Nolan to have received the explosion injury in the initial ambush so, more than likely, he would not have been able to drive away from the site given such a serious and debilitating injury.

John O'Mahony pointed out that further credence is given to this theory by the fact that the armoured car may have gotten lost as it left the Radio College. 'Mick Nolan was a corporal and, like the sergeants, he would have been briefed on all the routes and transit points around the city. If Mick was driving that night, he should have been capable of realising where he was – and how to get back to camp. But Pat, like myself and the other troopers, was never briefed on the roads around Elisabethville and the major routes to avoid. The truth is that Pat wouldn't have known where he was going that night and would have been looking for a landmark that he recognised to guide himself back to camp,' he added.

Brig-Gen. Pakenham advised the family that there is substantial evidence hinting at a major gun battle not far from a key Katangan gendarme base on 15 September. According to Pat's former colleagues, the main combat point was on an elevated roadway, with steep drainage ditches on either side, running directly parallel with the Lubumbashi River. Evidence of that gun battle came in information given to Art Magennis in the immediate aftermath of the battle from Katangan sources, from the army recovery team who found the Ford AFV in 1961 and from independent information supplied by Europeans who were working or living in Elisabethville at the time.

The Katangan police – not to be confused with the Katangan gendarmes who were effectively a paramilitary force – also reported a gun battle around that time in which two UN soldiers were killed. Unconfirmed police statements indicated that one of the bodies was taken to a local hospital and later buried in an Elisabethville cemetery. The other body had vanished from the scene by the time the police arrived. There were unconfirmed reports that this body may have been subjected to tribal rituals, with its remains being dumped in the nearby River Lubumbashi.

An unnamed Katangan doctor – in information given to Pat's comrades – reported a story he had heard from locals that two UN soldiers had been killed after a gunfight. He recalled the location as being on a route south of the Parc Zoologique and parallel to the River Lubumbashi – precisely the same location in which the shell-pocked armoured car was recovered by Captain Art Magennis and his team.

The review also found reference to bullet wounds on Pat Mullins' death certificate. Telexes in the UN archives had reported Pat Mullins 'Missing in Action', but there were no records relating to Pat in the UN file compiled from all Elisabethville mortuaries. This could be deemed to be a particularly relevant point given two things. Firstly, the civil administration, which operated to Belgian standards, was still operating relatively efficiently in Elisabethville in 1961. Secondly, had the corpse of a white person, particularly a UN soldier, been handled by a morgue, a hospital or police station, a mortuary record would inevitably have been kept. It would also, almost certainly, have been buried in accordance with European traditions as was done with the body of Michael Nolan.

The most difficult aspect of the army review was dealing with what had probably happened to Pat Mullins' body after his brave stand to protect his injured comrade was over. The family was advised that there is absolutely no evidence to confirm any single theory about what became of the remains.

However, while no concrete evidence was found, some disturbing reports have emerged. Captain Magennis had already determined for himself from his South African contact, Bill Williams, that there was speculation within the native Katangan population that one of the dead UN soldiers had been subjected to tribal rituals. The Katangan police – keen to distance themselves from the Katangan gendarmes – also hinted that the body of one of the UN soldiers had been subjected to tribal rituals by some of the younger soldiers following the gunfight by the armoured car.

Perhaps in an effort to conceal that fact, the body was later dumped in the river as one source implied. The reality is that cannibalism was relatively commonplace within certain Congolese tribal groups and there was a body of opinion amongst Irish and Swedish troops that it was still ongoing in Katanga during the deployment period of UN troops. However, it also happened that bodies were dismembered without such practices taking place. In some cases, the tribal ritual was as simple as removing the brave hand that wielded a sword in battle or the finger that pulled the trigger of a gun.

In the case of Pat Mullins, no one will ever really know what happened in that lonely ditch to the heroic soldier's body once he made the ultimate sacrifice to protect his friend and defend his armoured car. One possibility mooted at the February meeting was that Pat's remains may have been subjected to some ritual after he was killed in the gun battle. The family was advised that it is not considered feasible to offer them any hope that Pat's remains can ever be found.

Brig-Gen. Pakenham and his team gently informed the family that, given all the reports and evidence, there was simply no point in convening a formal court of inquiry at this stage. It was felt that such an inquiry would serve no additional purpose over and above the review process, either for the family or the military. Even should such an inquiry be held, there was only circumstantial evidence as to what actually happened. There are no records from the Elisabethville mortuary and, after a tribal ritual, a body was unlikely to be buried in the European manner. As some local reports indicated, it was quite likely to have been thrown into the local river.

As heartbreaking as it was for them to hear, the Mullins family simply nodded as they were told that the recovery of Pat's body was not a realistic hope at this stage. The remains of the heroic and steadfast eighteen-year-old will most likely never be found and brought back to the foothills of the Galtees. It was not the outcome that the family had prayed for but, sadly, the one they had feared all along.

However, Brig-Gen. Pakenham and his team were determined that the review should also address all the issues the family were concerned about. No UN force since the Congo has sustained the level of casualties suffered by the ONUC force in Katanga between 1960–64. Yet, in all the acts of heroism and courage shown over those five years by UN soldiers of many different nations, Pat Mullins' actions now stand tall.

To better recognise the sacrifice the eighteen-year-old made and the needs of his family, the Defence Forces are considering three additional measures:

* Glasnevin Cemetery – Pat's name is on a plaque at the cemetery and the impression is clearly given that he is buried there. That will now be corrected.
* Kilbehenny Memorial – to better commemorate the eighteen-year-old's memory in his home village, a special memorial will be erected to honour his courage in the Congo in September 1961. Pat Mullins will be remembered as a hero.
* Congo Trip – to offer the Mullins family some additional form of 'closure', a special trip could be organised for the family to Lubumbashi-Elisabethville, pending permission from the UN. It would allow Pat's loved ones to visit the places associated with his final hours and pay their respects at the spot last associated with him on earth.

The meeting in Mitchelstown where Brig-Gen. Pakenham outlined the circumstances leading to the death of Pat Mullins and the non-recovery of his remains, is perhaps what the family most wanted to hear. In particular, the Defence Forces will never forget soldiers like Pat who died in service overseas. To his family,

Pat was always a hero. They never doubted that the eighteen-year-old had shown the most incredible courage and selflessness in the hours leading up to his death – it was a part of Pat's nature that his family never for a single moment questioned. But now the country that they felt had forgotten Pat would properly remember both his heroism and his name. Fifty years after an eighteen-year-old had made the ultimate sacrifice by laying down his life through his courageous refusal to abandon a wounded comrade, Ireland would remember Pat Mullins.

It was a monument that meant more to his family than anything carved in marble or cast in bronze.

# APPENDIX A

## JOHN O'MAHONY

John returned from the Congo heartbroken at the loss of his friend, Pat Mullins. He decided that a career in the army was no longer for him and he transferred to the Defence Forces reserve list in 1962 and remained there until 1972. His last service in uniform came in August 1969 when he was called up as part of the Republic's response to the outbreak of 'The Troubles' in Northern Ireland.

After a brief period working in London, John returned to his native west Waterford and pursued a career in farming. A keen student of modern technology and foreign farming developments, he was at the forefront of the revolution within the Irish agri-sector, which was underpinned by mechanisation and crop growing technology. He successfully switched the focus of his parents' farm from dairy to tillage.

John rose to become chairman of the Irish Farmers Association's (IFA) powerful National Grain Committee and took part in major EU farm negotiations in France and Belgium. An avid student of nature, he also began compiling data on Irish weather conditions in the 1980s and is now one of Ireland's most respected 'self taught' meteorologists, regularly featuring on programmes including RTÉ's *Pat Kenny Show*.

John became active in the Irish United Nations Veterans Association (IUNVA) on its foundation and he has made it his life-mission to highlight the case of his friend Pat Mullins.

He has donated all his royalties from *Missing In Action* to IUNVA's Post 25 Fermoy branch.

Married to Sheila (née Healy), John has two sons, Brian and Desmond. Brian is based in Tulsa in the United States while Des lives in Tipperary and is a senior executive with Musgraves. John and Sheila have one grandchild, Maeve. John continues to farm at Kilmore outside Tallow, County Waterford.

## ART MAGENNIS

A native of Ardglass, County Down, Art Magennis served two tours of UN duty in the Congo as a captain, eventually commanding the Armoured Car Group of the final Irish detachment in the Congo at Kolwezi. He went on to serve on UN peacekeeping missions in Cyprus. He retired from the army in 1979 just as Ireland's UNIFIL deployment to Lebanon was escalating. Art retired with the rank of commandant after forty years loyal and dedicated service. To those who served with him, he remains an officer of rare ability and extraordinary loyalty. He has devoted his time since retirement to helping to highlight the courage shown by Tpr Pat Mullins that day in September 1961 and to the fact that the Mullins family deserved closure in terms of a renewed effort to locate his remains. Despite his years, Art Magennis annually attends all the ceremonies for Tpr Mullins, including the memorial Mass in the trooper's native Kilbehenny. Art Magennis' remarkable memoirs were an invaluable aid to this book. Art has five daughters, Carmel, Mary, Barbara, Maeve and Fiona. Maeve followed her father into the Defence Forces and, after serving on UNIFIL peacekeeping missions in Lebanon, retired with full military honours.

## TIM CAREY

The Skibbereen-born soldier successfully recovered from his wounds and returned to Ireland a hero for his actions in the Congo. Having joined the army in 1952, he decided to retire in 1967 and founded a successful windows and joinery business in Fermoy where he made his home after being based at Fitzgerald Camp for most of his army career. The business is still run by his family. Tim Carey eventually decided to enter politics and ran for election to Fermoy town council. He was elected and served as Mayor of Fermoy in 2006. He remains a regular attendee of Post 25 (Fermoy) Irish United Nations Veterans Association (IUNVA) functions and memorials. Along with Art Magennis, Tim Carey was instrumental in piecing together the true sequence of events of 14/15 September 1961. On 10 October 2009, Tim was amongst a huge crowd attending the unveiling of a special memorial wall by the Queen of Peace Church in Fermoy – the old Fitzgerald Camp barrack chapel – which commemorates all those associated with the former base who died while serving with the United Nations or the Defence Forces. A total of 114 names are inscribed on the memorial covering Ireland's UN operations from the Congo to Cyprus and from Lebanon to East Timor, Bosnia and Liberia. Trooper Pat Mullins is the sixteenth name on the list. Fittingly, the memorial faces out towards the now-vanished sports field where Pat Mullins once starred as a young army hurler.

## DES KEEGAN

A native of Dublin, Des joined the Defence Forces in February 1959 on his sixteenth birthday. After transferring to the 1st Motor Squadron in Fermoy, County Cork, he served in the army for twenty-one years before retiring with the rank of Squadron Sergeant. His career included three tours in the Congo, two tours in Cyprus and one tour in Lebanon. Having retired from the army, he was briefly employed in the private security sector before working for twelve years with electronics firm SCI in Fermoy and then retiring again – this time for good. He is one of the founder members of IUNVA's Post 25 in Fermoy and devotes a lot of his time to assisting retired soldiers. His son is currently serving in the Defence Forces and has undertaken tours of Lebanon, Chad and Liberia.

## THE MULLINS FAMILY

Denis (Dinny) Mullins took over the running of the family farm at Boher on the Cork-Limerick border. The farmhouse is much the same as the last day Pat saw it in 1961 – save for such modern 'innovations' as electricity and running water. As with all other Irish farms, the horse and plough is now a fast-fading memory and the entire holding is highly mechanised. Dinny married Marie and the couple have one son, Ned.

Tom Mullins, like Pat, worked for several farmers in the Kilbehenny area before getting a job with Mitchelstown Co-op. He married Mary and they have two children, Pat and Siobhan.

Mary and Tom Kent still live at Caherdrinna, midway between Kilworth and Mitchelstown, in the house where John O'Mahony and Pat Mullins enjoyed welcome breaks from training at nearby Lynch Camp in early 1961. Mary's son, Eamon, who Pat never met, has taken a keen interest in his uncle and the Congo. Mary and Tom have two other children, Joan and Pat.

Margaret Mullins married Jim Dwane (RIP). The couple were blessed with seven children, Patricia, Donie, Mary, Margaret, James, Catherine and Eamon.

Nelly Mullins married Mike Kelly (RIP). They were blessed with two children, Eamon and Anthony.

Theresa Mullins married Pat Healy and they have one son, Patrick.

# PATRICE LUMUMBA

The Democratic Republic of the Congo's first post-independence prime minister was dead within six months of making his inflammatory speech in front of King Baudouin in June 1960. Lumumba's fate echoed that of the Congolese people both past and future. Hunted like an animal, captured, tortured, humiliated, ignored by UN troops who could have helped him and finally handed over to his hated enemies in Katanga, Lumumba's killing still haunts modern Belgium.

Research by investigative reporter Ludo de Witte in the 1990s revealed that Belgium was deeply complicit in Lumumba's death and had the tacit support of the United States who viewed Lumumba as leaning dangerously towards Communism. His revelations prompted a parliamentary inquiry in Brussels – although four decades after the event, there was little left but rhetoric.

Even back in January 1961, Lumumba's killers realised that absolutely no trace of the prime minister's corpse could be allowed to remain after the execution. After the application of mining acid and funeral pyres, not a single physical trace was left of the Congo's charismatic leader. Yet rumours still swirled around the Congo that his killers – before destroying his body and those of two friends also executed – insisted on digging the bullets out of his brain to keep as grisly souvenirs. Lumumba's political career may have lasted just over two years, but he remains to this day one of Africa's most fascinating – and studied – post-colonial leaders.

Elisabethville, the city where he was flown to meet his brutal death, was eventually renamed 'Lubumbashi'. The city remains a wealthy mining outpost in a country still torn apart by poverty, bloodshed, corruption and tribal strife.

## CONOR CRUISE O'BRIEN

Just months after the vicious fighting involving Ireland's 35th Battalion at Elisabethville and Jadotville, Conor Cruise O'Brien resigned from his position with the United Nations in Katanga. To this day, debate rages over his role in the UN's switch from peacekeeping to peace-enforcing operations.

In 1962, O'Brien wrote *To Katanga and Back*, a book which offers a fascinating insight into both UN and African politics at the time – though it also justifies O'Brien's own position and actions. Throughout his life, O'Brien remained sensitive to comments about his role in the Congo – even using the letters page of *The Irish Times* to challenge some writings about Katanga and UN actions.

After a brief stint in academia in Ghana and then New York, O'Brien decided to return to Ireland and was elected a TD in 1969 for the Labour Party. He was later appointed as a cabinet minister in Liam Cosgrave's 1973–77 administration. O'Brien – who quickly earned the nickname 'The Cruiser' – proved a talented, effective, if controversial politician, who was always willing to speak his mind on issues, sometimes to the dismay of both his Labour and Fine Gael colleagues. He was particularly noted for his visceral opposition to the IRA and the growth of militant republicanism. It was ironic that, despite a family background in journalism, O'Brien was a trenchant supporter of the use of censorship to tackle republicanism in the 1970s.

Having left full-time politics, after losing his Dáil seat in 1977 following Jack Lynch's landslide Fianna Fáil victory, he burnished his reputation with an outstanding career in journalism both in Ireland and Britain where, for two years, he served as editor of *The Observer*.

His razor-sharp assessment of current affairs included coining the legendary Irish phrase GUBU (Grotesque, Unbelievable, Bizarre and Unprecedented) when a murder suspect was discovered in the Dublin flat of Charles Haughey's then attorney general.

O'Brien – a columnist with the *Irish Independent* – also found time to write several critically acclaimed books including a biography of Edmund Burke and his own best-selling memoirs.

However, in later life O'Brien shocked friends and contemporaries alike by publicly embracing Unionism and joining the UK Unionist Party. He would later resign. Three years before his death in 2008 at the ripe old age of ninety-one, he rejoined the Labour Party. O'Brien was also an ardent supporter of Israel's right to exist and defend herself from attack.

## JOSEPH MOBUTU

The former Christian Brothers student was the true winner of the brutal events of 1960–1964. Mobutu knew that the Force Publique or Congolese army was the key to the country's future – and he used it to sideline all the country's leading pre-independence politicians. His Katangan rival, Tshombe, did him a huge inadvertent favour by killing Patrice Lumumba. As Mobutu well grasped, the blood of the prime minister's assassination would forever stain Tshombe's rule.

On the withdrawal of the UN from the Congo in 1964, Mobutu allowed a brief interval before moving against Tshombe who fled into exile where he died.

Mobutu milked the Congo's riches for all they were worth and turned the country into his personal fiefdom. He knew that the key to the survival of his regime was proving a staunch ally of the West during the Cold War.

Mobutu sought to give the Congo a new start by renaming the country 'Zaire' and even funding the lavish, if gaudy, staging of the World Heavyweight Championship bout between Muhammad Ali and George Foreman in 1974. The fight went down in sporting legend as 'the Rumble in the Jungle'. All Mobutu actually managed to achieve was a lingering sense of exploitation thanks to his son who sped around the centre of Kinshasa in front of the world media in a series of expensive Italian and German sports cars.

The end of the Cold War spelled the end for Mobutu, though he managed to cling on to power until May 1997. However, his desperate attempts to bolster his regime are now blamed for helping trigger the genocide in neighbouring Rwanda.

Mobutu died just four months after fleeing to Morocco. He is buried in Rabat and the Congo has shown no desire for his remains to be repatriated.

## MOISE TSHOMBE

The execution of Patrice Lumumba tainted Tshombe's regime in Katanga, which from that point, was doomed. With Belgium and other pro-Katanga countries unwilling to fund mercenaries in a war against UN troops, the secession was effectively over.

Reinforced UN troops captured Katanga in 1963 and Tshombe fled into exile in northern Rhodesia. By 1964, when an all-inclusive political deal had been hammered out to settle the Congo's problems, Tshombe returned from exile in Spain. He quickly discovered that Mobutu and the Congo's titular head, Joseph Kasavubu, had no intention of allowing his long-term involvement in Congolese politics.

Tshombe was dismissed from the government within months and fled the country a second time after realising that Mobutu was about to charge him with high treason. In 1967, a Congo court imposed the death penalty on Tshombe. Two years later, Tshombe hit the headlines again when the plane he was travelling on was hijacked and diverted to Algeria. Tshombe was arrested and later placed under house arrest in Algiers. The Algerian government briefly considered deporting him to the Congo. But fear of western displeasure at such an effective death sentence stayed their hand and Tshombe remained under house arrest.

Tshombe died in 1969, reportedly from a cardiac condition that triggered a massive stroke. Belgium – where the authorities never forgot that he was a loyal ally – later agreed to have his body flown to Brussels for burial. Mobutu's regime maintained that Tshombe was en route to Africa, intending to take part in a military insurrection, when his plane was hijacked. Two earlier insurrections were brutally put down.

## BOB DENARD

After his exploits with the Katangan gendarmerie, the French mercenary continued to ply his trade throughout other war-torn parts of Africa.

Denard – whose real name was Gilbert Bourgeaud – served with the French navy, not the Foreign Legion as widely claimed. He became one of the world's best-known mercenaries.

By the time of his death on 13 October 2007 at the ripe old age of seventy-eight, Denard had fought in Indo-China, Algeria, the Congo, Angola, Zimbabwe, Gabon and the Comoros Islands.

Denard – who liked to be referred to as 'Le Colonel' – sired eight children through the course of seven marriages, several of which were polygamous. His story is widely credited as the inspiration for the Hollywood blockbuster, *The Wild Geese* and for Frederick Forsyth's best-selling novel, *The Dogs of War*.

Several years before his death, Denard converted to Islam. The scale of his precise involvement in both Katanga and the Congo remains shrouded in mystery to this day.

## DAG HAMMARSKJÖLD

The Swedish diplomat remains the only United Nations Secretary-General to be killed in office.

Hammarskjöld was only fifty-six when he died in the plane crash at Ndola on 18 September 1961. The reason for the crash of the Douglas DC-6 aircraft in which he was travelling remains a mystery – many are convinced that the plane was shot down. Conspiracy theorists have been aided in their suspicions by the bizarre manner in which the authorities in northern Rhodesia (now Zambia) initially responded to the crash. Several studies have indicated that if a more prompt response been initiated some of the passengers might have survived.

Only one man survived the initial crash, Sgt Harold Julian, and he told those trying to help him that there had been several explosions before the plane plummeted to earth. It was also discovered that there were bullet wounds on two of the UN leader's Swedish bodyguards. However, experts at the time discounted Julian's account as confused – while the Swedes' injuries were explained by ammunition 'cooking off' in the fire that followed the crash.

At the time of the tragic crash, Hammarskjöld was en route to Katanga to try and negotiate a ceasefire to end the bitter fighting which had erupted between UN forces and Katangan gendarmes. President John F. Kennedy – who also died violently within two years – described Dag Hammarskjöld as the greatest statesman of the twentieth century. He is now widely considered the finest UN Secretary-General in history.

## PAT CAHALANE

A native of Dundrum in Dublin, Cmdt Cahalane eventually recovered from the injuries he sustained to his hearing in the Congo. He was attached to Defence Forces headquarters where he gradually became involved in the training regime at the Irish Military College. He was later assigned by the army to assist Zambia (formerly northern Rhodesia) with the training of its army officers, spending some time in Africa in the process. After he retired from the army, he secured a job as a security consultant for a leading Irish bank. He died more than twenty years ago.

## KING BAUDOUIN I

The great irony of King Baudouin's June 1960 speech, which triggered Patrice Lumumba's scathing denouncement of Belgian colonialism, is that Baudouin was one of the most compassionate monarchs ever to have sat on a European throne.

Kind, generous, loyal and deeply religious, Baudouin was Belgian king for a period of forty-two years (1951–1993). Baudouin had not even wanted to accept the Belgian throne following the abdication of his father, King Leopold III, who abdicated under the twin clouds of his actions during the Nazi occupation of Belgium and a controversial romance with a commoner. However, Baudouin was warned that Belgium could not tolerate a second abdication in succession and that, if he refused to be king, the House of Saxe-Coburg-Gotha would likely fall and Belgium would become a Republic. He agreed to take the throne and proved one of the most diligent of Europe's royals.

He was so loved by his subjects that Belgium went into deep mourning when he died unexpectedly while on holiday in Madrid at the age of sixty-three. Baudouin's career was marked by a genuine concern for his subjects and the challenges posed by social disadvantage, which makes his actions in the Congo that summer in 1960 all the more difficult to understand given their obvious consequences.

The Belgian king was twenty-nine years old when he delivered that key address at the Congolese independence ceremony – and many now believe that his ill-judged speech was the combination of relative youth, the scheming of his political advisors and hard memories of his previous visit to Leopoldville when angry crowds threw stones at some of his supporters.

Baudouin had a happy thirty-three year marriage to the Spanish noblewoman, Doña Fabiola Mora Aragón. The couple never had children so, on Baudouin's death, the Belgian crown passed to the king's youngest brother, Albert II.

# APPENDIX B

## TIMELINE

- 1482 – First permanent European trading contacts established in the Congo with the formation of a Portuguese colony.
- 1680 – Slave trade begins in earnest, initially to feed booming British, Spanish and French plantations in the New World.
- May 1876 – Belgium's King Leopold II convenes the International African Association (AIA) with the aim of promoting exploration and colonisation. Leopold secures widespread support thanks to his promise to abolish the slave trade.
- September 1878 – Explorer Henry Morgan Stanley agrees to work with King Leopold to promote European interests in vast African regions.
- November 1884 – German Chancellor Otto von Bismarck organises the Berlin Conference to avert clashes between world powers over remaining unclaimed regions of Africa.
- February 1885 – King Leopold's organisation receives 2.34 million square kilometres of Congo territory, more than France and Portugal combined. But the region is allocated to the king's philanthropic organisation (AIA) not the Belgian state.
- 1889–1902 – The development of the automobile and perfection of tyre technology leads to an explosion in global demand for rubber. King Leopold's loss-making African possession rushes to sate the world's demand for rubber.
- 1900 – Anglo-French journalist, Edmond Morel, reveals King

Leopold's trade monopoly in the Congo and the fact that trade figures are being doctored.

- May 1903 – American missionary, William Morrison, makes damning allegations about atrocities in the Congo. The British public is outraged.

- June 1903 – Britain's consul in the Congo, Roger Casement, is asked to make a full report on alleged abuses of natives by Belgian overseers.

- December 1903 – Casement submits his report to Lord Lansdowne at the Foreign Office. The eighty-four-page document detailed appalling atrocities perpetrated against tribes who failed to adhere to Belgian rubber quotas. Most gruesome is the revelation that Belgian-employed African soldiers would sever and smoke the hands of Congolese workers – submitting basketfuls of smoked hands to the overseers to prove that they had not wasted rifle ammunition shooting them.

- 1904–1908 – The scandal over King Leopold's Congo operations finally forces the Belgian government to assume full control of the African territory. Conditions improve but the Congo natives are still subjected to effective apartheid.

- 1914–18 and 1940–45 – Belgium's occupation by German forces in both world wars effectively undermines their position in the Congo.

- 1913–1917 – Major mineral deposits discovered in Katanga with copper and diamond mining launched.

- 1941–1948 – Repeated disturbances in the Congo ranging from strikes to a mutiny by Force Publique, the Congolese national army.

- October 1952 – Governor-General Léon Antoine Marie Pétillon predicts that, without major civil rights reform, Belgium would lose the Congo.

- 1959 – Belgium's King Baudouin I pays his second visit to the Congo, which turns into a disaster when locals pelt him with stones after his perceived support for delayed independence. There are riots in Leopoldville.

- June 1960 – Belgium formally ends colonial links with the Congo, terrified of a savage civil war such as France faced in Algeria.

- July 1960 – Moise Tshombe comes to power in Katanga, the southern and wealthiest of Congo's provinces, and demands immediate secession. He is backed by European financial and mining interests but opposed by the Congolese government and northern tribal groups in Katanga including the Balubas.

- 2 July 1960 – Congo Prime Minister Patrice Lumumba appeals to the UN for support in the face of Katangan secession, which he describes as a military revolt.

- 11 July 1960 – Katanga declares unilateral independence.

- 13 July 1960 – The UN agrees to send troops to help keep the peace in the Congo and Ireland is one of a handful of countries asked to supply personnel. However, the UN insists troops are peacekeepers and not peace-enforcers – thereby refusing Lumumba's demand that the UN militarily force Katanga to rejoin the Congo.

- 27 July 1960 – Irish troops of the 32nd Battalion fly out to the Congo on the UN mission – the first major overseas deployment by the Defence Forces.

- September 1960 – Patrice Lumumba, Prime Minister of the Congo, is deposed in a coup secretly supported by Belgian interests.

- 9 November 1960 – Nine Irish troops are killed in an ambush by Baluba tribesmen at Niemba in northern Katanga. Just two members of the patrol survive.

- 17 January 1961 – Lumumba is flown to Katanga where, after being tortured, he is executed. Belgian soldiers are reported to have been present at his execution.
- 21 February 1961 – The UN passes a resolution to use force, if required, to get foreign political and military personnel to withdraw from Katanga.
- 28 August 1961 – Operation Rampunch is launched by the UN to strip the Katangese gendarmes of their European officers. Initially successful, the benefits of the operation are squandered.
- 13 September 1961 – UN troops are ordered under Operation Morthor to seize key positions in the city of Elisabethville with operations beginning at 2 a.m. Katangese mercenaries fight back amid claims Indian troops massacred combatants in the Radio Katanga building. (Sometime after the start of this operation Moise Tshombe flees the country).
- 14 September 1961 – A unit of the 35th Irish Battalion's Armoured Car Group is ambushed as they approach the communications centre in Elisabethville. Two men ultimately die. A third dies in a gun battle near a bridge junction.
- 15 September 1961 – Twenty-six Irish troops surrender at the Radio College in Elisabethville after the armoured car ambush. Katangan mercenaries threaten to execute the captured Irish commander, Cmdt Pat Cahalane.
- 17 September 1961 – UN Secretary-General Dag Hammar-skjöld is killed when his DC-6 aircraft crashes in northern Rhodesia (now Zambia) while he is en route to negotiate a ceasefire in the Congo. Speculation still persists that the plane was shot down to assassinate Hammarskjöld.
- 18 September 1961 – 155 Irish troops surrender at Jadotville after a courageous five-day battle. Outnumbered, with no

heavy weaponry, dwindling ammunition and food, their commander orders them to surrender to Katangan gendarmes to avoid further loss of life. A UN relief column is unable to fight its way through to them.

- 20 September 1961 – Ceasefire agreed between the UN and Katangan gendarmes. All captured Irish personnel are later freed unharmed. Tshombe returns to the country.

- 2 December 1961 – Conor Cruise O'Brien, the Irish diplomat who was the UN special representative in Katanga, resigns from his post. In 1962, he writes a best-selling book on his experiences, *To Katanga and Back*.

- September-December 1962 – UN forces, now substantially reinforced, launch an all-out assault on Katanga called Operation GrandSlam. The Katangan air force is wiped out on the ground by Swedish jet fighters.

- 10 January 1963 – Final pockets of resistance are mopped up in Elisabethville and Tshombe flees the country a second time.

- September 1963 – The Congolese parliament is suspended amid growing political rivalry between President Joseph Kasavubu and the Force Publique commander, Joseph Mobutu.

- April 1964 – The Congolese central government controls the country and feels sufficiently secure to allow Tshombe to return from exile and take a post in the coalition administration.

- 30 June 1964 – The last Irish troops leave the Congo as the UN mission is wound-up.

- July 1964 – Tshombe elected to serve as a minister in the new coalition government. Somewhat ironically, he is tasked with putting down regional rebellions.

- May 1965 – Tshombe sacked from government.

- June 1965 – Joseph Mobutu stages a successful coup to take over the Congo government and one of his first acts is to charge Tshombe with high treason. In November, he outlaws all political parties.
- July 1965 – Tshombe flees the country to northern Rhodesia and later Spain. In 1967, the Congo government sentences him to death *in absentia*.
- 1969 – Tshombe dies while under house arrest in Algiers. The Algerian authorities had stalled for over a year on deporting him back to the Congo amid fears over the international outcry that would be triggered by his inevitable execution by Mobutu's forces. Tshombe's body is flown to Belgium for burial.
- April 1971 – Mobutu begins to shift his foreign relations policy to a strong alliance with France while remaining a staunch US ally and 'anti-Communist strongman'.
- 27 October 1971 – Mobutu orders that the Democratic Republic of the Congo is formally renamed 'Zaire'. It means 'river that swallows all rivers'. Mobutu also takes to wearing a leopard-skin hat in public.
- 30 October 1974 – Legendary 'Rumble in the Jungle' heavy-weight fight staged in Kinshasa between Muhammad Ali and George Foreman. The fight is staged at the insistence of Mobutu who believes it will be a foreign public relations bonanza for his newly renamed Zaire. Apart from being one of the most iconic showdowns in world sporting history, the fight is remembered for Mobutu's son speeding around Kinshasa city centre in front of foreign reporters in various expensive sports cars.
- 1974–1978 – Mobutu nationalises dozens of foreign-owned companies – then promptly reverses his decision amid mounting economic chaos.

- 1989 – Zaire defaults on some international loans with disastrous consequences for development projects and the overall economy.

- May 1990 – Under increasing pressure at home, and now shorn of much of his former western backing due to the end of the Cold War, Mobutu finally agrees to lift the ban on all Congolese political parties.

- 1994 – The world is appalled as savage ethnic conflict suddenly erupts in Rwanda. More than one million people are butchered when Hutu death gangs attack Tutsis nationwide. Some Hutu clergy even help in the massacres. Sickeningly, most of those killed are slaughtered with machetes and axes.

- 1996 – Re-organised Tutsi rebels fight back and Hutus flee Rwanda in the hundreds of thousands. Tutsi militias end up controlling vast swathes of eastern Zaire/Congo. Cancer-stricken Mobutu is powerless to end the spiralling anarchy. Uganda begins to asset-strip eastern Congo.

- 17 May 1997 – Mobutu flees the country in the face of a widespread uprising and the advance of Tutsi-backed militias. The country is immediately renamed the Democratic Republic of the Congo by new President Laurent Kabila. Mobutu's thirty-two year rule had transformed one of Africa's wealthiest countries into a poverty-stricken state where central authority had collapsed. Despite this, Mobutu had formally renamed himself 'Mobutu Sese Seko Nkuku Ngbendu Wa Za Banga', which means 'the all-powerful warrior who, because of his endurance and inflexible will to win, goes from conquest to conquest, leaving fire in his wake'.

- 7 September 1997 – Mobutu dies in exile in Rabat, Morocco, from cancer. He is buried locally after the Congo rules out a Kinshasa funeral. Few mourn.

- 1999 – Belgian historian, Ludo de Witte, publishes his remarkable investigative work on the execution of Patrice Lumumba. The book reveals Belgian and US links to the killing. The Belgian parliament orders a full inquiry. No one is ever charged.
- 1997–2009 – The Congo suffers repeated wars, invasions and internal power struggles. Large parts of the country remain outside government control. The Second Congo War raged from 1998 to 2003, and eventually drags in seven African countries and twenty-four armed paramilitary groups. By July 2003, when an outline truce is agreed, the war has cost 5.4 million lives through fighting, disease and starvation. It remains the largest conflict of modern times on African soil and the world's greatest conflict since the Second World War.
- 2004–2006 – An estimated 1,000 people die each day in the Congo from malnutrition and diseases, most of which are easily preventable. Charities estimate that more than 200,000 women have been raped in the Congo's various conflicts. The UN was shocked in 2003 when claims emerged that the Mbuti pygmies – who live in northern Congo – were being hunted like 'game animals' and eaten amid the belief that their organs conferred magical powers.
- 2008 – An International Committee of the Red Cross study revealed that seventy-six per cent of Congolese have been directly impacted by warfare, either by having family members killed and injured or being displaced from their homes.
- 2010 – Boasting a land mass of 2,345,408 square kilometres, which is greater than that of Spain, France, Germany, the UK and Ireland combined, the Congo remains potentially one of the wealthiest countries on earth due to its diamond, mineral and timber resources.

Elisabethville – where the Katangan secession had first been masterminded – is now known by its new name, Lubumbashi. It remains a wealthy mining city by Congolese standards.

# APPENDIX C

Second Armoured Car Group, Irish 35th UN Battalion, ONUC Congo 1961:

Commandant Pat Cahalane, Capt. Mark Carroll, Capt. Seán Hennessy, Capt. Frank Lawless, Capt. Art Magennis, Lt M.G. Considine, Lt Kevin Knightley, C/Sgt Dan Carroll, CQMS Johnny Hamill, Sgt Tim Carey, Sgt Jim Flynn, Sgt C. Geary, Sgt Bill Hartley, Sgt Ned Keogh, Sgt Dan Morris, A/Sgt Mickey Rowland, Cpl Stan Cahill, Cpl John Ginty, Cpl Pat Holbrook, Cpl Jim Lucey, Cpl Eddie Nolan, Cpl Michael Nolan, Cpl Tommy O'Connor, Cpl Tommy O'Brien, Cpl John Joe O'Connor, Cpl Chalkey White, Tpr J. Byrne, Tpr P. Bolger, Tpr Michael Boyce, Tpr Dan Clancy, Tpr Mick Collins, Tpr Frank Featherson, Tpr Jimmy Harris, Tpr Des Keegan, Tpr P. Lynch, Tpr Jerry Lewellyn, Tpr Bill Maher, Tpr Pat Mullins, Tpr P. Murphy, Tpr Jerry Mallon, Tpr P. McCarton, Tpr J. McAuliffe, Tpr Dan McManus, Tpr M. Nolan, Tpr Ned O'Regan, Tpr B. O'Callaghan, Tpr Tommy O'Keeffe, Tpr Con O'Leary, Tpr John O'Mahony, Tpr Paddy Quinn, Tpr Jack Shanahan, Tpr Fred Sheedy, Tpr E. Tucker and Tpr J. Walsh.

# APPENDIX D

Official Defence Force classifications of Ireland's two missing soldiers, Tpr Patrick Mullins (1961) and Private Kevin Joyce (1981).

**Dáil Parliamentary Debate, Tuesday 21 June 2005.**
**Tpr Mullins:**
Minister for Defence, Willie O'Dea: 'I am advised by the military authorities that on September 15, 1961, Trooper Patrick Mullins and Corporal Michael Nolan were killed in action in the Congo when their armoured vehicle was hit by anti-tank fire from armed elements. While the remains of Corporal Nolan were recovered, those of Trooper Mullins were not. An investigation into Trooper Mullins' death by the military authorities at the time concluded on 29 January 1962 that he was killed in action at Avenue de Cuivre, Lubumbashi/Elisabethville, Katanga, in the Republic of Congo as a result of the hostile action outlined.'

Trooper Mullins is classified by the military authorities as: 'Dead, presumed to have been killed.'

**Pte Joyce:**
On 27 April 1981, an observation post in south Lebanon manned by two members of the Irish battalion serving with the United Nations interim force in Lebanon, UNIFIL, Private Hugh Doherty and Private Kevin Joyce or Seoighe, came under attack.

Private Doherty was later found dead from gunshot wounds

and Private Joyce was missing. Some equipment was also missing.

The attackers are unknown. Extensive diplomatic and military efforts to locate him have proved fruitless to date. Private Joyce is classified as: 'Missing in action, presumed dead.'

# BIBLIOGRAPHY

Arnold, Bruce, *Jack Lynch – Hero in Crisis* (Merlin, Dublin, 2001)

Coogan, Tim Pat, *De Valera – Long Fellow, Long Shadow* (Hutchinson, London, 1993)

De Witte, Ludo, *The Assassination of Lumumba* (Verso, London, 2002)

Doyle, Rose & Quinlan, Leo, *Heroes of Jadotville* (New Island, Dublin, 2006)

Dungan, Myles, *Distant Drums* (Appletree, Belfast, 1993)

Fisk, Robert, *Pity the Nation* (Andre Deutsch, New York, 1990)

Fitzgerald, Garret, *All in a Life* (Gill & Macmillan, Dublin, 1991)

Harvey, Dan, *Peacekeepers* (Merlin, Dublin, 2000)

Hickey, D. & Doherty, J., *A Chronology of Irish History* (Gill & Macmillan, Dublin, 1989)

Hogg, Ian & Adam, Rob, *Jane's Gun Recognition Guide* (HarperCollins, London, 1996)

Jenkins, Roy, *Churchill* (Macmillan, London, 2001)

Lee, Christopher, *The Sceptred Isle* (Penguin, London, 1997)

Meisler, Stanley, *United Nations: The First Fifty Years* (Atlantic, New York, 1997)

Meredith, Martin, *The State of Africa* (Free Press, London, 2005)

Nordass, Geoff & Riegel, Ralph, *Commando* (O'Brien, Dublin, 2009)

O'Brien, Conor Cruise, *A Memoir – My Life & Themes* (Cooper Square, New York, 2000)

O'Brien, Conor Cruise, *To Katanga and Back* (Hutchinson, London, 1962)

O'Donoghue, David, *The Far Battalions* (Irish Academic Press, Dublin, 2006)

O'Keeffe, Padraig & Riegel, Ralph, *Hidden Soldier* (O'Brien, Dublin, 2007)

O'Sullivan, Michael, *Seán Lemass – A Biography* (Blackwater, Dublin, 1994)

Pakenham, Thomas, *The Boer War* (Futura, London, 1979)

Pakenham, Thomas, *The Scramble for Africa* (Abacus, London, 1991)

Power, Declan, *Siege at Jadotville* (Maverick, Dublin, 2004)

Sharpe, Michael, *Attack & Interceptor Jets* (Dempsey-Parr, London, 1999)

Smith, Raymond, *The Fighting Irish in the Congo* (Lilmac, Dublin, 1962)

Trewhitt, Philip, *Armoured Fighting Vehicles* (Dempsey-Parr, London, 1999)


Newspapers: The *Irish Independent*, the *Sunday Independent*, *The Irish Press*, the *Cork Examiner*, *The Irish Times*, *The Avondhu*, *The Corkman*, *The Sunday Times*, *The Sunday Tribune*, *The Star*, the *Observer*, *The Daily Telegraph* & *The (London) Times*

Broadcast: RTÉ, BBC, TV3, NewsTalk, C103FM, Channel 4 and ITV